MYSTERIES AND SECRETS OF THE TEMPLARS

LIONEL AND PATRICIA FANTHORPE

MYSTERIES AND SECRETS OF THE TEMPLARS

THE STORY BEHIND THE DA VINCI CODE

THE DUNDURN GROUP
TORONTO

Copy-Editor: Lloyd Davis
Design: Andrew Roberts
Printer: Friesens

Library and Archives Canada Cataloguing in Publication

Fanthorpe, R. Lionel
    Mysteries and secrets of the Templars : the story behind the Da Vinci code / Lionel and Patricia Fanthorpe.

ISBN-10: 1-55002-557-0
ISBN-13: 978-1-55002-557-6

    1. Templars — History. I. Fanthorpe, Patricia. II. Title.

CR4749.F35 2005   271'.7913
C2005-900175-5

1   2   3   4   5   09   08   07   06   05

 Conseil des Arts du Canada Canada Council for the Arts Canadä ONTARIO ARTS COUNCIL
CONSEIL DES ARTS DE L'ONTARIO

We acknowledge the support of the Canada Council for the Arts and the Ontario Arts Council for our publishing program. We also acknowledge the financial support of the Government of Canada through the Book Publishing Industry Development Program and The Association for the Export of Canadian Books, and the Government of Ontario through the Ontario Book Publishers Tax Credit program, and the Ontario Media Development Corporation's Ontario Book Initiative.

Printed and bound in Canada.
Printed on recycled paper.

www.dundurn.com

Dundurn Press
8 Market Street, Suite 200
Toronto, Ontario, Canada
M5E 1M6

Gazelle Book Services Limited
White Cross Mills
Hightown, Lancaster, England
LA1 4X5

Dundurn Press
2250 Military Road
Tonawanda NY
U.S.A. 14150

MYSTERIES AND SECRETS OF THE TEMPLARS

TABLE OF CONTENTS

FOREWORD

Over its long life, the Christian faith has seen the rise of many influential movements and personalities. In the centuries yet to come, it will no doubt see many more. We can only wait in hope and expectation.

One such movement, coming early on in the history of the faith, would have limited appeal to most of us. Certain Christians, at that time, grew increasingly anxious about the wickedness of the world around them and the Church's apparent complacent acceptance of ever-lowering standards of behaviour. In the face of what they saw as such a fall from grace, they decided to take no further part in any of it — resolving to opt out of what, if they had known the phrase, they would have called the "rat race." They chose, deliberately, to isolate themselves, to live as hermits and adopt a lifestyle of extreme asceticism. To do so, they went into desert regions, hoping to live in isolation with God; but, in the event, many others who were like-minded were attracted to share their wildernesses. St. Anthony (AD 251–356) may have elected to live much of his long life in intended isolation, but over the years he had to share his desert life with others drawn to be part of the same experience. The way of life of these Desert Fathers, as they came to be called, led in later years to a worldwide monastic movement in which men and women vowed to a lifetime of obedience, poverty, discipline and chastity.

In a later century, other Christians took a very different attitude. Their resolve was not to distance themselves from their contemporary world but to stand and reason with it. Their aim was to overcome all false beliefs and behaviour with Christian logic and argument. Thomas Aquinas, a Dominican monk of the thirteenth century, steeped from an early age in the writings of Plato and Aristotle, accepted that Christianity came into the world by revelation and that, in the final analysis, some measure of faith would be needed to sustain it; nevertheless, he went on to contend that all Christian beliefs could be supported by reasoned argument. Aquinas was but one of a large company of Christian men and women, all of great intellectual stature, who devoted their gifts to the service of God and their religion.

We lesser mortals can never hope to reach the intellectual heights of such giants as Aquinas or Augustine. Still less likely are we ever to attain such contempt for material possessions as those in lifetime monastic orders. We are in genuine awe of the quality of life such men and women achieve, but it's not for us. Christian love, however, is not the preserve only of the great and gifted ones of this world. From that challenge none of us can hide. As the apostle Paul once wrote, "God has chosen the foolish things of this world to confound the wise and God has chosen the weak things of the world to confound the things that are mighty."

Rich, poor, strong, weak, old or young all are called to show the love of God and are capable of doing it. Of course, only the exceptional will ever go to such lengths of love as Father Damien, who devoted his life to an isolated leper colony until leprosy made him one of them. Few could easily follow Kagawa, a Japanese convert to Christianity, from his early life of affluence to a life of servitude in the worst slums of an industrial Japanese city, or Mother Teresa in her lifelong care of the decayed and destitute of the streets of Calcutta. The extremes of Francis, who began life in Assisi with much and ended with bare earth as his deathbed, are not for the faint-hearted. Such men and women with love that "knows no bounds" have always graced every generation and will be forever part of the great Christian landscape. If we can't emulate them, we can at least be proud of what, in our name, they have achieved.

During my years in Oxford, now over seventy years ago, my study was next door to a young man who could boast a well-known ancestor. He was descended from Sabine Baring Gould, who will forever be remembered, among much else, for his great hymn:

> Onward Christian Soldiers
> Marching as to war,
> With the Cross of Jesus,
> Going on before.

Apparently, the hymn was written originally for a gentle, routine Sunday School procession but, with its martial-sounding words and fine tune, it adapted easily as a marching song for militant Christians everywhere. As we have seen, there are Christians capable of great love; there are others of powerful intellect whose capacity to reason upholds the sometimes trembling faith of others. All seek with their differing gifts and temperaments to serve God and their fellows. There will always be, side by side with them, men and women of action, Christians muscular in their faith, those in the words of the old prayer we tend to call the "church militant." Such strong-minded Christians are always prepared, wisely or unwisely, to stand and fight for what they believe, or for the places they hold dear. Such were, and no doubt still are, the Templars. They came together originally to secure Jerusalem against invasion from equally militant Saracens, and to secure and maintain free access to all holy sites throughout the world. The Templars were the spiritual and intellectual spearhead of the Knights of St. John and the Crusades. They were active in the small Christian army that defended Malta in 1565 against the massive fleet and army of Suleyman the Magnificent. They were warriors for the faith at whatever the cost — and whatever the odds.

The writers of this book are both modern-day Templars who held high office in that movement. Co-author Lionel will forever look a muscular Christian, as will be apparent from the photographs of him in this book. He has practised martial arts for years, still works with weights (given the chance in so busy a lifestyle), swims many lengths of his local pool every day, rides a Harley Davidson motor bike and dresses in leathers. A priest, in every way larger than life. Nothing will ever undermine his faith. He will write about it in his many books, argue for it, debate with anyone and, if pressed too hard, he will even fight for it. A friend for many years, he seems to me to embody everything for which, historically, the Templars have always stood. The term "warrior-priest" would fit him very well.

But such a limited definition of the Templars would not satisfy either of the authors of this book. They have looked much deeper into the Templars' past and have identified there men of genius, scholars, inventors, explorers, navigators, engineers — people who enriched and advanced the world in which they lived. They believe their Templar for-bears discovered great truths, and held on closely to awesome, ancient secrets — sharing some of their discoveries with the few, but hiding them from others, leaving clues for future generations to decipher, if they can. Was Bérenger Saunière, the poor priest who became immense-ly rich in so mysterious a way, one of these lucky ones? Are some of their treasures, their stored knowledge, yet to be found?

Our authors believe the early disciples of the Templar movement were among the great ones of the world. They may persuade you; they may not. Lionel and his wife Patricia, the principal researcher of this and many of his other books, have written this work from the heart. They are proud to be Templars, and hope through this study to share with others what they are and what they believe.

Canon Stanley Mogford, MA
Cardiff, Wales, November 2004

(As always, the authors are deeply indebted to their highly esteemed friend, Canon Mogford, for his great kindness in providing this foreword. He is rightly regarded as one of the finest scholars in Wales, and it is always a privilege to have his help and support.)

INTRODUCTION

There are awesome, unsolved mysteries connected with the great and noble order of Guardians and Protectors who, for part of their long and honourable history, were known as the Templars.

The first of those mysteries is the enigma of their true origins and purposes. The second is the precise nature of the eerie, arcane secrets they protected long ago — and continue to protect to this day. The third is their system of codemaking and codebreaking: they were — and still are — expert semiologists and cryptographers. The fourth is the riddle of what happened to them after the treacherous and unprovoked attack launched against them by the odious and cowardly Philip le Bel (King Philip IV of France) in 1307.

In this volume, as co-authors, we draw on the knowledge that goes with the privileged positions we once enjoyed in the Templars (co-author Lionel was the honorary World Primate Archbishop of a Templar church as well as being a Knight Commander and Magnum Officialis of a Templar order, while co-author Patricia was a Dame Commander). This knowledge suggests to us an overall hypothesis encompassing all four of the great unsolved Templar mysteries.

The original hidden order of Guardians and Protectors is so old that its beginnings are lost in the intriguing mists of prehistory, myth and legend. The secrets of the order's ancient origins may be lost, but its purposes are not. It exists to guard, to protect and to preserve — perhaps, one day, in time of great need, to attempt to reactivate — something of immense importance to the future of the whole human race.

Trying to solve the mysteries of Templar codes is like searching for the Rosetta Stone: something that will provide vital clues to ancient, hitherto indecipherable, secrets.

Our research over the years has led us to examine the strange Yarmouth Stone in Nova Scotia and the curious symbols on the unusual slab of porphyry found in the Oak Island Money Pit in Mahone Bay, Nova Scotia. We've examined Norse runes and Egyptian hieroglyphs. In 1975 we interviewed Emile Fradin, who as a fourteen-year-old in 1924 found the mysterious alphabet — inscribed by a person, or persons, unknown — in Glozel, near Vichy, France. We have also studied the enigmatic symbols on the extraordinary Phaistos Disc from Crete.

The fourth and final Templar mystery is the strangest and most significant of them all. By miracles of courage, endurance and an ingenuity to rival that of Ulysses, hardy groups of the indomitable Templars defied Philip's mindless henchmen and made their way to freedom and safety — some by land; some by sea. Wherever these dauntless adventurers travelled — and some almost certainly reached the New World nearly two centuries before Columbus — they took their Templar spirit, and their secrets, with them.

As well as being superb warrior-priests, these medieval Templars were exceptional architects and builders. Their skill in designing and constructing fortresses was admired and acknowledged by the world. Clues as to where they went in order to evade the reach of the petulant and aggressive Philip IV and his successors may be detected in characteristic Templar architectural features in buildings dating from 1307 — the period that may well be termed the start of the Templar Dispersion.

As well as this dispersion, there were other, secret ways in which ingenious Templars went underground — in a figurative as well as a literal sense. Discretion, as the proverb reminds us, is the ally of valour — not an alternative to it, nor a substitute for it. An experienced craftsman working quietly and discreetly as an expert armourer for some local warlord would be too valuable to be questioned about his past.

As former Templars ourselves, we are convinced that, although the line grew thin at times between 1307 and our own twenty-first century, it never broke. The indomitable Templars are as much a part of modern life as they were of medieval life.

Lionel & Patricia Fanthorpe
Cardiff, Wales, 2004

THE TEMPLARS TODAY

Renewed twenty-first-century interest in the Templars and their mysterious, ancient secrets suggests that it would be helpful to begin any detailed study of them with a synopsis of who and what the Knights Templar were — and are. This very brief prologue is intended to do just that, and to provide a series of basic references as pointers to the detailed descriptions, analyses and hypotheses that comprise the later parts of this book.

In 1118, nine knights arrived in Jerusalem and, ostensibly, took on the role of protecting pilgrims from bandits. King Baldwin II made them welcome, and provided them with accommodation below Temple Mount in what were then called Solomon's Stables. What they really did, apart from protecting pilgrims, is central to the great Templar mystery.

With help and protection from the immensely influential Bernard of Clairvaux, the Templar Order was recognized by the Vatican and known formally as The Poor Knights of Christ and the Temple of Solomon.

It was a tremendous advantage to the Templar Order to be accountable to no one but the pope, and to pay no taxes to any secular ruler or local church official.

Their bravery in battle was deservedly legendary, and was reflected in their motto: "First to attack and last to retreat." Their enemies rightly feared their military prowess and unyielding ferocity. They were skilled architects and builders as well as supreme warriors, and their fleet was also widely renowned.

The Templars were betrayed by the evil and treacherous Philip le Bel, who ordered their strongholds attacked simultaneously on Friday, October 13, 1307. They were nearly wiped out, but a significant minority of them nevertheless escaped to carry on with their vital, secret work. The precise nature of that work is considered in depth later in the book.

The Templar fleet was never captured, and it is highly probable that significant numbers of resolute and indomitable survivors reached Scotland, the Scottish Islands and the New World.

It is difficult, if not impossible, to estimate the Templars' worldwide numerical strength in the twenty-first century. There are many different groups of Templars today — some are Masonic, others are not. Browsing Templar websites with a good search engine will give some idea of their diversity and numerical strength. Undoubtedly, there are a great many more Templar groups who, valuing their secrecy and privacy, prefer not to register their activities on the Internet. A conservative estimate would put Templar membership today at several thousand worldwide.

In addition to the many Templar commanderies and priories, there are also several Templar churches which are usually wide open and inclusive, theologically broad-minded, liberal, and very welcoming. Membership in several of these modern Templar churches is open to anyone of any denomination. Templar church members and clergy retain their own original church membership while adding their Templar church membership to it. In this way, those Templar churches that accept dual memberships of this kind are working towards unification of the church at large and doing what they can to overcome denominational boundaries.

A great many Templars today are deeply involved in charitable work, and contribute substantially to those in need — much as their forebears protected pilgrims in medieval times.

Chapter 1

THE MISTS OF TIME

Mysteries are inseparable from human curiosity. Questions are as natural to us as breathing. When they can't be readily answered, or they're argued over and then answered in strikingly different ways, they graduate to the realm of unsolved mysteries — and intrigue us more than ever. The more awesome and important the question, the greater the mystery that surrounds it.

Cosmology is one of these major areas of uncertainty. Is the universe finite or infinite? Is there an "outside" to it? If so, what *is* outside? Has it always been here? Will it always be here? Did it have a beginning? Was it created — and if so, who or what created it? Again, assuming it was created, how was it created? How does it operate? Did what we have come to know as the natural laws of physics, chemistry and biology just appear on their own as the thing developed and evolved — or were the rules of the game laid down by the Maker when he created the board and the players?

The original Hebrew name for the book of the Bible now known as Genesis was *Bereshith*, meaning "in the beginning." It's an intriguingly interwoven collection of narratives from at least four very ancient sources, and it sets out — within the limited terminology of its own cultural period — to answer a few of those philosophical, cosmological questions. The subtext beneath its allegories and etiological myths hints that there are some people — priests, prophets, princes and patriarchs — who know a lot more than others and who understand certain very important ancient secrets.

Oral traditions predated the written accounts by thousands of years, and although richly coloured by mythology and restricted by the educational and cultural limitations of their time, such oral traditions richly repay serious study today. What clearly and consistently emerges from studying these ancient traditions, and from the early written records such as Bereshith, is that there were strong, well-informed guardians, guides, protectors and leaders of their people who seem to have had access to knowledge and power sources that were not generally available.

Adherents of the great world faiths would argue that such leaders were appointed and inspired by their God (or by their gods and goddesses). Darwinian neurologists and psychologists would suggest that they had special — but perfectly natural and explicable — abilities arising out of genetic modifications and mutations that led to superior brain and body function. Everywhere, there were — and are — mathematical, musical and artistic prodigies who outperform the rest of us in their special fields. Leonardo da Vinci, Beethoven, Mozart, Einstein, Trachtenberg and Hawking are cases in point. The late and greatly admired grand-slam golfer, Bobby Jones (1902–1971), was an outstanding performer in his own fields. His brilliant legal mind was as magnificent as his skill on the golf course; such a man in ancient times — say, a uniquely gifted swordsman and statesman — would have been a natural leader and guardian of his people.

Other theories put forward to explain the charisma and superhuman qualities of some of these ancient guardians of humanity have included the idea that they were either extraterrestrials themselves, or the result of interbreeding between extraterrestrials and human beings. In this context, Bereshith (Genesis 6:2–4) poses the question inescapably:

> ... the sons of God saw the daughters of men that they were fair; and they took them wives of all that they chose.... The Nephilim [giants?] were in the earth in those days.... [W]hen the sons of God came in unto the daughters of men, and they bare children to them: the same were the mighty men which were of old, men of renown.

The account does not by any means preclude a simple and direct religious interpretation: the beings described as "sons of God" could be understood simply as angelic entities, or other benign, heavenly life forms. They might (in accordance with Occam's Razor!*) simply have been humanoid extraterrestrials with mental and physical abilities greater than those usually found among terrestrial humanoids at that time. They could equally well have been Atlanteans or Lemurians from one of those legendary "lost" or "submerged" civilizations with a high level of culture, technology and academic prowess.

Apart from the references in Bereshith that hint strongly at the historical existence of superhuman heroes (such as Nimrod, "the mighty hunter"), many other ancient texts describe the epic adventures of such heroic figures possessing attributes beyond those of "normal" *Homo sapiens*. Among the most famous of these records is the Epic of Gilgamesh. The narrative is believed to contain many strange secrets that could relate to the mysterious origins of the secret order of guardians and guides who were popularly known as Templars in the twelfth century. How does the Epic of Gilgamesh begin?

> Great is thy worthiness, O Gilgamesh, Prince of Kulab.
> You are the one who knows all things. You are the
> Emperor who understands all the countries of the world.
> You are the wisest of the wise. You know and understand
> all mysterious and secret things. You are he who knows
> about the World before the Flood.... You are the great
> architect and builder.... No man alive can rival what you
> have built.... Seven Sages laid its foundations.

The story of Gilgamesh is believed by many experts to be at least six thousand years old — and it is possibly much older. It tells the story of the semi-divine Sumerian King Gilgamesh of Uruk; his friendship with the powerful wild man, Enkidu; their joint conquest of the terrifying guardian of the forest, Humbaba; Enkidu's death; and Gilgamesh's inconsolable grief for his lost friend. Throughout the epic, Gilgamesh is

---

*William of Occam was a medieval philosopher who created a logical instrument for cutting out unnecessary complications: "One should not increase, beyond what is necessary, the number of entities required to explain anything." In theory, Occam's Razor shaves away "unnecessary" things and makes it easier to reach logical conclusions. Although admittedly helpful on occasions, it is frequently a hindrance in a universe that is almost incomprehensibly complicated!

seen as the defender and protector of his Sumerian people. He has numerous superhuman powers as well as great wisdom, and his word is law throughout his empire. In the broadest and most general sense, Gilgamesh can be understood as a Templar-type Guardian and Protector of something very powerful and deeply secret — and so, after his training by Gilgamesh, can Enkidu. It is almost as if Gilgamesh can be viewed as a prototypical Grand Master, with Enkidu as his trusted assistant and knightly bodyguard.

Selecting a sample of just nine such ancient and mysterious guardian-heroes provides a curious symbolic link with the nine traditional founders of their twelfth-century resurgence under the guise of Templarism.

Who are these nine entities? If the father-god figures of Odin, Jupiter and Zeus — known by different names in different cultures at different periods of time — are regarded as one being, and the war-gods Thor and Mars are also seen as one being, that accounts for two. If we add another Norse god, such as Ull (also called Ulir and Oller), plus Nimrod, Gilgamesh and Enkidu from the ancient Middle East, the total reaches six. The mysterious, but very powerful, Enlil of Babylonia is a strong candidate for one of the three remaining places, alongside Hermes Trismegistus (Hermes the Thrice-Blessed, also known as Thoth), the awesomely wise and powerful scribe to the gods of Egypt and controller of the famous Emerald Tablets. Last, but not least, comes the mysterious Melchizedek, the man "without father or mother — with neither beginning of life nor end of days." He appears

Board used to play the Royal Game of Ur.

in early sacred writings as the friend and benefactor of the great patriarch Abraham, who came from the ancient city of Ur.

Ancient pieces of the type almost certainly used to play the Royal Game of Ur.

The famous Royal Game of Ur was similar to chess in some ways, although very different in others. It is significant that a number of important Templar codes and ciphers can be encoded and decoded using a chess board. The links between this ancient game from Ur, chess and Templar codes will be examined in more detail in later chapters.

* * *

The nine great beings we've listed are merely a sample of the many divine and semi-divine figures, half-remembered through the mists of time and imperfectly recorded down the millennia that followed. But they provide a pointer to the central hypothesis at the heart of all real Templarism: ancient Protectors and Guardians existed long ago, and were involved in some type of warfare — like a cosmic chess game. It was a game that demanded the highest intelligence and indomitable courage — something like a war between good and evil, or order and chaos. These beings possessed what seemed to their contemporaries to be superhuman powers; they understood awesome mysteries and secrets; they held keys to forbidden knowledge. As the centuries went by, their arcane riddles were passed to others, to secret societies and hidden organizations — including the nine mysterious knights who searched below the ruins of what they believed to be part of Solomon's Temple in Jerusalem.

Who were these nine original Templar Knights? And what was their real reason for being in Jerusalem in the twelfth century?

First came Hugh (or Hugues) de Payen. Hugh had been in the service of another Hugh, Hugh de Champagne, and was also related through marriage to the St. Clairs of Roslin. This is particularly significant in light of the massive importance of Roslin (various later spellings exist) Chapel in Scotland and the meaning of the site it occupies.

André de Montbard was the uncle of Bernard of Clairvaux and was also in the service of Hugh de Champagne. Next came Geoffroi de St. Omer, one of the stalwart sons of Hugh de St. Omer; Payen de Montdidier, who was closely connected with the ruling house of Flanders — as was Achambaud de St. Amand. The other knights were Geoffroi Bisol, Gondemare, Rosal and Godfroi.

It is essential to make this initial jump of several millennia — from the ancient patriarchs and pantheons to the knightly adventurers in twelfth-century Jerusalem — in order to establish the connections between those ancient origins and what is popularly known today as Templarism. Now some of the intriguing gaps in those long millennia can be bridged.

* * *

Where had those first ancient heroes come from, and where had they acquired their secret knowledge and powers? They're worth looking at in more detail. The first is:

At least, that's what Bereshith calls him — the biblical Abram, later Abraham. According to the Genesis account, he was from Ur of the Chaldees and was the son of Terah, a descendant of Noah via his son Shem. With other members of his family, including his nephew Lot, Abraham moved from Ur to Haran, a renowned trading centre in the valley of the River Euphrates. Terah died there, and, according to the biblical account, Abraham felt a divine call to move on to a new land where God promised that he would become the father of nations and be a universal blessing.

A salacious episode involving Sarah (who was Abraham's half-sister as well as his wife) and their contemporary pharaoh is a strange one. Famine had more or less forced Abraham's nomads to seek food in Egypt, where, because of her great beauty, Sarah was likely to be acquired as an addition to Pharaoh's harem. It may have occurred to the politically astute Abraham that the inconvenience of a husband was unlikely to deter an all-powerful Pharaoh — his loyal guards could dispose of such an inconvenience swiftly and permanently, so that Pharaoh would be able to take on the unencumbered widow. Abraham therefore decided prudently to tell Pharaoh that Sarah was his sister — which was not entirely untrue.

This episode has raised doubts in the minds of some speculative historians as to whether Abraham and Sarah might actually have been Egyptian in origin, rather than Chaldeans from Ur. It has even been suggested by adventurous researchers and historians that Abraham and Sarah were originally from India — and were far more powerful and mysterious than the straightforward biblical accounts suggest.

A completely different — and equally probable — version of the Sarah and Pharaoh episode suggests that, far from attempting to deceive the Egyptian ruler about his real relationship with Sarah and meekly handing her over to Pharaoh, Abraham commanded so formidable a force of armed retainers that when Pharaoh *abducted* Sarah, her husband demanded her swift, safe return — or else Pharaoh would bitterly regret it! Confronted by the might of several hundred Chaldean warriors, Pharaoh swiftly handed the lady back.

But what if Abraham had fearless and skillful *Indian* soldiers at his command, as well as his Chaldean warriors? The Jewish scholar

Flavius Josephus, who wrote prodigiously during the first century of the Christian era, quoted Aristotle as saying, "The Jews are descended from great Indian Philosophers; they are called Calani in the Indian language." Clearchus of Soli, who was a disciple of Aristotle, wrote: "The philosophers are called in India Calanians and in Syria Jews. The name of their capital, Jerusalem, is very difficult to pronounce." There is also evidence that Megasthenes was sent to India by Seleucus Nicator in the third century BC. He reported back to the effect that the Jews had originated as a highly cultured Indian tribe known as the Kalani. Dr. Martin Haug, distinguished author of *The Sacred Language, Writings, and Religions of the Parsis,* argued that the Magi had referred to their own religion as Kesh-i-Ibrahim, claiming that all their religious wisdom had come from him, and that he had brought their scriptures from Heaven.

These very ancient Indian Cave Temples have Brahman connections, and could well date back to the period when Brahma and Sarai-svati — Abram and Sarai — supposedly left India and travelled to Ur of the Chaldees.

Voltaire, writing in the eighteenth century, believed that Abraham was closely connected with Brahman priests who had left India. He supported his arguments by pointing out that Chaldean Ur, traditionally associated with the Abramic patriarchs, lay near the Persian border on the road from India to the Middle East.

What other mysterious shades of meaning are associated with the original word *Chaldean*?

In these ancient cuneiform characters, the root word *cal* or *gal* is combined with another root word, *du*, and has the combined sense of "one who does great things" — a Chaldean, therefore, was "one with the power to do great things." If Abram and Sarai were Chaldeans — with great and mysterious power — where had they really come from in the beginning?

The general conclusion of this research is that the link between the Chaldean Abram and Sarai (later Abraham and Sarah) and Indian religious history seems to be more than coincidental. Some theorists have actually argued that the Indian god Brahma and his consort Sarai-svati are the same people as Abram and Sarai.

Was it from an ancient Indian temple like this one that Abram and Sarai came before they settled in Ur? What is the curious animal in the lower left corner: a hornless ram or a bull?

There are other intriguing etymological theories surrounding the name of Abram. These focus on the *ram* syllable, leaving the *ab/ap* prefix as the Kasmiri word for "father." In Hindu religion, the god Ram, known as Lord Ram, is an incarnation of Vishnu. It seems especially appropriate to identify him with the Chaldean patriarch Abram because Ram was regarded as the personification of all that is good, ethical and virtuous. Ram never lied. He was always respectful, kind and gentle with the old and the wise, no matter how frail their age had made them. He was never ill, and he never aged. He had the gift of eloquent and persuasive speech. He was omniscient, knowing especially the deepest and most secret thoughts of all whom he encountered. He was also described as an invincible warrior and the most courageous spirit on Earth.

It may also be significant that when Abraham was about to sacrifice his son Isaac, he realized his mistake and sacrificed instead a *ram* that was entangled in a thicket. The symbolism of the ram needs to be taken into careful consideration when taking into account this particular biblical episode, which played a major part in Abraham's life.

The ram has always been a symbol of power, authority and leadership.

The exciting Mexican author and researcher Tomas Doreste, writing in *Moises y los Extraterrestres*, ventures more widely than the Bereshith account and argues for a close and highly significant connection between Abram and Melchizedek. What if the name Melchizedek is derived from the Indian name Melik-Sadaksina? Traditionally, he was the son of a renowned Kassite (or Cassite) king, and the second part of his name, Sadaksina, can be traced through both Sanskrit and Kashmiri root words to mean "someone who has supernatural powers." Does this also tie in with Zadok, the priest who anointed the great and wise King Solomon? Was the name Zadok really a variation of Sadak? The possession of superhuman powers also ties in closely with the cuneiform *Galdu* — as described earlier, the ancient root words describing a Chaldean astrologer, wise man or magus.

This name Zadok, or Sadak, provides another intriguing link with the nine twelfth-century guardian-guides who surfaced as Knights Templar and dug in search of something under what they believed had once been part of Solomon's palace. Was that mysterious object that they sought connected with a wise and mysterious Chaldean, or an equally wise and mysterious Sadak from India — alias Zadok, Solomon's very powerful priest?

If Thoth and Melchizedek were actually one and the same superhuman entity, the strange legend of Sarah in the cave is particularly significant. According to various ancient myths and legends, Noah had access to the miraculous Emerald Tablet on which all the greatest secrets of "magic" (lost science? forgotten technology?) were inscribed. Having survived the flood, he hid the precious artifact in a secret cave at Hebron. One version of the story relates that Sarah found it there along with what looked, at first, like the incredibly well-preserved corpse of Hermes Trismegistus. He was, apparently, not dead: only in a state of suspended animation. When she took the arcane Emerald Tablet from his hand, he stirred and spoke to her. Understandably, Sarah fled from the cave.

One account says that she took the tablet, or tablets, with her and that they eventually became the mystical Urim and Thummim with which the oldest and most knowledgeable Hebrew priests determined the Divine Will. Another account says that she dropped it (or them) as she fled from the cave.

A subsequent chapter in the history of the Emerald Tablet — and a particularly interesting one in terms of the line of ancient Guardians — is that it came eventually into the hands of Alexander the Great when he explored the mysterious Hebron cave where Hermes lay sleeping. There are some researchers who would attribute Alexander's meteoric success to the knowledge he gained from reading the Emerald Tablet.

A contemporary image of Alexander the Great. Did the brilliant Macedonian emperor know the secrets of the ancient pre-Templar Guardians?

So we draw these strands together to pursue the hypothesis that there was a nexus between the early stories of the Hindu gods and the adventures of the widely travelled Chaldean hero Abraham, as recorded in Bereshith and elsewhere. This theory spreads the potent secret knowledge (which its hypothetical ancient Guardians such as Abraham and Melchizedek supposedly protected) much farther afield. Might it also shed some unusual light on Alexander the Great's exploits many centuries later — especially his conquest of Persia and his progress to India? Did the brilliant and humane Macedonian emperor have access to ancient secrets that were, for him, in his time, the key to world power?

Chapter 2

WAS ALEXANDER OF MACEDON ONE OF THE ANCIENT GUARDIANS?

Alexander III of Macedon, more widely referred to as Alexander the Great, was born in Macedonia in 356 BC. He was the son of King Philip II and his formidable Queen Olympias — who has been suspected of being responsible for the death of Philip, who was assassinated in 336 BC, an event that put Alexander in charge. With amazing military and political astuteness, and almost uncanny ability, Alexander acquired the Greek city-states and then set out to conquer the vast Persian Empire. Some researchers have regarded his unique abilities as having a paranormal component, and like the Pharaoh of Joseph's time, Alexander was certainly influenced by dreams. On one occasion, when he was attacking the city of Tyre in 332 BC, he dreamed of a satyr dancing on a shield. Aristander — who, like the biblical Daniel and Joseph, was an inspired interpreter of dreams — recognized one of the strange puns that are often found in dreams. (Some psychologists believe that such paronomasia are a feature of right-brain communication.) *Satyros* is Greek for "satyr," but it can also be split up to form *sa Tyros*, meaning "Tyre is yours." In due course, Alexander captured Tyre.

His aims and objectives were at least partly based in his desire to redress the Persian attacks on Greece. He hammered his way through Asia Minor, Syria and Egypt and was invariably triumphant. Of all the world's strategists, tacticians and military leaders, Alexander is arguably the only one who never suffered a single defeat. His greatest victory was achieved at Gaugamela, now part of northern Iraq. By the age of twenty-five, Alexander was overlord of Greece, emperor of Persia, ruler of Asia Minor and pharaoh of Egypt. From then onwards — until his untimely death at thirty-two — he and his invincible army covered nearly twelve thousand miles. During that time he founded close to a hundred cities over a two-million-square-mile territory that spanned three continents.

Although remembered mainly for his amazing military conquests and his personal courage in the field, Alexander was also a brilliant statesman, philosopher, theologian and metaphysician. If ever a leading thinker of the ancient world had a claim to belong to the mysterious line of timeless Guardians and Protectors, it was Alexander of Macedon. In 324 BC, in the Temple of Opis (alias Artemis), he made this enlightened oath which reached sublime ethical heights:

> Now that the wars are ending, I want all of you to live in peace and happiness. From now on all of you will live like one united people, enjoying a shared peace and prosperity.
>
> Think of the whole world as your own country with the same, shared laws, a land where the wisest and kindest rule, free of any regard for race or creed.
>
> I shall never separate people, as the narrow-minded do, into barbarians and Greeks. As your Emperor, I am not interested in the race of my citizens, nor am I interested in their origins. I categorize and distinguish my people by their virtue. Each good foreigner is a Greek as far as I am concerned, and each bad Greek is worse than what we once thought of as a barbarian.
>
> If differences arise among you, never resort to armed conflict. Resolve your quarrels peacefully. I will serve as your arbitrator, if you need me. Do not think of me as a dictator, but as father of all my people. Your conduct should be like loving brothers and sisters who live together within one strong and united family home.
>
> As for me, I consider all of you to be equal, white-skinned or dark-skinned. You are not subjects — you are citizens and shareholders — partners with me in our great Commonwealth.
>
> As far as it lies within my power, I shall always do my best to accomplish all that I promise you. We must keep this oath that we are now taking as though it were a Contract of Love.

Did that inspiration come from the ancient wisdom inscribed on the Emerald Tablet?

* * *

Other theories and speculations take the tablet's history in a different direction: they relate it to the famous, and as yet indecipherable, Phaistos Disk from ancient Crete, where the strange legends of the Minotaur mingled with the technological supremacy of Daedalus the maze builder.

King Minos of Crete was said to have received his instructions directly from the god Zeus in a deep, dark, secret cave. Were Zeus's instructions to Minos inscribed on the Phaistos Disk?

On the other hand, the Phaistos Disk may be completely innocuous — a cargo list from the Cretan mercantile marine, perhaps, or a pious prayer for rain, a good harvest or the continued health and fertility of a flourishing flock or herd. It might equally well be a skillfully coded repository — in the ancient pre-Templar Guardians' tradition — of secret, arcane knowledge: as powerful and relevant today as it was in the days of Minos.

Although infinite interpretations are possible, there were traditionally said to be thirteen magical teachings, or precepts, on the Emerald Tablets, and some inspired researchers believe that they have found what they think may be these same precepts on the Phaistos Disk. Could the two be identical, or is the Phaistos Disk perhaps a *copy* of the Hermetic Tablets?

Even more intriguing is the possibility that the precepts themselves — worthy as they are — served a double purpose. Was the making and collecting of such aphorisms an identifying code? Did those who were in on the great ancient secrets proclaim their status to other Guardians by quoting from the proverbs that the wise ones shared?

* * *

Is it more than coincidence or synchronicity that so many of the outstanding minds of the past have left proverbs and precepts behind

The mysterious Phaistos Disk from ancient Crete: never yet deciphered. Some researchers believe that it may be identical with the Emerald Tablets of Hermes Trismegistus — alias the Egyptian Thoth, scribe to the gods. Does it contain the Thirteen Precepts of Hermes in some strange pre-Templar Guardian code?

them? Many of these have a similar core and are very much in harmony with all that is best in legendary Arthurian chivalry and Templarism. The proverbs of Solomon, for instance, provide a capacious reservoir of distilled wisdom. To quote just a few examples, he writes, "A gentle answer turns anger away, but harsh words stir up fury"; "How much better it is to get wisdom than gold"; "Better is a dry morsel in happy company than a feast in a house full of stress." This same deep wisdom is also found in the Analects of Confucius when he writes, "Never do to others what you would not want others to do to you"; "He whose heart is set upon goodness will dislike no one"; "Be faithful, and keep your promises." Ancient Egyptian social wisdom also contains many excellent thoughts — for example, "Take care of the old; give the eld-erly man your staff to help him as he walks." The great Roman thinker Juvenal taught respect and care for the young in much the same way that the best Egyptian thought cared for the old. Juvenal wrote, "Great reverence is owed to a child." Anglo-Saxon wisdom proclaimed, "Death is better than a life of shame." Wise and fearless old Vikings taught, "Anything is better than treachery." The humanitarian wisdom of ancient Hindu writers maintained, "Children, the old, the poor and the sick should be treated as though they were the Lords of the Air."

In view of the current sharp focus on Leonardo da Vinci — his codes and ciphers, his encyclopedic knowledge and his involvement with Templar secrets, as well as the ancient wisdom of the pre-Templar Guardians — his keen interest in proverbs and aphorisms might be very significant. It is as though by creating new ones himself, and collecting what he considered most noteworthy in the wise sayings of others, Leonardo was quietly hinting that this kind of condensed wisdom was the hallmark of those who understood the secrets of the Templars and of the ancient Guardians who had preceded them. Examples from Leonardo's collection include "Iron rusts from disuse"; "Stagnant water loses its purity and in cold weather becomes frozen — even so does inac-tion sap the vigour of the mind"; "The acquisition of any knowledge whatever is always useful to the intellect"; "Ask advice from him who governs himself well."

So, the aphoristic precepts of Hermes Trismegistus — whether or not they are inscribed on the Phaistos Disk — may well have a part to play in unravelling the mystery of the ancient Guardians and Protectors: as well as passing worthwhile behavioural, moral and ethical wisdom to those who would listen, the sharing of aphorisms acted as a badge of identity.

The first of the thirteen precepts that some researchers think may be inscribed on the Phaistos Disk refers to the concepts of certainty and truth, which are represented geometrically by the origin, or centre, of a circle — the circumference being the locus of a point always equidistant from that central and certain truth.

The second precept is the one for which Rosicrucianism is best known: "As above — so below." This is made within the mystical circle codes by drawing two diameters that intersect each other at right angles in the centre, designated as *o*, the *origin*. It can also symbolize the Templar Cross within the mystic circle.

An equilateral triangle can be drawn within a circle, each of its equal angles touching the circumference. This is the third precept: the triune nature of God — Father, Son and Holy Spirit; Creator, Sustainer and Redeemer of the Universe and all that lives within it.

The fourth precept is the square within the circle — the old four-element theory (earth, air, fire and water) that is central to alchemical theory.

The pentagon and pentagram unite within a circle — all five of their points touch the circumference. This is the fifth precept. Followers of the mystical Hermetic theories regard these regular, five-pointed shapes as particularly powerful symbols of strength and perfection. It is almost certainly more than coincidence, for example, that the American Pentagon is built that way. Dr. Tim Wallace-Murphy's superb book on Templarism in America provides very convincing evidence for Templar influence in the New World after 1307.

The hexagon and hexagram constructed inside a circle are, according to the sixth Hermetic precept, symbols of dynamic power. They, in particular, are symbols of earthly power of the kind that Alexander the Great wielded.

If the six-pointed figures represent earthly, or temporal, power, the seventh precept, symbolized by heptagrams and heptagons, represents mental and spiritual power. This seventh precept is concerned with thoughtfulness, wisdom, prudence, ethics, morality and simple goodness. The age-old idea that the number seven is lucky and a powerful benign influence is linked to this seventh Hermetic precept. The number seven is also associated with the star Sirius, and in olden times only seven planets were known — this, too, gave extra significance to the number seven.

When the octagon and octagram are drawn inside the circle, they symbolize the eighth Hermetic precept: the idea of ascending to Heaven, acquiring heavenly wisdom and knowledge, then returning to Earth to make use of it for the benefit of others — an idea that can be demonstrated both in the Alexandrian oath in the Temple of Opis and in the highest of Templar ideals.

The ninth Hermetic precept is echoed in Tolkien's Middle Earth, where there were nine Rings of Power. Drawing a nine-sided figure inside the mystic circle represents the special strength that is associated with endurance. This is the ninth precept: the fortitude that never gives up — unbreakable determination and an iron will.

The cyclic decagon with its ten regular sides symbolizes creation, the making of good and powerful things. It symbolizes the formation of the universe itself in Hermetic thought. The Ten Commandments of Judaic Law were brought down from the mountain by Moses, the hero who led his people out of Egypt — that same wise hero who knew every secret of Pharaoh's court.

The eleventh Hermetic precept goes, appropriately enough, with the mysterious Phaistos Disk theory of the Emerald Tablet of Trismegistus: the eleven-sided figure within a circle such as the Phaistos Disk stands for wonders and miracles. Eleven is a strange number that intrigued the classical Pythagoreans as well as the brilliant twentieth-century mathematician Trachtenberg. One of the oddities associated with the number is that, to discover whether a large number is exactly divisible by eleven, one need only add every second digit of that number, then subtract the total from the sum of the digits left behind. If the result of that subtraction is zero, eleven, or a multiple of eleven, then the large number will divide exactly by eleven. For example, consider the number 13,580,237. On the one hand, by adding 1+5+0+3, we get 9; on the other, we get 3+8+2+7, for a total of 20. The difference is 11, so 13,580,237 should divide exactly by 11. And it does: dividing 13,580,237 by 11 yields exactly 1,234,567 — solved in seconds with a pocket calculator today, but Trachtenberg didn't have one. Eleven was the Hermetic miracle number, the number from which wonders and marvels came. Considering the Ten Commandments, eleven could be considered as the miracle that went beyond the law, that *transcended* the law.

The twelfth precept was particularly and specifically Hermetic in nature: it was the thrice-blessed aspect of Trismegistus. Each of his three great blessings was itself divided into four portions. His philosophical blessing was his understanding of time and space, the nature of the universe, and humanity's place within it; his scientific and technological blessing was his practical knowledge and wisdom: technology, physics, chemistry and biology — the pragmatism that made his temporal life successful and enjoyable. His personal blessing was his knowledge that love is the greatest good, and that the surest path to happiness is to bestow upon others that unselfish love that enriches and blesses both the giver and the receiver. Alexander's Oath in the Temple of Opis came very close to this twelfth Hermetic precept.

The thirteenth Hermetic precept was the concept of completion and fulfillment, satisfaction and totality — the recognition that accomplishment and achievement were the ends towards which all life strove. The sun, moon and planets in their apparent movements through space, and the cycle of the earthly seasons, all had this Hermetic sense of realization.

Was all of this Hermetic symbolism to be read from the Phaistos Disk? One more curious fact about the artifact deserves careful consideration: each individual character was pressed into the clay using a stylus *with that character carved into it.* Some bygone craftsman — or woman — had gone to a great deal of trouble to produce a complete set of styli to create such disks. It seems like a reasonable assumption that the intention was to produce many more inscriptions using those same styli. So, where are the others?

There is a great deal that is good and worthwhile about those old Hermetic teachings: it is reflected in both medieval and contemporary Templar thought and in the teachings of the ancient Protectors and Guardians who preceded them. It is also central to traditional Arthurian chivalry, as delineated in the adventures of the Knights of the Round Table, and there may well be significant connections between ancient Guardian codes, Templar codes and Arthurian codes. In addition to their former Templar ranks, the authors belong to the Fellowship of the Knights of the Round Table of King Arthur (Membership Numbers 0460 and 0461), with its headquarters in King Arthur's Great Halls, Fore Street, Tintagel, Cornwall, England.

The famous Arthurian Round Table in King Arthur's Great Halls, Tintagel, Cornwall, England.

Close-up of Sir Galahad's place at the Round Table. Note especially the Templar Cross on Galahad's shield.

The strange old fountain at Couiza Montazels near Rennes-le-Château. Do these weird statues represent quinotaurs?

Detail of one of the mysterious aquatic creatures from the ancient fountain at Couiza Montazels near Rennes-le-Château in France, with its enigmatic Templar connections. Could this be a quinotaur?

Chapter 3

TEMPLARISM AND THE MYSTERY OF THE MEROVINGIANS

One of the most intriguing and mysterious characters in history is Merovech the Twice-Born, also known as Meroveus or Mérovée, the king who gave his name to the Merovingian Dynasty. These Merovingians traced their origins back to a tribe called the Sicambrians, who were part of a larger association known as the Franks. They were a powerful force in French and German affairs during the turbulent years of the fifth, sixth and seventh centuries.

If Arthur, and the myths and legends surrounding him and his Knights of the Round Table, can be placed realistically in the period that coincided with the fall of the Roman Empire and the dark aftermath of that fall, then the Arthurian period coincides with the rise of the mysterious Merovingians.

Clodius, known as the "long-haired king of the Franks," married Princess Basina of Thuringia, and legend insists that, after conceiving Mérovée, young Queen Basina went for a swim in the Mediterranean. During that swim she encountered a mysterious aquatic creature often described as a "Quinotaur" — or, in full, *bestea Neptuni Quinotauri similis*, meaning literally "an animal belonging to Neptune and resembling a Quinotaur." Neither title conveys much information, and precise descriptions of quinotaurs don't appear to exist. Apparently, the creature was not totally unattractive, and the nubile young queen was said to have been either seduced or raped by it.

There are two etymological possibilities behind the *quin* part of quinotaur. The obvious one is the simple, numerical connection: the idea that *quin* means five, hence the thing presumably had five limbs. However, the extremely wise Pythagoreans, who were likely to have been involved with the ancient Guardians, had a much subtler and sophisticated understanding of *quin*. They thought that, in addition to the four widely accepted elements (earth, air, fire and water), there was a fifth element — something purer, rarer and infinitely stronger and more dynamic than normal, terrestrial fire. This fifth element could transcend the Earth and fly up to the highest heavens: it was, in fact, the distilled essence of fire from which the stars themselves were built. Because of this mystical, stellar connection, calling the creature that helped to father Mérovée a quinotaur was a coded reference to his true origins: quinotaurs came from the stars.

The result of Basina's aquatic sexual encounter was that in some mysterious way, genetic material from the amorous quinotaur got into the future Mérovée while he was still in the womb. He therefore had *two* fathers: the Frankish King Clodius and the mysterious quinotaur! In this context, serious consideration might also be given to the myths and legends of highly intelligent and super-powerful water deities known variously as Oannes, Ea, Neptune, Poseidon, Atergatis… What if there are shreds of strange truth behind the legend of Basina's marine encounter? Is it remotely possible, especially in view of modern genetic technology, to accept the possibility that mysterious and magical King Mérovée was a hybrid between his normal earthly parents and something very strange, alien and aquatic?

Some other researchers into the mysteries of Mérovée have seen a connection between the riddle of Basina's impregnation by the quinotaur and the old legends about Jesus being the husband of Mary Magdalene and the father of her children. According to these tales, Mary escaped to the south of France after the crucifixion, ably aided and abetted by the loyal and courageous Joseph of Arimathea. In these versions she is herself depicted as the living Holy Grail, the woman who carried the bloodline of Christ by bearing his children. As she reached France from over the Mediterranean, the quinotaur legend lost all significance other than its marine nature. This hypothesis then goes on to suggest that Christ's descendants via Mary Magdalene intermarried at some early stage with the Merovingian ancestors — possibly even with Basina's Thuringians.

* * *

Thuringia has its own curious mystery centred on the legends of Tannhauser and the haunted Horselloch Cavern. This legend could in turn be linked with the Merovingian mysteries.

According to legend, Tannhauser was a combination knight and minstrel — who could well have been in the Templar tradition, and party to the ancient secrets of the Guardians. One day as he rode through Thuringia close to Mount Hörselberg, where the weird Horselloch Cavern is situated, Tannhauser heard singing more beautiful and alluring than any siren could have produced to tempt Ulysses. He also saw an exquisitely beautiful woman, and her almost equally irresistible attendants, making their way towards the Horselloch. Entranced, he followed. The woman was none other than the goddess Venus — or Aphrodite. Like a man in a dream, Tannhauser followed Venus and her beautiful handmaidens down into the eerie depths of the Horselloch.

For the next seven years, the legend recalls, Tannhauser enjoyed a sex life that the wealthiest eastern emperor would have envied — not only with her attendants but with Venus herself. At last it dawned upon him that he was, after all, supposed to be a devout and dedicated Christian knight, and that he should not really be having the time of his life with the pagan goddess of physical delights and her equally enthusiastic entourage.

With almost unbelievable strength of mind, and the greatest regret, Tannhauser tore himself away from the unlimited sexual delights of the Horselloch and made his way to the nearest priest to confess his sins and beg for absolution. The horrified priest refused. Tannhauser was referred from one sacerdotal officer to the next clerical rank above until — bishops, archbishops and cardinals all having referred him to higher authority — he begged absolution from the pope himself. His Holiness refused, saying that to absolve a man who had spent seven years enjoying the sexual favours of a pagan goddess and her nubile minions was beyond even his powers. He added, just to make the point unmistakably clear to Tannhauser, that the dry, polished, wooden staff of papal office that he held was more likely to bear shoots and leaves than was Tannhauser to find forgiveness.

Resigned to his fate, Tannhauser decided — sensibly and logically enough, given the circumstances — that if, as the pope declared, he had no chance of sharing the Christian Heaven, he might as well go back to the Horselloch and enjoy the unsurpassable female company down there until Judgment Day. And three days after he had left, the pope's staff blossomed! A fast rider was dispatched to recall Tannhauser to be absolved after all — but by the time the messenger got to Thuringia, Tannhauser was well on his way down the Horselloch. Presumably, he's still there.

There are curiously coded, symbolic links between the behaviour of the sprouting papal staff in the Tannhauser legend and the one that Joseph of Arimathea planted at Glastonbury (Mary Magdalene myths and legends almost invariable involve Joseph of Arimathea as well), tying Glastonbury in with King Arthur yet again. Tannhauser was perhaps not technically a Templar, yet he was undoubtedly a man in the Templar tradition. Mary Magdalene, referred to as a sinner (with the sexual connotations that fascinate puritans) and traditionally a reformed prostitute, links germanely with Venus-Aphrodite, in whose temples the prostitute-priestesses were often available for sex with worshippers. And the Arthurian affair between Lancelot and Guinevere connects symbolically with Mary Magdalene yet again: Venus-Aphrodite, Guinevere and Mary are seen from the same perspective.

Mary Magdalene in a mysterious cave: painting from the Rennes church.

The Lancelot figure of Arthurian romance is symbolically another Tannhauser — drawn on by irresistible sexual temptation, but possessing massive strength, courage and nobility. Whatever real or imagined wrong he may have done his friend King Arthur, Lancelot, the greatest warrior of his day, rides back to save Guinevere from the flames kindled by her hypocritical, self-righteous accusers. This also ties in with the biblical account of the "woman taken in adultery" whom her self-righteous, narrow-minded, judgmental accusers would have enjoyed stoning. There is far more to that episode than appears on the surface.

Her accusers ask Jesus for his opinion. The old Mosaic Law advocates stoning, but if Jesus agrees with Moses in this particular instance, his cunning and unscrupulous enemies will tell the Roman occupiers (who reserved the death penalty exclusively for their own overriding authority) that Jesus is a dangerous insurgent who has contravened Roman Law. To disagree with Moses is to lose Jewish support; to support Mosaic Law is to risk serious trouble with the Romans. Jesus solves the problem by saying, "Let him who is without sin among you cast the first stone at her." One by one, her accusers leave.

Christ rescued that hapless girl as surely as Lancelot rescued Guinevere. Some adventurous biblical scholars have even suggested that the girl accused of adultery and dragged before Jesus could have been his own wife, Mary Magdalene.

Her accusers in that case would have expected him to become furiously angry and make some rash statement

Statue of St. Mary Magdalene in the church in Rennes-le-Château.

about stoning her that would have given them an opportunity to accuse him of sedition against Rome.

The third strangely symbolic parallel is the loving, accepting and understanding relationship that apparently existed between Clodius and Basina. When her intimate encounter with the quinotaur is known, there is no word in the Mérovée legend of any hurt or angry reprisal on Clodius's part: no rejection of his queen.

Is there even a fourth parallel when we re-examine the Sarah-Pharaoh episode?

What it all boils down to is that, deeply hidden among the tantalizing pre-Templar Guardian codes and ciphers, there seems to be a highly significant incident involving a love triangle. In purely and simplistically moral and ethical terms, the central teaching is love, understanding, reconciliation and acceptance. This fits well with the theory that the Guardians used epithets, maxims and proverbs as part of their identification system. Taking the incident all the way back to Bereshith, are there yet further, much older, parallels with the story of Adam, Eve and the Serpent in the Garden of Eden?

Artist's impression of the sinister Serpent in Eden.

* * *

One of the great Templar mysteries seems to be that their mysterious, precursor Guardians do indeed go back to the very dawn of time.

The mystery of the Merovingians begins with Mérovée the Twice-Born and ends with the supposed death of the infant Sigebert IV, son of Dagobert II, in AD 678. If the ancient pre-Templar Guardians were involved with the episode of Basina and the quinotaur, the Templars themselves were involved with the enigmatic treasure of Rennes-le-Château and the ancient church dedicated to St. Mary Magdalene.

There are many controversial accounts of the shadowy Merovingian genealogical tree, but Dr. Gaston Sirjean's definitive, scholarly version is the most reliable. We have broadly followed his theory, but in our view, the actual succession of the Merovingian Dynasty probably consisted of:

> Clodion/Clodius (husband of Basina), 428–448
> Mérovée the Twice-Born, 448–457
> Childeric I, 457–481
> Clovis I, 481–511
> Clotaire I (Clotaire the Old), 511–561
> Chilperic I, 561–584
> Clotaire II (Clotaire the Young), 584–629
> Dagobert I, 629–639
> Sigebert III, 639–656
> Dagobert II, 656–679
> Sigebert IV, 679–? (or 676–678?)

Among the many highly controversial historical riddles that centre on the strange mountain top village of Rennes-le-Château, which we have researched in depth since 1975, are some curious — and rather suspect — coded parchments. When decoded, they seem to indicate that the mysterious treasure of Rennes-le-Château is buried alongside the body of Dagobert II — thought by some researchers to be secreted deep within a maze of tombs below the ancient foundations of the Church of St. Mary Magdalene in Rennes-le-Château.

Co-author Lionel in the pulpit of the Church of St. Mary Magdalene in Rennes-le-Château.

If Mérovée the Twice-Born was himself one of the ancient Guardians — or a trusted servant who understood their codes and secret symbols — it seems logical to assume that his descendants were also party to those great secrets.

Life for the Merovingians was precarious in the extreme. Their Dark Age centuries were times of uncertainty and constant war. It seems probable that, for safety, young Dagobert II was spirited away to Ireland and brought up in the distant monastery of Slane. Upon coming of age he married a lovely young Saxon princess named

The ancient Church of St. Mary Magdalene at Rennes-le-Château.

Mechtilde, who bore him at least three daughters and a son: the last recorded Merovingian monarch, Sigebert IV.

The account of Mechtilde's untimely death is recorded in some rather dubious documents referred to as *Dossiers Secrets*, which purport to cover various episodes and incidents in Merovingian history. The Dossiers Secrets were reportedly deposited in the Bibliothèque Nationale by one Henri Lobineau — a name that was almost certainly an alias. Some researchers have suggested that he was really Leo Schidlof, an Austrian art expert, who died in 1966 — and cannot now be questioned. Other investigators have suggested that Lobineau was really Henri de Lenoncourt, a French aristocrat using the Lobineau pseudonym for reasons of security. The most likely explanation, however, is that an unknown Jesus and Mary Magdalene bloodline enthusiast simply deposited the fictional Merovingian papers using the name Lobineau. There are, unfortunately, some devoted enthusiasts who will go to extraordinary lengths to modify the evidence in order to support cherished theories. One pyramidologist, for example, was caught sawing off a piece of ancient stone at Gizeh because the measurements did not fit the calculations he had worked on for years!

In George Orwell's grimly realistic *Nineteen Eighty-Four*, the Thought Police serving the totalitarian dictatorship can play havoc with history — and "reality" is only what the state allows it to be. Orwell's dystopia is not a million miles away from the techniques used by prejudiced politicians and their time-serving, sycophantic court historians to modify reality to fit in with the whims of the powerful. It would have been very convenient for some theories for Mechtilde to die young so that Dagobert II could remarry. This alleged remarriage was to Giselle de Razès, part of a noble ruling family said to be connected to the Jesus and Mary Magdalene bloodline via Mérovée.

We may reasonably discard the flimsy Lobineau evidence for Mechtilde's death, and go instead with mainstream historical theory that includes the death of Dagobert II, leaving her as a young widow. We then find that there is also some reasonable doubt about the death in infancy of young Sigebert IV, Dagobert II's son and heir. The boy and his mother are left in a politically precarious position. The ruthless new Carolingian Dynasty will not feel safe until the last Merovingian claimants are well and truly gone. What could be safer for Dagobert II's family than to spread the story that the infant Sigebert IV (and Mechtilde herself) are dead? What if, disguised as one of her own loyal servant girls, Mechtilde takes her children back to her Saxon homeland — a place where she and they are protected?

There are strong and persistent rumours that Dagobert II and his infant son (who did *not* predecease him) were ambushed. The king entrusted the infant — and the secret of the mysterious Rennes Treasure — to a servant whom he trusted absolutely. Dagobert then fought off the attackers as long as he could while his son was carried away to safety. What evidence is there for this interpretation of the end of the mysterious Merovingian Dynasty? The enigmatic *Dalle du Chevalier* provides a strange but compelling clue.

The mysterious Dalle du Chevalier found at Rennes-le-Château.

This curious old carved stone was discovered in the floor of the ancient Church of St. Mary Magdalene in Rennes-le-Château during the late nineteenth century. As far as can be discerned, it seems to show a lone warrior on the left, and two figures — perhaps a man and a child — on another horse on the right. The two archways in the old carving are remarkably similar to the archways in the ancient Château at Rennes which gives the village its name.

Are these ancient archways in the Château at Rennes connected symbolically with the archways carved into the Dalle du Chevalier?

Is the ancient Dalle du Chevalier telling those who can read its strange symbolism that the secret of the Rennes Treasure lies somewhere below the Château rather than under the church?

The ancient ruined Château Hautpoul at Rennes, which gives the village its name.

Is it also saying that the infant Sigebert IV *did* escape from his enemies and grow to manhood? If he did, what place does he have in the mysterious Merovingian bloodline and its claims to be related to Jesus and Mary Magdalene — not via Giselle de Razès, who never married Dagobert II, but via Mechtilde, who retreated to safety in Saxony with Sigebert IV, the boy who carried his father's mysterious Merovingian genes? And where does the strange tale of Basina and the quinotaur fit into all this? Is it meant to be understood literally or symbolically?

The questions remain. Where do the Merovingians feature in the mystery of the pre-Templar Guardians? What strange truth lies behind the legends of Mérovée the Twice-Born? Did Mechtilde and Sigebert IV escape to Saxony? What does the Dalle du Chevalier really tell us?

Chapter 4

WHO SENT THE TEMPLARS TO JERUSALEM — AND WHY?

The case for the existence of an older, far stranger and more powerful order than the twelfth- and thirteenth-century Knights Templar is a strong one. The earliest written records, ancient religious manuscripts, sagas, myths and legends from the dawn of prehistory, all point in similar directions. In their different ways — and taking into account the cultural and ethnic differences distinguishing the creators of these records and stories — much of the evidence seems to point in seven clear and converging directions:

1. There were beings with greater strength, greater power and greater intelligence than early humanity — and they apparently coexisted with us from the very beginning.

2. These beings were believed to have originated from some other realm (Paradise, the stars, caverns at the Earth's core, seas and oceans) or from some very advanced and powerful society. Some researchers might venture to suggest the legends of Atlantis or Lemuria in this connection.

3. A number of the beings were benign, didactic, paternal, protective and altruistically concerned with guiding and improving human morality and ethical behaviour. Others were malign, destructive, unpredictable, hostile and negatively intrusive.

4. Biologically, these beings were sufficiently similar to us to have sexual relationships with our ancestors and, as a result, to produce remarkable, hybrid offspring — usually possessing some of the non-human parent's advanced characteristics.

5. These superior beings and their quasi-human descendants enjoyed greater longevity than ours — perhaps even immortality.

6. There were frequent reports of wars, battles and conflicts among various groups of them, and between those prominent individuals who led the super beings. Such conflicts involved aerial combat and awesome weaponry — such as Zeus's thunderbolts and Indra's darts.

7. These beings seemed able to control vast forces that nevertheless worked systematically and were governed by consistent rules and principles. Were their superior powers merely based on an advanced technology that only *suggested* the idea of magic to our earliest ancestors? Or did they actually *have* powers that were truly paranormal?

* * *

At this point, we need to digress into behaviourist psychology, and in particular, Skinner's rats and pigeons. The great American psychologist B.F. Skinner lived from 1904 until 1990. Born in Susquehanna, Pennsylvania, he took his doctorate at Harvard in 1931. This was followed by a distinguished academic career that led to the Edgar Pierce Professorship in Psychology in 1958. His behaviourist psychology hypothesized that human and animal behaviour can best be understood in terms of the physiological responses of organisms to external stimuli. The central points of the behaviourist hypothesis were that learning took place when the organism acted upon — or responded to — its environment — hence the famous behaviourist phrase *operant conditioning.*

Working with rats and pigeons, Skinner invented the famous Skinner Box — a device in which a rat learned to press a lever to obtain a food reward. Rewards and stimuli were therefore central to behaviourist learning theory. His lengthy and impressive work in academic psychology can best be summed up by one memorable statement: "The consequences of behaviour determine the probability that the behaviour will occur again."

Whoever the ancient Guardians and superior beings actually were, and wherever they originated, their interactions with early human beings often seem to have taken on the characteristics of behaviourist psychologists — with normal terrestrial humanoids (like us) serving as their rats and pigeons. The central behaviourist idea that the presence or absence of rewards and punishments determines our future behaviour figures prominently in much of the religious thinking of antiquity.

A common scenario has Character A defying the gods in some way by breaking an important taboo concerning territory, clothing, food, drink or sexual behaviour. Character A is killed by a thunderbolt, stricken with leprosy, bitten by a venomous snake, gored by a bull or eaten by a lion. The taboo is, therefore, powerfully reinforced for all observers. Character B prays and worships regularly, gives generously to the priests and carefully observes all the local god or goddess's religious rules and regulations. Character B is prosperous, lives to be over 100 and enjoys excellent health. Once again the behaviour is reinforced. Early priests, prophets and religious leaders proclaim that sin leads to trouble, while exemplary behaviour leads to rich rewards — and naturally reinforce their arguments by reference to characters A and B.

The fly enters the behaviourist-learning ointment when a good and innocent Character C (like Job in the Old Testament) leads a perfect life, endures abject poverty, suffers abominably and dies prematurely, while Character D (selfish, arrogant, vicious, totally untrustworthy and immoral) is observed to have the swiftest chariot, the most luxurious palace, the finest foods and wines and the most delectable harem in the known world. He seems immune from all disease and degeneration and is apparently all but indestructible. When he finally dies, it is comfortably in bed at the age of 120. The newest and loveliest of his innumerable slave girls is in his arms, and there's a broad, contented smile on his face.

This blows a hole wider than the Pacific Ocean through the religious operant conditioning of the day. The link between desired, socially approved behaviour and appropriate rewards is snapped like a paper garland. How are the ancient Guardians — assuming that they exist — going to train and educate us, when the reward-and-punishment system so clearly fails to reinforce the behaviour they want us to acquire? The pigeons are flying away! The rats are gnawing their way out of the box!

Perhaps the deep, dark secret of those who were *really* in the know was that the ostensible links between human behaviour and life's material rewards and punishments were unreal. The Guardians knew perfectly well that when those who were religiously "good" benefited from earthly rewards, it had nothing to do with their devout religious behaviour or their observance of religious rules, regulations and taboos. Similarly, when those who were notoriously, religiously "bad" enjoyed the best temporal things that earthly life could offer them, it had nothing to do with their disregard of religious or social mores. Suppose that, in ancient times, the cognoscenti knew that. The vital information the Secret Guardians had access to was the *real* connection between temporal cause and effect; their dilemma was that their control of primitive terrestrial humanity depended largely upon "religious" operant conditioning.

At a deeper and far more important level, the Secret Guardians also knew that blatant temporal rewards were not all that they appeared to be. The good, honest, unselfish, caring and loving individual who had none of this world's goods — nor any of its secular pleasures — had an inner peace, a deep spiritual satisfaction and sense of true fulfillment that was, in the scale of eternal verities, worth infinitely more than luxurious palaces and all-conquering armies. Such individuals could live with themselves: their consciences were clear, and that was of inestimable value. Such individuals also knew that the true and total lifelong love and commitment of one permanent and faithful partner brought infinitely greater happiness than any harem, however full.

* * *

At some time around the end of the eleventh century and the early years of the twelfth, it seems that the ancient Guardians, in whatever form they then existed, saw the need to locate and protect something of major importance — something associated with the ancient power, wisdom and wealth of King Solomon.

A key figure in this aspect of the twelfth-century Templar mystery — and one whose critical role is all too often ignored, overlooked or drastically underestimated — is the mighty and knowledgeable Bernard of Clairvaux, one of the most significant powers behind the Knights Templar.

Bernard was born in 1091 at Fontaines, near Dijon, in Burgundy. His father, Tescelin Sorrel, also known as Sorus, was a Burgundian knight who was said by some historians to have died during the First Crusade (1096–1099). He is also said, by other sources, to have been a convert to a religious way of life, and to have accompanied his famous son to a monastery. If the theories are amalgamated — and it may be suggested that Tescelin survived the First Crusade before entering Bernard's order — it raises the question of what he found out in the Holy Lands and communicated to his son before death overtook him.

Bernard's mother, Aleth de Montbard, had a great reputation for piety, and she is believed to have been the central religious influence on Bernard's subsequent life and spiritual thought. Aleth was the daughter of Bernard Montbard and his wife, Humberge de Taillefer.

St. Bernard's father, Tescelin, is something of a mystery man. Genealogical research into his ancestry runs into the buffers, apart from recording his birth as circa 1050. Did Tescelin have any curious links with the lost Merovingians, Dagobert II and Sigebert IV? Tescelin must have been someone out of the ordinary to rise as he did to the highest ranks of eleventh-century Burgundian nobility and to be considered as a suitable spouse for the high-born Lady Aleth of Montbard — with Taillefer connections on her mother's side. It is fascinating to note this probable link between Bernard's mother, Lady Aleth, and William Tallifer (the spellings of Taillefer and Tallifer were not consistent in the eleventh century) — he was William III, Count of Toulouse, and these counts of Toulouse were connected with the mysterious Cathar heretics, who were also called Albigensians.

Assuming for the sake of argument that Tescelin did ride out on the First Crusade and there, in the Middle East, encountered strange, esoteric knowledge that he brought back to Fontaines, how much of that strange data did he share with his brilliant young son, Bernard?

The Crusaders were accompanied by a French monk and mystic named Peter Bartholomew, who claimed that he began having strange visions of St. Andrew during the Siege of Antioch in 1097. In the course of that First Crusade, Catholic European forces helped the Byzantine Empire to fight the Seljuk Turks, as well as to regain control of Jerusalem, which was in Muslim hands at the time.

After the Crusaders had succeeded in capturing Antioch, Peter Bartholomew proclaimed that he had been told, in yet another mystical dream or vision, that the Lance of Longinus — otherwise known as the Spear of Destiny — was hidden under the floor of the ancient church of St. Peter. Bartholomew duly led Raymond IV, Count of Toulouse, to the spot — where together they recovered the miraculous lance. This discovery inspired the Crusaders to ride out triumphantly against the Muslim army that had begun besieging Antioch almost as soon as the Christian forces had captured it.

The concept of divine, magical weapons goes much further back than the Christian era: Zeus's thunderbolts, for example, and Indra's dart were lance-like, aerial projectiles. It is also interesting to note that the priests of Baal, who confronted the prophet Elijah on Mount Carmel, also cut themselves "with knives and lances" (I Kings 18:28) — did they believe that their lances had some magical or religious significance? It is possible that a pre-Christian legend of some powerful, magical spear was Christianized into the legend of the Lance of Longinus, the Spear of Destiny.

In Christian-era myth and legend, this lance or spear of destiny, was averred to be the one that had pierced the side of Christ — according to the account of the crucifixion in John's gospel (Chapter 19, Verses 31–37). The Roman soldier who was said to have used it at the crucifixion was thought to have been a certain Gaius Cassius Longinus — a man of the same name was associated with the conspiracy to assassinate Julius Caesar. The spear was said to have been exhibited in the Mount Zion Basilica in the sixth century. When the Persians occupied Jerusalem in the seventh century, the lance allegedly broke and its head was incorporated into a sacred icon in the Church of Hagia Sophia in what was then called Constantinople (now Istanbul).

This legendary Spear of Destiny was credited with the ability to give its holder power to conquer the world: Constantine, Justinian, Alaric the Visigoth, Charlemagne and Barbarossa were all said to have used it. In relatively modern times Kaiser Wilhelm II of Germany and Adolf Hitler were both said to have had control of it at critical moments.

It was also part of the lance's legend that if its holder *lost* possession of it, he would die swiftly. In March of 1938, Hitler had taken it from the Hofmuseum in Vienna; technically, therefore, he was then its controller. However, as Germany collapsed at the end of World War II, an American lieutenant, Walter William Horn, formally took possession of the lance in the name of the United States government. The date was April 30, 1945 — the same day that Hitler, supposedly, committed suicide.

General Dwight David Eisenhower, who was then running the show, insisted on the lance being returned to the Habsburgs who had owned it during their days as Holy Roman Emperors. Accordingly, it was sent back to the Hofburg Treasure House.

Another pretender to the role of the original lance, or Spear of Destiny, is said to be held at Etschmiadzin in Armenia, and there's yet another reputedly ancient Holy Lance in Krakow.

How much did Tescelin the Crusader know about the lance? He was very probably at the Siege of Antioch when it was discovered. Is the lance possibly one of the strange and mysterious things that the twelfth-century Knights Templar dug for near the site of Solomon's Temple in Jerusalem?

There are interesting connections linking Bernard of Clairvaux with the Languedoc and the Counts of Toulouse who ruled it — and who were almost certainly related to his mother, Aleth. Bernard also encountered the Cathar sect, which was prominent and influential there. While almost every other church leader was criticizing the Cathars and condemning them as heretics, Bernard found them quite likable and spoke of their genuine piety and virtue. His fiercest criticisms were levelled at the corruption and laxity within the hypocritical Church, which pompously regarded itself as the orthodox defender of the real faith.

Is it possible that Bernard himself had some secret sympathy for the dualistic gnosticism of the Cathars? This suggestion must be treated with caution. Bernard enjoyed nature and the natural environment, much as Francis of Assisi did. Cathars, on the other hand, disliked nature because they believed that all physical matter was the creation of the evil demiurge. Their theology was based on a type of cosmic dualism in which the good God was pure spirit, while physical matter had been created by evil.

Bernard's cryptic comment rings down the centuries: "I know with certainty, so you must believe me: you will find something greater and more important in the forests than in any books. Trees and stones can teach you far more than the wisest men can teach you."

Did the wise and subtle Bernard mean more than he seemed to be saying? When he referred poetically to stones and trees, was he actually hinting that there were coded, symbolic clues in *certain* stones and trees — clues that could well lead to a mysterious treasure or a vast, ancient power source? Had this arcane knowledge come down to him from the ancient, secret Guardians?

* * *

Rennes-le-Château in the Languedoc features prominently in the medieval Templar treasure mysteries, and so does the neighbouring village of Rennes-les-Bains. When the mysterious Bérenger Saunière was priest at Rennes-le-Château, an equally mysterious character named Henri Jean-Jacques Boudet was the priest at Rennes-les-Bains. Boudet wrote, published, and then, surprisingly, tried to recall all the copies of an enigmatic book entitled *Le Vraie Langue Celtique et le Cromleck de Rennes-les-Bains,* which translates as *The True Celtic Language and the Cromlech of Rennes-les-Bains.* What was so strange and mysterious about that ancient stone? Was it, perhaps, one of the special "teaching stones" to which Bernard referred?

In addition to the strange old cromlech that captivated Boudet, there were two other very significant stones in the vicinity of Rennes-le-Château. The first was the gravestone of the last of the Hautpoul line: Marie de Negre.

The mysterious coded tombstone of Marie de Negre. The inscription was erased by Father Bérenger Saunière, priest at Rennes-le-Château.

The ruined Château that gives Rennes its name today is the venerable Château Hautpoul. There are many researchers who concur with the theory that this stone was once engraved with an epitaph to Marie de Negre, and that this epitaph was itself part of a very complex Templar-style code. Whatever was once written on her stone was deliberately destroyed by Saunière well over a century ago.

The second of the enigmatic stones in the Rennes area was a table-type tomb identical to the tomb painted by Nicholas Poussin as part of *Les Bergers d'Arcadie*. It shows three shepherds and a shepherdess deciphering the grim inscription *Et in Arcadia ego* cut into the stonework of the tomb.

The Tomb of Arques near Rennes-le-Château, which replicated the tomb in the Poussin shepherds picture. The upper parts of the Tomb of Arques have now been destroyed. Why?

Experts have argued over this Arcadian theme for many years. It can be taken to mean, "Although my body lies here, my spirit is in Arcadia, the perfect land of eternal joy." It can also mean, "Even here in Arcadia, the perfect land, I, Death, am present." Another school of thought prefers the idea of the fabulous Arcadian treasure as the subject of the inscription. For them, the painted tomb is saying, "I, the treasure, am hidden in Arcadia."

The challenge, then, is to find Arcadia: where and what, exactly, does Poussin the painter mean by Arcadia? Painters such as Poussin and da Vinci tended to have their own secret codes — some of which were shared by members of the profession, while others were not.

Part of the answer may lie in, or near, Shugborough Hall in Staffordshire, England, where a curious monument — like a mirror image of another version of the Poussin shepherd painting — is carved in the grounds. That Shugborough monument provides yet another curious stone clue. Who erected it? What does the enigmatic code below it mean?

The curious Shepherd Monument in the grounds of Shugborough Hall. Does it carry a secret Templar code?

The table-tomb near Rennes — resembling the ones in the painting and the carving at Shugborough — was recently situated at Arques. The modern part of it was barely a century old, but it had been erected by the Lawrence family, who were originally from America, over a much older subterranean tomb that could well have been familiar to medieval Knights Templar. We examined this tomb thoroughly on our visits to Rennes-le-Château, even photographing the interior.

Other Rennes researchers have recorded finding a strange wheel-and-chain device in the older part of the Tomb of Arques, deep below the relatively recent table-top. The Tomb of Arques stood close to the River Sals, and this leads to another theory regarding its original purpose.

The foundations of the ancient church dedicated to Mary Magdalene at Rennes are believed to be Visigothic. It was the Visigoths' practice to bury their leaders below the beds of rivers. The river would be dammed; a tomb would be dug in its bed and made watertight. The dead ruler would then be laid there with his armour, his weapons, his horse and his treasure. The tomb would next be covered to make it indistinguishable from the rest of the riverbed. Finally, the dam would be destroyed, allowing the waters to flow back over the tomb as though nothing had ever disturbed the river's natural course. It created an almost perfect hiding place.

A sample page from the intricate research work undertaken by M. Fatin, the brilliant sculptor from Rennes-le-Château. In his opinion, the village itself has been laid out as a gigantic "Ship of the Dead" conveying the body of some truly awesome warrior-leader. Does that leader now lie below the River Sals, close to the Tomb of Arques at Pontils?

If some great and important person from Rennes-le-Château's Visigothic past — or even earlier — had been buried in the River Sals, might not the mysterious Tomb of Arques at nearby Pontils have provided a secret route into that sealed, submerged tomb?

Early-twentieth-century coffins deep in the Tomb of Arques. But what ancient mysteries lie below these decaying coffins? Does a tunnel lead from this tomb to another under the riverbed?

Co-author Lionel measuring the Tomb of Arques

A few years ago, however, the upper part of the tomb of Arques was entirely destroyed. There had to be a reason for that — just as there had to be a reason why Bérenger Saunière destroyed the allegedly coded inscription on the tombstone of Marie de Negre, the last Hautpoul.

That great supporter and reinforcer of the Knights Templar, Bernard of Clairvaux, may well have meant something of great significance when he referred to what could be learned from trees and stones. Did the Languedoc Cathars in and around the Rennes area share some of their strange secrets with Bernard, who was clearly both good and trustworthy? Did that information, along with what Tescelin had told him after the First Crusade, inspire Bernard to create the Templar Order, whose quest was to search out and protect some deep, awesome, ancient secret? To what extent were the Arthurian stories of the Grail Quest a symbolic, coded message pointing to what the Templars were doing in Jerusalem in the twelfth century?

There can be little doubt that the Templars of Languedoc knew the Cathars well, and sympathetic Templars may also have been party to the Cathar mountaineers' escape from Montsegur in 1244.

The Cathar stronghold of Montsegur in southwestern France. What ancient secrets did the Cathar mountaineers escape with in 1244?

Co-author Patricia inside the ruined Cathar fortress of Montsegur.

In a nutshell, the Cathars of the Languedoc fell victim to the Church's accusation of heresy, and the formidable fortification at Montsegur was one of their last strongholds. Just as Bernard had been sympathetic to their high social and moral principles, so too had some of the noble and generous-hearted Templars of Languedoc.

The attacks on the Cathars began at the start of the thirteenth century. There were three basic motives for them. The Cathars had grown so strong and numerous that, by 1167, Bulgarian Bishop Nicetas arranged a meeting for the Cathar Bishops at St. Félix de Caraman, near Toulouse. Their religious enemies could no longer spurn or ignore them as a mere minor sect comprising a few quaintly deluded heretics: they had grown into a flourishing and prosperous rival church! The jealous northern knights and other aristocrats wanted the prosperous Cathar Languedoc for themselves. They welcomed any excuse for an attack which offered such potentially rich plunder. The church felt that both its basic teachings and the power it derived from feudalism were threatened by the egalitarian Cathar doctrines, which were sincerely held and incorporated into their everyday lives by the Cathars and their followers.

Their enemies also suspected that the Cathars possessed ancient secrets and powerful, mysterious artifacts — which both the feudal lords of the north and the rulers of the church naturally wanted for themselves. There were whispers among their greedy, jealous enemies to the effect that the Cathars might well be guarding the Holy Grail, the Ark of the Covenant, Urim and Thummim and the Emerald Tablets of Hermes Trismegistus. The Cathars were accordingly in very grave danger.

The oldest parts of Montsegur had at one time been more of a shrine and place for prayer, meditation and worship than a fortress. Sensing their peril, the Cathars and their supporters now fortified it. They successfully repulsed a number of attacks, but in 1244, after a gallant struggle that lasted for months, the defenders of Montsegur finally surrendered.

Surprisingly, their enemies offered very lenient surrender terms. Provided that no one left the fortress or attempted to take anything away from it, the garrison could more or less go home quietly as if nothing had happened — but if anyone attempted to leave prematurely, they would all be burned. Despite this grim threat, four Cathars, including Amiel Aicart, were lowered down the precipitous west face of the huge rock on which Montsegur stands. They carried with them "the treasures of their faith" — whatever that meant. There is no record of these four men or their treasure ever having fallen into the hands of the authorities. In Zoe Oldenbourg's definitive work *Massacre at Montsegur*, this mysterious treasure is referred

Memorial to the Cathars who were burned alive in Champs de Cramatchs at Montsegur in 1244.

to as *pecuniam infinitam* — literally, unlimited (or infinite) money. Even as these four desperate Cathars escaped with what to them was more important than their friends' lives or their own, more than two hundred other Cathars were being burned alive in what is still known today as *Champs de Cramatchs* — the Field of the Burned Ones. It is marked today by a solemn memorial stone.

Even today, Montsegur has not yielded all its ancient secrets. Contemporary accounts referred to a labyrinth of caverns and passageways beneath the fortress. The phrase *infra castrum* is used in the testimony of Bérenger de Lavelanet. In his *Histoires des Albigeois*, Peyrat gives credence to this theory.

In attempting to suggest answers to the question with which this chapter began (the question of who sent the Templars to Jerusalem and why), we are left juggling several tantalizing possibilities. Bernard of Clairvaux and his family were unquestionably good and powerful people, but it seems likely that they had access to some of the strange and mysterious knowledge associated with the ancient, pre-Templar Guardians.

There are tenebrous, camouflaged connections linking Bernard's people, the Cathars, the Counts of Toulouse, the missing Merovingians, and the strange secrets of Rennes-le-Château — to which some of the Templars were almost certain to have been party. Bernard was one of those who saw the need for the right heroes — his indomitable Templars — to be in the right place at the right time. But there were other reasons for them to be there. To appreciate those equally mysterious factors, we need to explore the history of Rennes-le-Château and its environs in greater depth.

Chapter 5

THE TEMPLARS AND THE SECRETS OF SEPTIMANIA

The first inhabitants of Rennes and its area of the Languedoc were Neolithic or even earlier. Archaeological finds at or near Rennes have included flint arrowheads, basic hand tools, primitive pottery and simple beakers. The next detectable inhabitants seem to have been the Tectosages, a Celtic people whose name meant "wise builders" or "skillful builders." Later, as the Roman Empire spread out to the Languedoc, the Tectosages were driven away. The Romans left behind a great many traces of their presence — including the famous thermal baths that gave Rennes-les-Bains its name.

Before the Romans were supplanted by the Visigoths in the early years of the fifth century, they set up what was destined to become one of the most interesting and intriguing parts of the whole Languedoc: Septimania. Its original purpose during the reign of Augustus Caesar was to provide a settlement for veterans of the Roman Seventh Legion — hence its name, derived from the Latin word for "seventh." Septimania was later to include Roman citizens with Jewish backgrounds, and their highly beneficial presence in the territory contributed enormously to the culture and commercial prosperity of the Languedoc in general. In the truly multicultural Languedoc of those days, Jews and Arabs, Franks, Gauls and Romans seemed able to live together with tolerance, and, in many cases, with genuine friendship. It was an idyllic situation while it lasted, and one which our own turbulent, tragic and intolerant world could learn from.

Geographically, Septimania was situated between the Pyrenees and the Cévennes mountain ranges and was bounded by the Rhône and Garonne rivers. It is now organized into the French administrative departments of Aude, Gard, Hérault and Pyrénées-Orientales.

The Visigoths were very much in evidence — in fact, this was their last Gallic territory. They had originally been driven westward by the advance of the Huns from the east, and it was to the Visigoths that the Rennes-le-Château area owed its early name of Rhedae — a word connected with the idea of "travelling chariots." To that extent the Visigoths were not unlike the nineteenth-century American pioneers moving resolutely across the continent from eastern cities in covered wagons. The Visigoths set up an entrenched fortification all around their living wagons.

Arabian conquerors from Africa travelled by way of Spain and Gibraltar and quickly overran most of Septimania. This made the Visigoths retreat into their well-fortified defences at Rhedae, which some authorities believe then became the capital of Septimania. The Franks rose to prominence, drove back the Visigoths and the Arabian invaders, then ran Septimania themselves for a few years in the eighth century before it became part of Carolingian Aquitaine. By the end of the ninth century, however, it was under the jurisdiction of the counts of Toulouse — including William III, the Tallifer with probable family connections to Aleth, mother of Bernard of Clairvaux.

Co-author Lionel at the site of the Battle of Hastings, where the Norman hero Taillefer died in 1066. Was he related to Taillefer, Count of Toulouse?

Another Taillefer, or Tallifer, was a brilliant warrior-minstrel who accompanied William the Conqueror to England in 1066. He struck the first blow in the Battle of Hastings and died fighting during that battle. The fearless Taillefer is honoured on the Bayeux Tapestry, and tradition maintains that he led the Norman attack, singing about the exploits of Charlemagne and Roland as he went. Apart from his immense courage and inspirational leadership, almost nothing is known of him. He could well have been one of the aristocratic Languedoc Taillefers and, as such, a forerunner of the noble and indomitable Templars of that region.

Memorial plaque to King Harold, who died in the Battle of Hastings in 1066, during which the Norman hero, the warrior-minstrel Taillefer, also died.

* * *

In Septimania, the combination of ancient Jewish wisdom from the Cabala and the strange, mystical secrets of the Cathars created a volatile mixture of arcane knowledge that the Templars eagerly explored. It is perhaps possible to envisage the secret workings of the ancient Guardians in bringing cabalistic Jewish wisdom and Christian gnosticism together in Septimania. And dedicated numerologists smile knowingly at the name of the territory: the number seven is very significant to them.

What exactly was this cabalistic knowledge that the Templars eventually acquired in Septimania? The word, which can be spelled in many ways, including Qabbala and Kabbalah, actually means "received" — implying that the data contained in the Cabala has been handed down from the remote past. The heart of cabalistic teaching is an esoteric doctrine centred on the nature of God and of the universe. Its very existence supports the theory of an elite, exclusive order of ancient Guardians to whom the mysterious truth has been revealed. One important mystical text, as far as students of the Cabala are concerned, is known as the Sefer Yetzirah. Its contents were regarded as vitally important by the Maskilim, meaning those who were wise in the ways of the Cabala. They emphasize the distinct importance of every single letter and every separate word in their mystical text — even accents and numbers have their special significance. It is the most detailed of all codes — and one of the hardest to decipher and interpret.

Although "Cabala" originally referred only to those portions of Hebrew scripture and oral traditions that were *not* in the Pentateuch (the books of Genesis, Exodus, Leviticus, Numbers and Deuteronomy), the definition changed and developed over time until it came to encompass the whole of the deep, ancient, mystical and secret Jewish knowledge.

Because of their interest in subtle wordplay, the cabalists might just possibly have optimized the pun available in the noble Languedoc name Hautpoul — one-time owners of the ancient Chateau Hautpoul in Rennes-le-Château. Hautpoul literally translates as "high chicken" — implying the most important one, the most famous one, or the dominant one. In French argot, *poule* was the affectionately possessive term that a pimp used for the working girls he organized and protected — "*mes poules.*" If this idea is attached to the tradition of Mary Magdalene ("the woman who was a sinner") being a prostitute before her conversion — synonymous, perhaps, with "the woman taken in adultery," then she becomes the highest, or best known *poule*: the "hautpoul," in fact. Did the ancient Hautpoul family claim descent from her? The cabalists often called themselves *hen*, meaning "grace," which was a clever Hebrew acrostic for "secret knowledge" or "secret science." Were they also thinking of "hen" in the sense of *poule* or "chicken"?

They also referred to themselves as "the wise," or "the people who understand," and an example of this special cabalistic usage of the phrase is found in the strangely coded, symbolic and apocalyptic book

THE TEMPLARS AND THE SECRETS OF SEPTIMANIA

of Daniel (Chapter 12, Verse 10): "… none of the wicked shall understand, but *the wise shall understand…*"

The Cabala falls naturally into two distinct sections: theoretical and practical. Its followers believe that the second part, the practical part known as *ma'asit*, is tantamount to a very powerful and effective form of white magic involving the use of the secret, sacred names of God. In cabalistic codes these names are cautiously referred to as "the Crown." Close analysis of cabalistic magical practices reveals that their most erudite leaders issued strict warnings about the use of magic — even the "white" variety that was supposedly used to aid prayer and meditation. Some cabalists found it difficult to draw a clear line between "white" and "black" magic, and this was particularly the case when they undertook exorcisms, the creation of amulets, and even necromancy.

Another variant line of cabalistic thought focused on the concept of "God's Throne" as described in the Book of Ezekiel, which is also full of strange mysticism, codes, ciphers and symbols. For example, in Chapter 1, Verses 26 and 27, Ezekiel describes something that sounds very like the pilot's command module in a spaceship — except that Ezekiel describes what he can see in magical rather than in technical terms: "And above the firmament that was over their heads was the likeness of a throne, as the appearance of a sapphire stone: and upon the likeness of the throne was the likeness as the appearance of a man above upon it. And I saw as the colour of amber, as the appearance of fire round about within it, from the appearance of his loins even upward, and from the appearance of his loins even downward, I saw as it were the appearance of fire, and it had brightness round about." Here is an honest and observant man describing the unknown in terms of the known. Things are *as* other things; they have the *appearance* of other things; they have the *likeness* of other things.

Cabalists use the term *Merkabah* to describe their concept of God's Throne, and the dangerous ascent to it via various mystical, planetary spheres guarded by hostile superior beings. More than one serious researcher has concluded that Ezekiel was in contact with extraterrestrial aliens — but the evidence for and against that hypothesis deserves a volume or two in its own right!

In simple, physiological, anatomical terms, there are cabalistic references to *yorde merkava* — literally descending, or going down, to the Throne — which could imply that the mystics who underwent the experience assumed a stylized, meditative posture with their heads down in order to induce a trance, or altered state of consciousness.

Another important symbol for the cabalists is the orchard, particularly — as referred to in the highly symbolic Song of Solomon in the Old Testament (Chapter 6, Verse 11) — an orchard of nuts, vines and pomegranates.

The cabalistic secrets were hidden like the seeds of the pomegranate, or the kernel inside the nutshell.

The Song of Solomon also contains symbolic references to the physical size, splendour and strength of the body of the "beloved" — he can be compared to a kind of Iranian *urmensch* or super being, and there are ancient Coptic and Hellenistic writings dating back almost two millennia which describe a parallel figure. Are the cabalists here simply referring to a magical, heavenly being such

Curious cabalistic symbolism of the pomegranate in the Song of Solomon.

as Metatron — who in their thinking was second only to Yahweh — or have they made contact with a gigantic, alien humanoid with vast technological power? The fact that in the Song of Solomon this superior being has an Earth girl as a lover links to the ideas in Bereshith (Genesis 6:2): "That the sons of God saw the daughters of men that they were fair; and they took them wives of all that they chose."

Botnim, or pistachio tree — a cabalistic symbol used in the Song of Solomon.

The so-called "Book of Clarity," otherwise known to the cabalists as *Sefer Bahir*, can confidently be traced to Provence, to Septimania and to the Languedoc. The Sefer Bahir contains many references to magic, and much of it seems to be based on another, older work called *Raza Rabba*, which translates as "The Great Mystery." This volume apparently reached Provence from the east, and was also well known among German cabalists of the period.

What does emerge from this effervescent maelstrom of secrets, ciphers and symbols is that in the twelfth and thirteenth centuries there was a very complex and volatile mixture of Templars, cabalists, Cathars, Bogomils, Paulicians and Manichaeans operating in Provence, the Languedoc and Septimania — together with a strong suspicion that the Essenes had also had a hand in matters.

* * *

The daughters of men were fair.

Philo of Alexandria (30 BC–AD 40) wrote at first hand about the Essenes, and regarded them as extremely wise and virtuous. The prolific first-century Romano-Jewish historian Josephus Flavius (AD 37–100) wrote during the reigns of Vespasian, Titus and Domitian. Josephus also had a high opinion of Essene virtue and maintained that they had the Cabala, and guarded it to the best of their ability. But who, exactly, were these Essenes?

Interest has been focused on them since the discovery of the Dead Sea
Scrolls just after World War II. Regarded by scholars as one of the most
important archaeological discoveries of the twentieth century, the first
scrolls came to light when a boy threw a stone into a cave near Qumran
and heard a jar smash. Climbing up to the mysterious cave, he discovered
the first batch of Dead Sea Scrolls. From 1947 until 1956, eleven caves were
discovered by the northwestern shore of the Dead Sea. The region, barely
a dozen miles from Jerusalem and a clear 400 metres above sea level, is very
dry and arid — a climate that undoubtedly helped to preserve the scrolls
for two millennia or more. In any case, nearly nine hundred of them must
have been there originally. Many are written on animal skin; some on
papyrus; and one very important and remarkable scroll is on copper. The
writers used a carbon-based ink, wrote from right to left, and were innocent of all punctuation. Some of the scrolls are biblical; others are not.
Almost every Old Testament book is represented among the fragments,
and there is a special emphasis on Messianic prophecy — the belief that a
great leader, the Messiah, is coming to save the Hebrews. Many are written
in Hebrew, some in Aramaic, and a few in Greek.

It looks as if the motive for hiding the scrolls during the First Jewish
Revolt (AD 66–70) was the inexorable advance of the highly disciplined
and effective Roman army. The ancient scroll village of Qumran was
excavated during the 1950s, and it provided ample evidence of being
closely connected to both the mysterious Essenes and the Dead Sea
Scrolls. Qumran may also have been closely connected with the Cabala,
and may have housed a number of those Maskilim who understood its
deep riddles. Were copies of those cabalistic secrets also hidden in a
labyrinthine maze of secret caves deep below the Dome of the Rock,
where the first nine Templars dug and searched so industriously? Did
later Essenes — or former Essenes who had left the sect's base in Qumran
shortly before the troubles of AD 66 began in earnest — make their way
with other Roman Jews to the relative peace and stability of Septimania?

Essenes were preachers of peace and lovers of peace. Did their cabal-
istic secrets somehow blend with the gnostic dualism of the Cathars of
Septimania? Was that the main source of the arcane information that the
Languedoc Templars gleaned from Septimania? What were these strange
Cathar doctrines, and can we trace their history and development from

the Essenes of Qumran to the twelfth- and thirteenth-century contacts between the Templars and the Cathars in Languedoc?

To understand Cathar teachings, it is necessary to look back at Mani and the doctrine, known as Manichaeism, which he founded. Mani, otherwise known as Manes and Manichaeus, was born in Babylonia in 215. His father's name was Patek, and through his mother Mani was related to the Parthian royal family. His lineage did him little good; they were deposed while he was still a child.

Mani's teachings were based on two mystical experiences in which he described being visited by an angel who commanded him to start a new religion. He travelled extensively — including visits to India — which may account for the Indian theories about the origins of Abraham and Sarah. Finally, Mani ran into fierce opposition from the Zoroastrian priests, was imprisoned, and died after a few days' incarceration at Gundashapur.

Mani taught that light and darkness were opposed, just as good and evil were opposed, but he compounded those ideas so that light itself was good and darkness was evil. Mani taught that the Spirit — or light — was equated with love, wisdom and loyalty. Darkness, from which Satan and the demons had emerged, was equated with hatred, illness, suffering and treachery.

This strange Templar carving from Royston Cave in Hertfordshire, England, may be meant to represent Manichaean gnosticism. Was gnostic dualism one of the ancient pre-Templar secrets?

Human beings were seen as being under the corrupting power of Satan, but the God of Light intervened to help and redeem us. According to Mani, a string of prophets (the ancient Guardians again?) ranging from Noah through Abraham and including Jesus, had all done their best to carry this work of salvation forward, but Mani now regarded himself as the last and greatest of these saviour-prophets — the one who would put everything right. Because Mani saw the world of matter as largely an evil place from which the light and goodness trapped inside sinful human beings had to escape, his teachings favoured strict asceticism and self-denial. Because the created world was largely a dark place, Mani's followers wanted as little as possible to do with it. Similarities with Catharism are already significant here — and the Manichaeans shared a love of secrecy, mysticism and symbolism with the later Cathars.

Having first gained ground in the east — Persia and Mesopotamia — in the third and fourth centuries, Manichaeism moved westwards throughout the Roman Empire. It had a massive influence on the Paulicians and Bogomils, who in turn passed much of its esoteric gnostic dualism and many of its other secret teachings to the Cathars and Templars of Languedoc.

The Paulicians themselves were a Manichaean-Christian group that took root in Armenia and Asia Minor. They acquired their name from Paul of Samosata, although they themselves regarded Constantine of Mananali (an area west of the River Euphrates), as their real founder. The Paulicians accepted only the Gospels and Pauline epistles as their inspired books; they had no time for priests or for the Catholic Church. Their doctrines were blatantly heretical by the theological standards of their time: they denied the virgin birth of Jesus and insisted that God was not the ruler of this world but of the world to come — the only things he had created were the angels. For the Paulicians, it was the evil demiurge who had made this world and all living things. They were opposed to the Eucharist, and did not venerate the cross. In view of the accusations of this type which were levelled against the Templars when they were treacherously attacked by Philip le Bel in 1307, it seems highly probable that, among the secrets they had gleaned, the Cathars had included this item of Paulician doctrine.

Peter's repentance was not accepted by them — his denial of Christ put him outside the pale as far as the Paulicians were concerned. These and their other doctrines were included in their handbook, called *Key of Truth*. Perhaps one of the strangest of their beliefs was that it was possible to attain a level of religious perfection that would put a truly pious and dedicated believer on a level with Christ, so that the believer actually became a miniature "christ" himself and, as such, was venerated by the other members of groups like the Paulicians, Bogomils and Cathars.

By the time the Templars and other crusaders reached the area, the Paulicians were flourishing in Syria and Palestine, but they disappeared from their bases in Armenia rather mysteriously at the end of the eleventh century and did not appear there again until the eighteenth century.

Curiously, the Paulicians protested against Mani himself — but enthusiastically adopted many of his Manichaean ideas.

* * *

Just as the Paulicians had encapsulated much of their doctrine in *Key of Truth*, so the Essenes before them almost certainly had copies of the mysterious Book of Jubilees, which some of its devotees claimed was Mosaic in origin, but which was almost certainly written during the reign of John Hyrcanus I. In due course the mysterious information it contained would inevitably have reached the Templars of Septimania via the cabalistic Jews and their Cathar associates in the Languedoc. John Hyrcanus (175–104 BC) was the Jewish priest-king from 135–104 BC, and under his rule the Hasmonean kingdom of Judea attained great power and prosperity. Meanwhile, the Essenes were flourishing in Qumran.

The youngest son of Simon Maccabeus, whose ancestor Hasmoneus gave his name to the dynasty, John Hyrcanus was a gallant warrior, an effective administrator, a wise statesman and a successful ruler. Whatever its precise date or authorship, the Book of Jubilees is of particular interest because of its pointed references to beings called the Watchers. How much did the writer know about the ancient, secret Guardians, the precursors of the Knights Templar?

Having considered the Manichaean influence on the Paulician predecessors of the Cathars, it is important to refer to the Bogomil influence as well. Secret Bogomil teachings and their arcane knowledge would also have filtered through to those Templars who knew the Cathars of Languedoc. The Bogomils were a religious group centred in the Balkans for close to five hundred years. The movement, whose origins can be traced back to the tenth century, seems to have started in Bulgaria when dualistic neo-Manichaean Paulicians from Armenia and Asia Minor teamed up with reformist evangelicals who were opposed to the Bulgarian Orthodox Church. The founder of the Bogomils was a priest of that name, which was actually a Slavonic translation of the Greek name Theophilus — one who loves God.

Like the Manichaeans, Paulicians and Cathars, the Bogomils had no time for ordained priests, and they based their cosmological theology on the idea that the good God was pure spirit. All physical matter and physical beings were, therefore, the work of the devil, or demiurge. They denied the incarnation of Christ, baptism and the Eucharist, and were scornful of the cross. They did not believe in miracles and had no time for ornate church buildings. Their morals and ethics stemmed from this dualism; so for them, any contact with physical things — especially "the flesh" — had to be avoided. This put vegetarianism on the same pedestal as chastity, as far as the Bogomils were concerned. Marriage, meat and alcohol were all anathematized. In his tenth-century "Sermon Against the Heretics," a Bulgarian priest named Cosmas described the Bogomils as "social anarchists."

Yet, behind all their curious, hyper-puritanical behaviour, Manichaeans, Paulicians, Bogomils and Cathars guarded some vitally important ancient secrets — which the Templars gleaned from them — especially in the Languedoc. What they didn't learn from those ascetic gnostic groups, the Templars may have retrieved directly from the cabalists. It seems likely that only the *leaders* of each group knew the most significant parts of the cabalist magic, the gnostic ciphers, Dualistic symbols and Cathar codes. What did the Templars do with the arcane knowledge that they had acquired?

Chapter 6

THE TEMPLARS AND THE MYSTERY OF PRESTER JOHN

How much historical truth is there in the account of St. Thomas (one of Christ's twelve disciples) going to India as a missionary? Absolute proof is hard to come by, but the tradition is strong — and strong traditions are frequently supported by an irreducible core of truth. What if Thomas knew, or suspected, that the great patriarch Abraham had actually come from India in the very beginning, before moving to the Chaldean city of Ur? This would surely make India an ideal place for missionary work in the apostle's eyes. Inasmuch as it's possible to make any sensible estimate of a man's character and motivations at a distance of two thousand years, what little is known of Thomas is that he was a rational, thoughtful man who asked for proof. He was also a dynamic and decisive character, who — upon having obtained the proof he needed — was prepared to act on it. The New Testament account (John 20:24–29) makes it clear that all of Thomas's doubts about Jesus being miraculously resurrected after the crucifixion were completely dispelled. This news had to be broadcast as widely as possible to those who would be wise enough to understand. Where better, then, in Thomas's mind than in distant, magical India — a land that was accustomed to strange mysteries? Surely the mystery of Christ's resurrection would be accepted and understood there.

Thomas is said to have landed at Kodungallur, on today's Kerala coast at the southwestern tip of the Indian subcontinent. The Arabian Sea off that coast is also known as the Lakshadweep Sea. Tradition recounts that Thomas persuaded many of the leading Brahman families of Kerala to accept the Christian faith, and that he established seven churches there — the mystic number seven comes into the story once again, just as it did with the tale of Septimania. In addition to his preaching, teaching and pastoral work in the Kerala coastal fishing villages and small inland settlements, Thomas was a man of frequent prayer and profound meditation who often went alone to the Malayattoor hills — now home to an important shrine dedicated to his memory. After Thomas's martyrdom in AD 72, he was buried at Mylapore, not far from Madras.

The southwestern tip of India, known as Malabar in Roman times, provides ample evidence of trade with Roman merchants — often in the form of the old Roman coins that are dug up there. There is also evidence that King Solomon, builder of the Jerusalem Temple and keeper of many strange secrets, had traded there almost a thousand years before the Christian era began. (Could the nine original Templars excavating below the Temple Mound in Jerusalem have been looking for something that Solomon's men brought back from Malabar?)

Further information about the importance of Malabar in Roman times comes from the great Roman historian and scientist Caius Plinius Secundus, generally known as Pliny the Elder (AD 23–79). His love of proof matched Thomas's. By a curious coincidence, Pliny made a special study of the Celtic language while he was in France (Gaul) and Spain — and this links up rather strangely with the unusual book that Father Boudet wrote: *Le Vraie Langue Celtique et le Cromleck de Rennes-les-Bains,* which translates as "The True Celtic Language and the Cromlech of Rennes-les-Bains." Did both Pliny *and* Boudet — nearly two thousand years later — suspect that the Celtic Tectosages from the Rennes-le-Château area knew strange secrets that made a knowledge of their language vitally important? The name "Tectosages" literally translates as the wise builders, or the skillful artisans — people with practical ability as well as theoretical knowledge. They were part of the Volcae, a large, free and independent Celtic community that once occupied present-day Languedoc. The headquarters of the Tectosages was Tolosa, which is now the modern city of Toulouse.

Pliny complained that the Phoenicians — Rome's serious, long-term trading rivals — were buying spices, silk and precious stones from India. His writings also made it clear that merchant ships from Malabar were trading with the Egyptians and other customers in the Persian Gulf. There is evidence that Jewish colonies were established in India before the Christian era, and that Rome enjoyed diplomatic networks with various Indian governments earlier than the first century AD. All this evidence of regular contacts between India and the Mediterranean increases the possibility that Thomas really did reach India as a missionary.

Further evidence that Thomas reached India and established churches there comes from Eusebius Pamphili (AD 260–340), the Bishop of Caesarea in Palestine, often referred to as the "Father of Church History." Jerome (AD 340–420) and Eusebius both refer in their writings to a journey to India made in AD 190 by Pantaenus, who was sent there by Bishop Demetrius of Alexandria. What were then steadfastly referred to as the "Thomas Christians" were reported to be flourishing in India.

An old sailing ship of a type that could have carried merchants from the Mediterranean to India.

* * *

What connection might there be between Thomas, the apostle and missionary to India, and the so-called Gospel of Thomas that turned up among the ancient records in the Nag Hamadi library? Writing in his *Refutation of All Heresies* during the first quarter of the third century, Hippolytus (AD 170–235) mentions the Naasenes, who were gnostics and who used the Gospel of Thomas. The Nag Hamadi library was discovered in Egypt in 1945 in the area between Cairo and Luxor. The mysterious old codices there consisted of a thousand pages in Coptic.

ⲁ Β Γ Δ Ε Ϛ Ζ Η Θ Ι Κ Λ Μ Ν Ξ Ο
Π Ρ Ϲ Τ Υ Φ Χ Ϙ Ⲱ ⲱ ⳋ ϥ ⲡ ϩ ϫ ϭ †

The thirty-two letters of the Coptic alphabet, which is partially based on the Greek alphabet.

The Coptic letters have the sounds of: *a, b* or *v, g, d, e, s, dz* combination, long *ei, th,* short *i, k, l, m, n, ks* combination, *o, p, r, s,* long *t, u, f, kh* combination, *psi* combination, long *o* or long *u,* yet another alternative form of *s,* another *f, h,* a lighter version of *dz* which borders on *ds, ts* and finally a light *ti* sound. The addition of so many seemingly unnecessary alternatives for what are practically — and almost indistinguishably — the same sounds suggests a number of possibilities about the Coptic language:

1. It was originally spoken by people with a different hearing range, or subtler-than-average powers of phonic discrimination.
2. There were complicated orthographic rules for using particular Coptic letters in particular circumstances; for example, one kind of *s* might be used exclusively for word endings, and another type for their beginnings.
3. The apparently unnecessary letters were an essential part of subtle Coptic codes, or ciphers. For example, the use of one type of *f* could tell the initiated reader that there were coded messages hidden in the manuscript, while the other type of *f* meant, "Don't bother to look — there's no code here. Just take the words at face value."

It's worth noting in passing that when a mysterious coded stone was discovered deep in the Oak Island Money Pit in Mahone Bay, Nova Scotia, Professor Barry Fell ventured the very interesting idea that it was inscribed in Coptic and bore a religious message. This suggested that Coptic refugees had sailed to Nova Scotia centuries ahead of Columbus's epochal transatlantic voyage. Other cryptographers have suggested that it referred to the location and value of buried treasure.

Although closely related to Greek letters, Coptic is normally accepted as the final stage of the written version of the Egyptian language — one which appeared in the second century BC, but didn't come to prominence until two centuries later. The oldest form of Egyptian writing is at least six thousand years old — and probably considerably older.

The earliest hieroglyphs and ideograms were intricately designed and beautifully painted, so the artists who had the laborious task of creating them inevitably looked for shorter and simpler forms. These were introduced over the centuries, concluding with the Coptic script as we know it today.

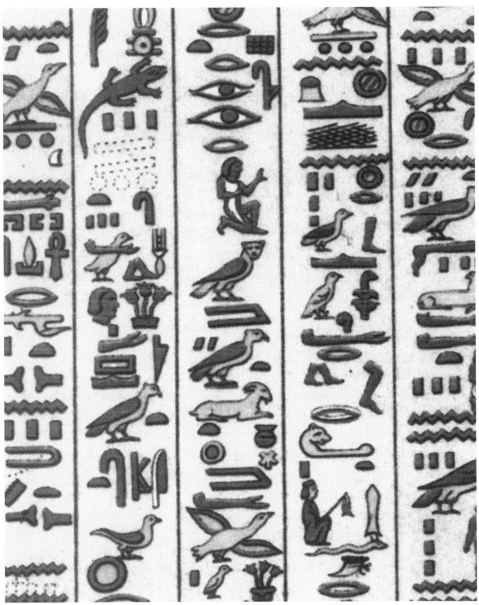

Examples of ancient pre-Coptic Egyptian writing.

The copy of the Gospel of Thomas discovered at Nag Hamadi is not a gospel narrative — it is merely a collection of 114 sayings attributed to Jesus. Some of them accord harmoniously with the main Christian teachings as recorded by the accepted gospel writers; others are strange, controversial and perceptibly gnostic in tone. The central theological thinking of the Naasenes who relied on this Gospel of Thomas seems to have been the old, basic, gnostic view that the physical world is evil and that the good God with a group of like-minded spiritual powers (angels?) sent Jesus as an *appearance* (rather than a person) in order to enable captive humanity to return to the higher, spiritual plane of existence — thus escaping from physical matter and all its attendant evils.

Many textual scholars tend to date the Gospel of Thomas from around AD 150, and regard it as having no link with the apostle of that name. The strong possibility that Thomas the Apostle did reach India and establish churches there, and that Thomas may have selected India because of what he believed to be its mysterious connection with the origins of Abraham and Sarah, are useful starting points in the quest for the mysterious Prester John. If Abraham and Sarah had an Indian background, and if the apostle Thomas visited India, too, was Prester John an Indian priest-king?

* * *

How did the Prester John story really begin?

Otto, Bishop of Freising, wrote in his *Chronicles* in 1145 that he had heard via Hugo, Bishop of Gabala (Jibal in Syria?), that there was a Nestorian* Christian priest-king in the Far East who had overcome the Medes and the Persians, conquered Ecbatana and headed for Palestine to assist the Christian forces there. Unfortunately, if this was indeed Prester John, his otherwise invincible army had failed to cross the flooded waters of the Tigris, and he had reluctantly gone back home. It

---

*Nestorius (circa AD 380–451), patriarch of Constantinople from 428–431, argued against the use of the term *Theotikos* (Mother of God) to describe Mary the Mother of Jesus. See: J.F. Bethune-Baker, *Nestorius and his Teachings* (Cambridge: The University Press, 1908).

is psychologically understandable that hard-pressed defenders would welcome stories that promised help from semi-mythical, heroic rescuers — Arthur of the Britons, Wenceslas of Bohemia, and Drake in his hammock all fall into this category. In the hour of their people's greatest need it is said that the sleeping heroes will wake again and return to save them.

The geography of the twelfth century was such that India, the Indies, the Far East, Abyssinia and Ethiopia were frequently conflated and confused. Tales of Thomas's Christian churches in Malabar in southern India could easily be distorted into tales of Prester John and his huge army of rescuers for the beleaguered Crusaders of Palestine.

In 1165 a letter describing Prester John's untold wealth, invincible armies and amazing kingdom was widely distributed. Another letter, attributed to Pope Alexander III, went out on September 22, 1177. According to this letter, the pope had heard of Prester John via Philip, the papal doctor, who had in turn gleaned his information from "trustworthy and reliable citizens of Prester John's Kingdom." John requested a church in Jerusalem, and Alexander III responded by saying that humility rather than pride would help John to achieve this ambition.

In the thirteenth century, news arrived in Western Christendom that a huge army was wreaking havoc on the Muslim forces — and fresh hopes were kindled that these were Prester John's long-awaited Christian reinforcements. To the great disappointment of the battered, retreating Crusaders, the huge army attacking their enemies turned out to be Jenghiz Khan (1162–1227) and his awesome Mongol horde.

Despite conflicting reports and contradictory versions of the whereabouts of Prester John and his mysterious kingdom, the Indian hypothesis recurred persistently. Christians travelling in India tried hard to find a local ruler who would fit Prester John's profile.

An old Catalonian map published in the late fourteenth century showed Christian kingdoms in India. Marco Polo wrote of a place called Abascia which he claimed was part of India, but this was almost certainly a misunderstanding on his part: he may well have meant Abyssinia. Certainly the Abyssinian priests referred to their country as the Kingdom of Prester John, and Portuguese explorers went looking for Prester John's kingdom along the whole of the North African coast.

Yet another map dating from the start of the sixteenth century places Prester John's mysterious Christian kingdom in or near India as geographers know its borders today, and a note accompanying the map says that Prester John was a good king who ruled most of India and owned mountains full of precious stones and other treasures.

Many of the Prester John myths and legends coincide with the Templar ascendancy of the twelfth and thirteenth centuries. Part of the great medieval Templar mystery seems to be that they were well aware of — and possibly in regular contact with — a mysterious Christian ruler in charge of a powerful state in India or North Africa. The Templars' sea power would facilitate such contacts.

On the other hand, the whole concept of the kingdom of Prester John may have been a carefully constructed Templar symbol, code or cipher, to represent the secret power of the Templars themselves. Every Templar commandery and fortress was, in effect, part of that "hidden" kingdom — one that couldn't be located geographically because it was *everywhere*.

Chapter 7

TEMPLARS AND TROUBADOURS

Of all the places where codes could be hidden, the songs and stories of the minstrels and troubadours were among the safest. Troubadours, *jongleurs*, minstrels, *trouvères*, *minnesingers* and *meistersingers* all flourished throughout Europe — and beyond — at the same time as the Templars. Nor were they a new phenomenon: the Romans had referred to such welcome travellers as *jocucators*; Anglo-Saxons had entertainers known as gleomen; early Germans had named them *gauklers* or *scops*. In Italy they were called *giocolinos*, and in Spain *juglars*. In addition to the musicians, singers, storytellers and poets, many of these peripatetic entertainers were acrobats and tumblers. These latter skills were closely allied to early forms of wrestling, boxing, unarmed combat and rudimentary martial-arts techniques — very useful acquisitions for undercover espionage agents and confidential messengers.

The elite among them — especially the troubadours and minstrels — were very well paid and highly placed in society. Although Danny Kaye and Glynis Johns' brilliant 1956 film *The Court Jester* was primarily an outstanding *comedy* success, it also shed interesting and accurate historical light on the role of a court jester, as well as those like the top minstrels and troubadours who fulfilled similar — if more nomadic — roles. Like the jester in that 1956 film, minstrels and troubadours were very much aware of the internecine politics and power struggles of the day. They knew a great deal about the religious controversies, mercantile rivalries and other social upheavals that were bedevilling the areas through which they travelled.

Because of the nomadic nature of their work, the minstrels and minnesingers would have been invaluable carriers of news — and of secret, coded, Templar messages. Furthermore, like the sinister jester whom Danny Kaye's character replaced in the film, there could have been those among the minstrel and troubadour fraternity who were both willing and able to dispose of inconvenient rivals. Their very calling made it relatively easy for troubadours and jongleurs to infiltrate an otherwise secure medieval court or well-fortified stronghold and surreptitiously slip poison into a victim's drink or a stiletto between a victim's ribs.

It is also important to remember that these highly skilled travelling entertainers could constitute a formidable fighting force in their own right. For example, in 1212, it is recorded that Earl Randulf of Chester was besieged in Rhuddlan Castle, but he managed to send a desperate plea for help to Roger de Lacy, the formidable Constable of Chester. Roger — nicknamed "Roger from Hell" because of his awesome prowess in battle and his notorious lack of clemency — ordered his son-in-law Dutton to organize an army from among the jongleurs who were then entertaining in large numbers at the annual Chester Fair. When Dutton led this fearsome band to within sight of Rhuddlan Castle, the besiegers took one look at what they were up against — and very wisely fled. Dutton and his team were rewarded in perpetuity with a Royal Charter.

The songs the French jongleurs performed were known as *gestes* or, in full, *chansons de geste*. They were long, epic tales of heroism and adventure that acclaimed the leading warriors of the day. It is particularly significant that the fearless minstrel-soldier Taillefer (who probably had family connections with the Counts of Toulouse *and* Bernard of Clairvaux) sang "The Song of Roland" as he led out the Norman soldiers against King Harold's men at Hastings.

What exactly is this "Song of Roland," and what curious codes and ciphers might it contain?

In 778, Charlemagne, King of the Franks, was on his way back from Spain when the Basques — through whose territory he was passing — attacked his rearguard and defeated it. The great Frankish hero Roland was prominent in this engagement, and many troubadour songs were soon being written about him. The historical Hrodland, also known as Roland, was Count of the Marches of Brittany, and the songs seem probably to have been first performed among his Breton people. The travelling troubadours soon took them all over France, however, and Roland became a national hero rather than just an acclaimed Breton. The story changed dramatically in its minstrel form from what probably happened historically. For instance, the real Charlemagne was only a young man in his thirties when the Basque victory over his rearguard at Roncesvaux actually happened, yet the song gives him a long white beard and an equally long and successful military and political career. The Basques have been replaced in the song by Saracens, and a traitor named Ganelon — whose activities do not seem at all historically accurate — is brought in to explain the defeat!

An extract from the "Song of Roland" clearly illustrates its characteristics — and the possibilities of using such poems to conceal codes and ciphers:

> Blancandrin was a courtier wise
> And lord beneath Val Fonde's skies.
> Wise and valiant, a loyal aid,
> "O great King Marsil, be not afraid.
> Swear fealty now to Charlemagne
> And long shall be King Marsil's reign.
> Give Carl a splendid and royal gift:
> The bear, the lion, the greyhound swift,
> Hundreds of camels, laden with gold
> And silver bars. This wealth untold
> Will all of Charlemagne's soldiers pay —
> Contented, his army will march away.
> So here in Spain all shall yet be well
> When Charlemagne rides to his own Chapelle..."

The Blancandrin of this pasage was a valiant, wise and loyal counsellor to King Marsil of Saragossa, and he knew well that the Saragossans would have no chance at all against Charlemagne's vast Frankish army. His advice to make peace and submit to Charlemagne was, therefore, politically and militarily sensible. But the extract could also be full of symbolism and codes: the bear, the lion and the greyhound are fascinating ciphers. The King Arthur legends, for example, are also associated with the Bear Clan.

The references to generous gifts of gold and silver are clear indicators not only of the treasure that is to be given to buy Charlemagne's favour in this supposed story of Roland, but of other hidden treasure elsewhere. And why does the minstrel sing specifically of Chapelle? Does the cipher say that there is a vast treasure concealed at Aix-la-Chapelle (modern Aachen)?

Take the twelfth-century version of the "Song of Roland" with its probable troubadour Templar modifications, and dare to ask whether the symbolism goes far deeper. Charlemagne is phonetically close to Solomon: each is a great emperor. If the Charlemagne of the "Song of Roland" stands for Solomon of Jerusalem, does Chapelle represent some far greater place of worship — the Jerusalem Temple, close to which the nine pioneering Templars dug in secret? This is pure speculation, of course, but this brief extract from the "Song of Roland" serves to illustrate the importance of the gestes, as well as their code-carrying capacity.

Early Anglo-Saxon poetry was noted for its starkly compressed metaphors known as kennings; its dramatic caesuras breaking the flow of the narrative; and its overall use of alliteration. Centuries of more recent English poetry had consistent end-rhyme schemes and characteristic iambic pentameters. Gestes such as the "Song of Roland," however, were readily recognizable in their original forms by their assonance — their internal "vowel rhymes" — and it is possible that such assonant phrases would also have lent themselves readily to medieval cipher builders and codemakers such as the troubadours and Templars. Is it reasonable to envisage a scenario in which the minstrels and troubadours undertook a dual function for the Templars, first encoding the secret messages that the Templars wanted to send, then incorporating those encodings into their gestes?

Because the Templars are associated first with valiant military prowess and second with castle architecture, it is all too easy to overlook their third, equally important, role as international bankers. Their system was centuries ahead of its time: a pilgrim could deposit money with one Templar Commandery near his or her home, take a secure receipt, and ultimately draw cash from another Templar Commandery a thousand miles away. It was a far safer system than carrying cash along lonely, bandit-infested roads that were little better than tracks. Just as twenty-first-century credit cards have security features such as PIN numbers and microchips, so the Templar bankers would have had their own security system — and a previously-agreed-upon, special line from a troubadour geste would have served their purpose well enough.

In addition to the codes that could be secreted in letter formations and words, poetic meters also offered ciphering opportunities to minstrels, troubadours and minnesingers. The keen eyes and ears of a professional troubadour would swiftly detect any irregularity in the rhythm of a poem, and minstrel code makers could use such irregularities to good effect.

Prosody — the study of the laws, or rules, of poetry — recognizes poetic feet (like the bars in music) and categorizes poetry by the way these feet are constructed and then incorporated into lines and stanzas. Many of the sophisticated twenty-first-century techniques of prosody and the modern taxonomy of poetry were not around when troubadours like Raimbaut of Vaqueiras (circa 1150–1210) were composing and singing. It is, nevertheless, possible to find significant rudiments of modern prosody in their work, and a brief descriptive analysis of contemporary prosody provides a magnifying lens through which to study the detailed structure of the works of the troubadours and minstrels.

Poetic feet are recognized by the arrangement of accented and unaccented syllables within them. Here, we use the letter A for accented, meaning an emphasized or stressed syllable, and the letter U for unaccented, meaning a light, or weak, syllable. Following that labelling system, an *iambus* is a foot with a UA structure; a *trochee* is AU; an *anapaest* is UUA; a *dactyl* is AUU; and an *amphibrach* is UAU. Allowing for slight and occasional differences in emphasis between Canadian, American and British pronunciation, the following examples may help to illustrate the different types of feet: UA = *remove*; AU = *deeper*; UUA = *to the left*; AUU = *happily*; and UAU = *excitement*.

An older metrical device — and possibly a more significant one for would-be code builders among the medieval fraternity of minstrels and troubadours — was what can best be described as *syllabic versification*. Examples of this turn up in Italian, Spanish and Provençal. It consisted simply of counting the number of syllables that were used prior to the final stressed syllable in a line: surely a gift for any poetic codemaker?

* * *

An early example that may well contain a particularly subtle troubadour double-code can be found in "Kalenda Maya," one of the many works of the redoubtable Raimbaut de Vaqueiras. He was knighted in the service of the Marquis de Monferrat, and was, for a time, blissfully happy as the courtly lover of Lady Beatrice, the marquis's sister.

Tragically, there seems to be a mean, toxic motivation in the corrupted hearts of some despicable, jealous people to interfere with the blissful happiness of young lovers. Such, apparently, was the case here. Time and again these poisonous court gossips rebuked Lady Beatrice for "dishonouring" her brother, and her own high rank, by accepting a mere knight like Raimbaut as her lover. Seemingly, Beatrice was finally influenced by their vicious slanders against Raimbaut and turned away from him. He no longer smiled and laughed in court; he no longer sang his magnificent troubadour songs. Outwardly, he was as miserable as Hamlet the Dane.

When two superb jongleur violinists turned up at Monferrat, even their brilliant playing of a superb *estampida* failed to reach Raimbaut's broken heart. Knowing what was wrong, the sympathetic marquis pleaded with his sister to show Raimbaut some kindness again — which she finally did, and the result was his composition and performance of "Kalenda Maya."

That's as far as the superficial history of the episode takes us. But what if the two visiting jongleur violinists from France were really important secret couriers, sent to find out what political and military news there was to be gleaned from Monferrat? Raimbaut has several vital points to make, and he conceals them in the "Kalenda Maya" — ostensibly nothing more than a fashionable courtly love song. What if the marquis and Lady Beatrice are party to what is happening, and have connived to create the love-story camouflage that Raimbaut needed to hide the vital political and military message?

The poem "Kalenda Maya" itself is an *estampida*, a fast medieval dance: the Spanish word can actually be translated literally as "stampede," carrying idiomatic overtones of "to go in a great hurry, like an arrow from a bow, like a flash of lightning." If we apply a simple numerical code to the words of the "Kalenda Maya," we find that every seventh line, with an occasional continuation into the line which follows it, produces what could be a singularly important coded message — a very long way from the simple song of courtly love in the troubadour tradition that it appears to be on the surface. Here are the translations of those seventh lines:

> Until I receive a swift messenger (Lines 7–8)
> And I hurry to you (Lines 14–15)
> God forbid that the envious/evil one (Lines 21–22)
> Two such loyal/true companions (Line 28)
> I would die (Line 35)
> In secret thoughts (Line 42)
> Exposed/revealed/naked (Line 49)
> Fair/good/worthy knight (Line 56)
> I know (Line 63)
> Gratitude/thankfulness (Line 70)
> Lady Beatrice (Line 77)
> Eloquence/oratory/convincing speech/diplomatic words
>   (Line 84)
> Without a doubt/certainty (Line 91)
> Whoever forgets [you?] (Line 98)
> Perfectly virtuous/absolutely right and honourable
>   (Line 105)
> Finished (Line 112)

This simple example of seventh-line cipher theory is, of course, again a purely speculative one — but *seven* was a very significant number to the medieval mind, and when an every-seventh-line code formula is applied to "Kalenda Maya," as demonstrated above, a coherent message emerges:

> Somebody needs a swift messenger who has to hurry to whomever the message is meant for. A dangerous enemy is in the vicinity, and is threatening two good and loyal companions. There is a very real danger of death involved, if this enemy's plans are not thwarted. The matter must, therefore, be kept absolutely secret. It can be revealed only to the good and trustworthy knight

who is known to Raimbaut the troubadour, composer of this *estampida*, and encoder of its secret message. Much gratitude is owed to this knight for his services to Lady Beatrice. In addition to his fighting prowess, loyalty and trustworthiness, he is an eloquent orator and a skillful diplomat. The certainty of his noble and reliable character is emphasized again: this extra reassurance is understandable if Raimbaut, Beatrice and her brother are placing their lives in his hands.

Rambaut then terminates the message: finished.

Like all coded messages, this one depends on knowledge already held by the encoders and decoders. We can safely assume that they would know to which king or prince it had to be sent if urgent military help was needed. They would also know the identity of the dangerous enemy who was threatening two loyal companions. Those could have been the two jongleur violinists, or even Lady Beatrice and her brother, the marquis. The good, valiant and trustworthy knight could, perhaps, be Raimbaut himself — or a Templar hero of his acquaintance who would save them. The idea of speed and urgency might suggest the characteristic, precipitous courage of a Templar knight. The saviour, whoever he is, has diplomatic skills as well as military ones — and these are apparently needed to persuade the recipient of the message to send whatever help is needed in Monferrat.

* * *

No survey of the importance of the minstrel role would be complete without reference to King Richard the Lionheart and his faithful minstrel, Blondel. Some historians describe the episode as apocryphal, but others regard it as having a factual basis. Treacherously imprisoned by a Christian king who should have been a loyal ally and staunch fellow crusader, Richard's place of imprisonment is kept secret so that his men cannot storm it to rescue him. Blondel, however, safe behind his troubadour camouflage, is able to roam from castle to castle, singing one of Richard's own songs. Eventually, the imprisoned Lionheart hears it and joins in, and once his location is known, his freedom is not far away.

Chapter 8

THE TEMPLARS AND THE BLACK MADONNA MYSTERY

Several medieval minstrels and troubadours were involved with a secret cult generally referred to by researchers and historians as the cult of the Black Madonna. There are complex, interwoven theories about this sect and its beliefs, some of which vary so widely as to be almost diametrically contradictory.

A number of profound Jungian psychologists and academic mystics see the Black Madonna as synonymous with the Earth Mother, or ancient matriarchal goddess. To their school, she is the primordial female principle — but at the same time she is a very real, suprapersonal entity in her own right. Perhaps *because* the interpretations of the intricate meanings of the Black Madonna vary so widely, the Jungian researchers into her cult see part of her power as the reconciliation of opposites, the bringing together of things as different as heat and cold, or darkness and light. For them she represents wisdom and, through wisdom, the resolution of life's conflicts and paradoxes.

Almost all the ancient pantheons contained powerful goddesses, and in a sense the Black Madonna theology perpetuates their myths. She is Isis; she is Artemis; she is Venus-Aphrodite; she is Diana; she is Gaia. Essentially, she is all of them — and more. It may be appropriate, perhaps, to think of her as the golden chain on which the named goddesses are threaded pearls.

In a completely different sense, she is said to comprise every aspect of human femininity: incomprehensibly, she combines virginal purity, protective, affectionate maternity and the free-loving, wanton, sexual passion and willingness of the ever-available goddess of physical love. Metaphorically, she is said to create life as the Earth Mother goddess: all life comes from her, and all life returns to her. She cares for and protects her dependent children with fierce, maternal loyalty. She never fails to satisfy the strongest sexual desires of her most ardent lovers. She is supremely honoured, respected and guarded with their very lives by her valiant protectors and worshippers, the members of the cult of the Black Madonna. How many of the Templars and troubadours were also her secret followers? Her cult was widespread throughout the Languedoc during their era, and a number of Cathars may also have been secretly involved.

There is also a sense in which the Black Madonna is identified — at least in part — by some of her worshippers as being tantamount to the Kundalini fire. According to some ancient legends and traditions, the original Kundalini was a fire goddess who wound her serpentine way up from the centre of the Earth and thus reached the biosphere. Accordingly, the concept of the Kundalini fire involves the theory of chakras, and a special form of yoga in which the power of the metaphorical "curled serpent" chakra at the base of the spine, also called Kundalini, is released. According to this theory, the power spreads throughout the body like cold fire, or a powerful electric current.

Because of its dangerously heretical nature in medieval times, when the Inquisition regarded torture and execution as the ideal cure for anything in the least unorthodox, the cult of the Black Madonna was spread and sustained secretly by word of mouth — written evidence was far too dangerous because it was so vulnerable to the inquisitors. Nevertheless, some remarkably ambiguous inscriptions appeared in surprisingly prominent places. "Darkness precedes light and she is mother" is inscribed on the altar of Salerno Cathedral in Italy. Completed in 1084, the cathedral was built by Robert Guiscard, Duke of Apulia and Calabria. He was a Norman adventurer who had a great deal of military success in Italy before he died in his seventieth year in 1085. The strange altar inscription may possibly reflect the secret influence of highly placed members of the Black Madonna cult in Salerno at that time. It was part of their belief that wisdom was dark, feminine and secret, and that this Dark Wisdom had existed before the coming of light.

In the Mediterranean world of the first century AD, Sophia was the goddess of wisdom. She was regarded as beautiful and as an ideal counsellor and companion for all who had the good sense to seek her out. In her profound and fascinating 1991 book *Sophia: Goddess of Wisdom*, Caitlin Matthews points out that Sophia is in one sense the great lost goddess. Sophia is described as veiled and darkened — often forced into shadowy corners at the edges of traditional worship, ignored and undervalued.

Is this darkly beautiful Mediterranean goddess of wisdom connected in any way with the strange religious carvings known as Sheela-na-gigs? Unlike the realistic beauty of Greek and Italian carvings, the Sheelas are little short of grotesque. Their bodies are unattractively thin to the verge of emaciation — almost skeletal; their eyes and ears protrude; their hands clasp their genitalia and display them. Some theorists have suggested that they are fertility cult symbols, but this seems rather unlikely. If anything, they resemble the "lean kine" of Pharaoh's prophetic dream. A more likely interpretation — and one that would link them with Mediterranean Sophia, the gnostics and the Cathars of Languedoc — is that their display of genitalia is intended to symbolize a return to the womb after death. The Sheela is saying that Mother Earth absorbs the dead, but is also the source of their new life: rebirth and reincarnation. This is a parallel theme to the idea of the Dark Wisdom that both precedes and follows the light of life in an endless series of cycles. Sophia says, "We are born to die and we die in order to be reborn."

Because of this widespread early belief, the mother goddess was also connected in popular thought with the underworld. She was a dark goddess of death as well as a dynamic goddess of fertility and new life. It is difficult, if not impossible, to get very far inside the minds of the earliest religious thinkers, but it seems probable that they viewed their goddess as entirely external and objective. She was the land and the sea, the lakes and the rivers, the deep valleys and the lofty mountain peaks. She was seedtime and harvest — queen of all seasons. Unlike the Christian concept of an indwelling Holy Spirit, or the internal aspect of the Kingdom of Heaven as Christ taught it, worshippers of the great mother goddess — followers of the cult of the Black Madonna — had little or no concept of internalizing their deity, or taking any of her powers into themselves, and subsequently using them to improve their lives.

There was, however, also an element of fate and destiny attached to both Sophia the Wise — who counselled her worshippers about how best to deal with what lay ahead — and the Earth Mother, who set the parameters for famine or plenty, for death and rebirth.

* * *

Another interesting sidelight on the Black Madonna is the Irish goddess Bridgit, also spelled Bridget, Brighid and Bride. Like the Black Madonna, Bridgit is a triple deity, and, like Kundalini, Bridgit is a fire goddess. Her original name was Breo-saight, which meant "arrow of fire" or "blazing arrow." As with Sophia, Bridgit can be a goddess of wisdom, learning and knowledge. In her maternal aspect she's also a goddess of hearth and home and is frequently seen as Danu, the great mother goddess of Ireland. Thirdly, she can also be the beautiful, virginal, white maiden goddess of Ireland. This triple nature also made it possible in different myths and legends for Bridgit to be wife, sister and daughter of the mighty Dagda — almost every version of the story associated them, but rarely in the same way!

When the Irish pantheon was Christianized, the former goddess Bridgit became St. Brigid, but her original incendiary powers were not quite forgotten; as a consequence, her sacred fire was never extinguished. (Then along came Henry VIII, who made life difficult for all monks and nuns in his domain — including St. Brigid's nuns, whose fires he terminated. Happily, they have since been rekindled by the faithful.) Not quite knowing how to incorporate "St. Brigid" into traditional Christianity, a compromise was reached by making her Christ's legendary "foster mother" and the midwife who assisted Mary when Jesus was born. A further myth swapped Bethlehem for Glastonbury, thus "explaining" why an Irish midwife was present. Although a difficult trip in the first century, Ireland to Glastonbury was a less formidable journey than Ireland to Bethlehem! Full marks for ingenuity and imagination — zero for historicity.

* * *

The ancient vodun religion, practised in parts of Africa, dates back at least six thousand years and possibly longer — it was contemporary with ancient Egypt. Vodun is also known by various other names including voodoo, vodoun, vodou, lucumi, macumba, sevi lwa and candomble. The Yoruba people of West Africa practised vodun, and they brought it with them to the Caribbean and parts of America during the era of slavery. When it reached South America it mutated into candomble, which is also known as umbanda.

In these religions, the dark and mysterious maternal goddess is known as Iya-mi-Osoronga, which translates as "Osoronga-my-mother." This idea is symbolized by a gigantic basin, sometimes called *igba*, which is a totality — both the container and its precious contents. It stands for the growing child within the womb. In the candomble creation myth, a very powerful, magical bird is found in this vast basin. Its name is Atioro, and it represents both the wonderful, active, dynamic power of fertility and reproduction, *and* the latent, potential power of the new entity that is being created.

The diverse nature of this fertility goddess and her ambivalent powers are encapsulated in the candomble myth of Iya-mi-Eleye, the women-birds who were there at the beginning of the world. According to candomble legend, they settled on seven trees — yet another example of the ancient magic number seven. Those on three of the trees did good works; those on three more trees were evil and malicious. On the seventh tree, good and evil alternated — like chaos and order, darkness and light, mercy and cruelty.

The candomble myth also involved a great mother figure, known as Iya-mi. Like the women-birds, the Iya-mi-Eleye of the seven trees, she was both good and evil, both creator and destroyer. The name of Oxum — sometimes symbolized as a fish goddess — also inspires awe among candomble believers, and here once again the bringing together of opposites, the resolving of paradoxes and the reconciliation of contradictions are essential parts of her functions. Because the Iya-mi-Eleye play such a prominent role in the candomble mythology, Oxum is not only a fish but a gigantic bird as well: she has scales as well as feathers.

* * *

Passing from the South American mysteries of the candomble beliefs to the enigmas of ancient Sumeria and the Chaldean city of Ur on the far side of the world, we find yet another ambivalent Earth Mother goddess:

Inanna. She leads Chaldean warriors to victory by day, and by night becomes their goddess of physical love, fertility and pleasure: a situation close to the Viking paradise of Valhalla. Inanna's priestesses were the temple prostitutes who, symbolically, could not belong to one man because they belonged to *all* men. Inanna was the Chaldean equivalent of Babylonian Ishtar, and she also had a strong affinity with Isis and Neith of Egypt. Neith was always regarded as the oldest and wisest of the Egyptian female pantheon — the feminine equivalent of Thoth or Hermes Trismegistus, the all-knowing scribe of the Egyptian gods whose vast knowledge was inscribed on the Emerald Tablets.

The cult of the Black Madonna also had ties with Cybele and Demeter of Greece, while in classical Rome she was Ceres, or Tellus. By whatever name she was venerated, her pre-Christian roots indicated that she was always a very powerful deity — always dark, always mysterious and ambivalent.

Bearing in mind that the strange wisdom of the Celtic Tectosages of early Languedoc would have included the worship of Annis, a Celtic mother goddess, it is easy to understand why the cult of the Black Madonna flourished there in the centuries that followed. They would also have had contacts with Cretan worshippers who venerated the mother goddess.

Co-authors Lionel and Patricia setting out for the Cretan Cave of Zeus.

Picturesque stalactites inside the legendary Cretan Cave of Zeus.

In this Cretan aspect of her worship, caves were always associated with her, especially the Cave of Zeus.

Mysterious symbolic birds, sacred to the Earth Mother goddess, on an ancient Cretan artifact in the Nikoiaos Museum.

There is also a special sense in which she is regarded as the goddess of birds, beasts and aquatic life — often as their protector, but sometimes (as in the real symbolism behind the popular legend of the Minotaur) she is the one to whom the great bull, symbolic of male fertility, is sacrificed.

Cretan bull.

The famous Cretan double axe is also associated with her ceremonies.

Co-author Patricia with a huge Cretan double axe.

Co-author Patricia at the Minoan Labyrinth, Knossos, in Crete.

Cretan representation of the Earth Mother goddess.

In the Cretan tradition, the Earth Mother goddess and her priestesses were depicted as bare-breasted, and this ties in particularly well with the idea of the nourishment of the infant Zeus in his secret cave. It is widely accepted that this original Earth Mother cult — of which the cult of the Black Madonna is almost certainly a more sophisticated descendant — goes right back to Palaeolithic times.

Despite her ancient origins, the Earth Mother goddess was only one member of whichever pantheon any specific culture recognized. Almost all the old gods in these classical pantheons began to shrink and fade as Christianity spread and flourished — especially after the reign of the Roman Emperor Constantine (AD 306–337), when Christianity became legitimate and official. Erstwhile worshippers of the Earth Mother adopted a Machiavellian strategy, succinctly summed up in the aphorism, "If you can't beat 'em — join 'em!" Their ancient mother goddess became the Black Madonna: to those who knew the great secret, she was still herself and venerated as such, but she was now disguised under a Christian veneer that kept her cult, and its secret, safe.

It is significant to note that three prominent versions of the goddess — Isis, Diana of the Ephesians, and Cybele — were all depicted as black. Of the three, Isis is especially interesting because some scholars conjecture that the very earliest Black Madonnas actually represented Isis and Horus rather than Mary and Jesus.

For several centuries, Isis was venerated in Paris, but was replaced (or subtly Christianized?) by St. Genevieve, who began life as a fifth-century shepherdess. (Was she also the inspiration for Poussin's enigmatic shepherd paintings and the Shugborough Hall monument mystery?) There are intriguing ramifications here.

The cult of the Black Madonna also has enigmatic connections to the Merovingian dynasty, founded by Mérovée the Twice-Born. It seems to be suspiciously more than coincidence that a mysterious holy woman referred to as St. Genevieve is credited with exerting a profound influence over Mérovée when he took Paris. According to the legend, it was solely because of her that Mérovée was so merciful to the vanquished citizens of Paris. There are also said to be strange links between the saintly cult of Genevieve and the riddle of Dagobert II, who was the last known member of the Merovingian line. Do those alleged connections really relate to a strange nexus between Dagobert II and the Black Madonna cult? Is it the black goddess Isis, rather than the Parisian St. Genevieve, who ought to be linked with Dagobert II and the mysteries of Rennes-le-Château, the Templars and Cathars of Languedoc?

There are probably more arguments about the inscrutable Priory of Sion than about any other sector of the intricate Templar enigma. Contradictory theories about the priory range from whether it ever existed at all (other than as a figment of somebody's overwrought and unscrupulous imagination) to the idea that it is a very, *very* old, powerful group of Guardians with abilities and secret knowledge that still transcend what most of us can do, and what most of us think we know. It is often referred to as the Priory of Our Lady of Sion — whoever she may be — and could be dedicated to Mary Magdalene, to Mary, the mother of Jesus, to Isis, to some other Earth Mother goddess, to some nameless Black Madonna, or even to the exquisitely beautiful Black Girl who is one of the two ecstatic lovers in the Song of Solomon (Chapter 1, Verse 5). Could this same delightfully sensuous woman also have been the mysterious Queen of Sheba who is known to have visited Solomon? The true identity of the Lady of Sion deepens an already unfathomable mystery.

Whoever she was, and whatever the priory is — or was — there seems to have been a series of important interfaces and interactions between the priory, the Templars, the Cathars, the Black Madonna cult and the troubadours in the Languedoc during the twelfth and thirteenth centuries.

Another fascinating candidate for the mysterious lady's role is the black St. Mary of Egypt, who lived from 344–421. As in some traditions of Mary Magdalene, Mary of Egypt had supposedly been a prostitute. Allegedly, she had worked at the oldest profession in Alexandria for close to twenty years before being miraculously converted.

* * *

Another intriguing candidate is the mysterious St. Sara la Kali. The "Kali" part of her name means "black," and this seems to connect strongly with Marie de Negre — Black Mary — of Rennes-le-Château fame. Kali is also the name of an Indian goddess who is often depicted as a black woman with four arms. In one of her four hands she holds a severed head; in another, a sword; the remaining two are waving approvingly to give confidence to her worshippers. She has a necklace of skulls and a girdle of severed hands, is smeared with the blood of her enemies, and she stands on her husband's passive, supine body. Just like the inexplicable Sheelas of the United Kingdom, Kali's tongue protrudes, and her eyes bulge.

The statue of St. Sara la Kali, by contrast, is life-size and depicts a singularly beautiful black girl. It was originally found in the crypt of the ancient church of Saintes Maries de la Mer on the Île de la Camargue in France, at the mouth of the River Rhone. Sara la Kali's shrine was closed to all except Romanies until 1912, when it was opened to the general public. As a pilgrim enters the shrine, on the left is a very old pagan altar — possibly erected for sacrificing bulls as part of the Mithras religion. This links yet again with the Cretan bull cult and the Minotaur legends. Some scholars think that the Roman Mithras is derived from the Persian god Mithra, but it is Ahriman — the Persian god of evil — and not Mithra who slays a bull in their legends.

Whether the present shrine of Sara la Kali was ever a Mithraic site is debatable, but it is undoubtedly very old — almost certainly pre-Christian. Romany women and girls think of Sara as a wise woman who is able to pass secret knowledge on to them. They venerate her by constantly supplying her statue with fresh garments, and they kiss her face reverently as part of their devotions. In the darkness of her shrine, Sara is surrounded by hundreds of candles. Trophies of her healing power, such as abandoned crutches and leg braces, and letters of gratitude attesting to her healing miracles are stored in the shrine.

Sara la Kali's origins are retold in numerous legends, but one of the most interesting versions says that she was the black servant of Mary, the mother of James and John, and she saved their lives when their boat was in serious trouble not far from the French coast. In another romantic version she was the powerful chieftain of a Romany group who lived in the area, and was instrumental in saving the lives of Peter and Paul when their ship was in trouble near the mouth of the Rhône.

* * *

Other mysterious Black Madonnas in hagiography are traditionally accompanied by black animals, especially black lions, that have the power to destroy evil. Because of their early Mediterranean connections, the Spanish traditions of the Black Madonnas and Earth Mothers have crossed the Atlantic to Latin America. In Brazil, for example, in the early eighteenth century, a fisherman found one in the Paraiba River. It was a small, black female statue, and the lady was resting on a crescent moon. It was so miraculously heavy for its relatively small size that he had great difficulty in getting it out of the water. Today it is known as Our Lady Aparecida. She's the patroness of Brazil, and a city is named after her.

* * *

Although highly secretive and clandestine, the cult of the Black Madonna still thrives on both sides of the Atlantic. The Templars played no small part in disseminating knowledge of her. Many of them returned to their own countries from the Middle East, carrying with them small statues of the beautiful Black Madonna. Another secret closely associated with her cult may well have been that the legendary "Holy Grail" of the Arthurian romances was, in fact, a woman and not a sacred cup — yet another version of the old idea that Mary Magdalene had been married to Jesus and borne his children, hence she herself carried his sacred blood and was a living vessel, grail or chalice.

Whatever the true connection is, there are strong arguments that favour the conclusion that the medieval Templar mysteries include the ancient secrets of the Black Madonnas.

King David escorts the Ark into Jerusalem. Notice the musical instruments, especially the trumpets.

Chapter 9

THE TEMPLARS AND THE MYSTERY OF SOLOMON AND SHEBA

One interesting solution to the mystery of the Black Madonnas is that they represent the enigmatic Queen of Sheba and her visit to the Hebrew emperor Solomon, who came to the throne of Jerusalem in 922 BC. He consolidated the empire that his father, David, had founded, and he reigned in relative peace and prosperity by virtue of a series of alliances, which often involved royal weddings. When Solomon died, his son Rehoboam failed to hold the territory together. The ten northern tribes of Israel rebelled against him under the leadership of Jeroboam, the son of Nebat, and Rehoboam was left with only the smaller southern kingdom of Judah.

Solomon's empire was four times the size of twenty-first-century Israel. It stretched from Tiphash, on the River Euphrates, in the north all the way down to the Red Sea port of Elath, on the Gulf of Aqaba, in the south. Egypt and the Arabian Desert lay to the south of Solomon's empire, and the Hittites' territories were to his north. He controlled a significant coastal boundary along the eastern shore of the Mediterranean, and his fleet of merchant ships sailed far and wide to western Mediterranean lands — and south to all the trading ports that were accessible via the Red Sea.

It was in what had once been Solomon's peaceful and prosperous lands that the Templars and their fellow crusaders experienced the challenging vicissitudes of success and failure: hard-won victories and bitterly resolute defeats. In fight after fight the indomitable Templars lived up to their proud maxim: "First to attack and last to retreat!" It was in those war-ravaged, Middle Eastern territories that they would have heard stories of Solomon's power, wisdom and wealth — and they would also have heard of his famous meeting with Makeda, the beautiful black queen of Sheba.

There are controversies surrounding not only Makeda's personal name and actual identity, but also the location, size and nature of her land of Sheba, which occupied not much less than 500,000 square miles and comprised a potent topographical mixture of mountains, valleys and deserts. Sheba, also referred to as Saba, meant "the heavenly host." Latin speakers knew it as Arabia Felix, meaning "happy Arabia" or "fortunate Arabia."

What made Sheba so blessed? Commercially, it was her natural resources. The territory had great quantities of gold and gemstones, but more importantly it had the ideal soil and climate for growing spices. Dionysius, a Greek traveller and historian writing in the first century of the Christian era, said that the Arabian air was permanently filled with the scents of delicious spices and of myrrh and incense. Dionysius also commented admiringly on the prolific flocks of sheep and flights of birds that he had seen there. He even commented that the birds brought cinnamon with them in their beaks.

The inhabitants of Sheba possessed advanced technology and had remarkable civil-engineering skills — well ahead of their time. Can they be explained rationally in practical, common-sense terms, or do they provide fuel for wider and more exciting speculations? Had Sheban skill and knowledge been imported from somewhere like legendary Atlantis? Is it even remotely possible that the Shebans had received extraterrestrial help? Was that one of the strange secrets that the Templars discovered via the cult of the strange and mysterious Black Madonna?

Sabaean, or Sheban, success with spice cultivation depended to a great extent on their advanced irrigation systems. They had constructed dams nearly twenty metres high in places. One such impressive structure had controlled the Sheban River Adhanat for fifteen centuries, effectively irrigating the spice fields around Marib, the capital, before it finally succumbed to some major disaster (probably an overwhelming flood) in 542 BC. Until then, the Shebans had had the production of precious herbs and spices well in hand; after their main dam went down, however, the inexorable desert stole in.

During the long centuries before the crops failed, a period that included Solomon's reign in Israel, there was the all-important question of *marketing* the Sheban herbs and spices. Sheban caravans travelled north along the spice roads until they reached Solomon's territory. To go farther, to cross Israel and use the Mediterranean seaports, they needed Solomon's permission.

Each nation's economy stood to gain a great deal from a trade agreement: Solomon's treasury would profit from the sale of merchants' licences, while Sheba's merchants could expect to profit from being able to reach more distant customers without let or hindrance. When Makeda went to visit Solomon, taking with her the fabulously expensive gifts listed in the Bible, some of the "difficult questions" she put to him were likely to have been commercial in nature: "How many of my caravans may pass through your territory in a given period? What percentage of our herbs and spices will you want in return for granting us traders' licences? Will you allow adequate numbers of Sheban soldiers to accompany my spice merchants, because there are bandits along the route? If we bring you spices and herbs, what goods will you give us in return? Do you prefer bartering goods for different goods, or trading with gold and silver coins?"

One legend of her encounter with Solomon may well have some historical truth in it. Almost like an Aesop's fable, it illustrates the Odyssean shrewdness of the man reputed to have been the world's wisest emperor. The legend relates how Solomon, anxious to sleep with the beautiful black queen, extracted a solemn promise from her that she would take nothing of his without first asking his permission — and that, should she break this promise, she would have sex with him. He then arranged a particularly salty evening feast, and thoughtfully called for a vessel of drinking water to be placed conveniently in Makeda's room before she retired for the night. Overcome with thirst, the Sheban queen drank the water without first asking Solomon's permission — and, consequently, he insisted that she should fulfill her promise.

There is another interesting and significant section of the Solomon and Sheba story, one which concerns some of the writings found in the Kebra Negast — the Book of the Glory of the Kings of Ethiopia. It stated that, according to ancient laws, the monarch of Ethiopia in those days had to be a virgin queen. After her encounter with Solomon, Makeda no longer fulfilled that requirement, and yet she continued to reign. Was it in the minds of the compilers of the Kebra Negast that, as she had no official husband in Ethiopia, Makeda had experienced some form of parthenogenesis? Or did her loyal supporters consider that she was still notionally and legally a virgin as far as ruling the country was concerned? Was there also an echo here of the idea that the "son of a virgin" was going to be a very special sort of man indeed? Was this at least part of the authority that Menelik, whose name means "son of the wise man," exercised over his Ethiopian people when he became the founder of what they always refer to as their Solomonic Dynasty?

This "son of a virgin" concept could help to account for Makeda's association with the cult of the Black Madonna. In pre-Christian times, perhaps, statues of a beautiful black woman holding an infant in her arms represented Queen Makeda and Prince Menelik — not Mary and Jesus. Legendary and speculative, but what light could archaeology throw on the Sheban myths and legends?

In 1951 the American Foundation for the Study of Man financed the Wendell Phillips expedition from the University of California. Their plan was to excavate the ruins of Marib, on the southern end of the Arabian Peninsula, 2,000 metres up in the mountain range beside the Red Sea. The well-equipped and effectively led Phillips expedition got as far as Mahram Bilqis, which translates broadly as "the throne of the Queen of Sheba." What they had located was actually the ancient Ilumquh Temple of Awwam. Ilumquh was a moon goddess, and was associated with a moon-bull whose image was remarkably similar to the Cretan Bull of Knossos. What was the connection between the two ancient and mysterious sites?

The building the Phillips team investigated at Mahram Bilqis was elliptical in shape and approximately 100 metres long. Just as the bull motif had been almost identical to the Cretan one, so the design and architecture of this big oval structure bore an uncanny resemblance to the ancient ruins of Zimbabwe and Mozambique. Art and architecture together were suggesting that something from the remote past had made its presence felt in Crete, Arabia *and* Africa.

The Mahram Bilqis work came to a sudden end when the political situation changed dangerously and dramatically in Marib; but Professor Allbright commented that what Phillips and his team had found, supplemented by the work of two or three succeeding expeditions, made it clear that Sheba was a dominant power in the area from 1000 BC onwards — coinciding neatly with Makeda's visit to Solomon.

As well as the biblical evidence concerning Sheba, reference can be made to the interesting old records in the Kebra Negast. The earliest known copy of the Kebra Negast is scarcely a thousand years old, but the oral traditions from which it is drawn are much older, and, like the Dead Sea Scrolls, there may well be pristine manuscript versions of it hidden away in ancient caves, just waiting to be rediscovered. The Kebra Negast purports to tell how the Ethiopians (Shebans?) were converted from their earlier worship of sun, moon and stars to Judeo-Christian monotheism.

A substantial body of scholarship suggests that the Kebra Negast dates from the time of the Templars, and places its origins somewhere after the restoration of the Solomonic Dynasty (identical to the "House and Lineage of David") in Ethiopia, which would relate to the reign of the Ethiopian monarch Yekuno Arnlak, who was in power from 1270 until 1285.

Early knowledge of the Kebra Negast came to Europe via Francisco Alvarez, who was sent by Emmanuel, King of Portugal to visit King David of Ethiopia. What Alvarez learned there was published in Portuguese during the 1530s. James Bruce of Kinnaird, a dauntless eighteenth-century British explorer, was given a copy of the Kebra Negast by Ras Michael the Vazir before leaving the beautiful and historic Ethiopian city of Gondar.

Much of the Kebra Negast's mysterious and intriguing contents found their way into Bruce's *Travels in Search of the Sources of the Nile*, and may now be consulted in Oxford University's Bodleian Library. The heart of this mysterious old document is its account of Queen Makeda's visit to Solomon, how she became pregnant by him, and how their son, Menelik (various spellings exist), grew up and went back to Israel to see his royal father.

Before she went back to Ethiopia, Solomon had given Makeda a very precious ring from his own hand and told her to give it to their son in due time. This she did, and Menelik wore it when he went to Jerusalem, where he showed it to his father, Solomon. The Kebra Negast also tells of how Solomon recognized and honoured the young Ethiopian prince and invited him to remain in Jerusalem. Solomon also told Menelik that he bore an amazing resemblance to Solomon's own father, David.

Despite Solomon's warm invitation, Menelik declined, and returned to his own homeland accompanied by a group of young Israeli nobles and courtiers. His main reason was that Rehoboam, another of Solomon's sons, was older than he was, and Menelik felt that it was Rehoboam's right to inherit his father's empire one day. It was also reported that Menelik and his Jewish companions took the Ark of the Covenant with them when they left Israel, and that it was finally lodged in a sanctuary in Axum.

Controversy rages continually over whether the mysterious object guarded in the temple next to St. Mariam's Church in Axum in Ethiopia is in fact the biblical Ark of the Covenant. Traditionally, only one holy guardian at a time is allowed to see the Ethiopian Ark. Keshe, a former protector of the Axum Ark and now a centenarian, described it as "a gold-lined wooden box, with a solid gold lid, surmounted by two cherubim with outstretched wings." Keshe also maintains that the Ark protects the original stone tablets containing the Law. He is in great awe of these tablets and says that you can feel their power when you approach them.

If there is any validity to the theories that the Ark of the Covenant is an exceptionally powerful and dangerous technical artifact, it should be borne in mind that gold is more effective than lead at shielding out radioactivity, because it is denser (gold has a density of 19.3 grams per cubic centimetre, whereas the density of lead is only 11.3 g/cm^3). Dare it be suggested that the gold lining and solid gold lid of the Ark might be there as protection against something inside which is highly radioactive?

The monks of Axum have also exhibited ancient musical instruments which they believe came from Jerusalem when Menelik brought the Ark of the Covenant to Axum. Comparing these ancient Ethiopian instruments with those depicted on the famous triumphal Arch of the Flavian Emperor Titus (AD 79–81) shows close similarities; does this to some extent authenticate the age and origin of the ancient instruments at Axum? If the historic silver trumpets at Axum are of the same design as the ones shown on Titus's Arch in Rome, it is not unreasonable to conjecture that they probably came from the same location.

Other arguments in favour of the Kebra Negast account of Makeda's pregnancy by Solomon, and the subsequent birth of Menelik, are: the presence of the Ethiopian Falasha Jews in large numbers, prior to their emigration to Israel in 1980; their claim to be the descendants of the Jewish protectors of the Ark who left Jerusalem with Menelik; their use of rituals from Solomon's era; the presence in Ethiopia of Christian churches dating back to the fourth century — churches that were almost certainly Judeo-Christian in origin; the probability that the Ark left Jerusalem after 955 BC but well before 587 BC, when Nebuchadnezzar captured Jerusalem but never found the Ark. If Nebuchadnezzar failed to find it, it had either gone from Jerusalem before he got there, or it was hidden so deeply and secretly that only its guardians could have recovered it.

Sometimes described as being as powerful and effective as that much later conqueror Alexander of Macedon, Nebuchadnezzar was never a man to take no for an answer. He had smashed the power of Egypt at the Battle of Carchemish in 606 BC and brought both Syria and Phoenicia under his control. With peace established, Nebuchadnezzar undertook a vast building program — with Babylonian bricks, each bearing his name. He made Babylon into a dream city and constructed a network of canals, reservoirs and aqueducts to support it. Nebuchadnezzar was well over eighty when he died in 561 BC after a reign of more than forty years.

He regarded himself as the favourite mortal under the protection of the Babylonian god Nebo, and his name actually meant "Nebo, protect my boundaries." A man with such a high opinion of himself would have gone to great pains to locate the Ark of the Covenant in order to enhance his power and prestige. So the questions remain tantalizingly unanswered: Was Menelik really the son of Solomon? Is the Ark of the Covenant still in a sanctuary at Axum in Ethiopia? Do some of the Black Madonnas represent Makeda and Menelik — of the house and lineage of David?

A curious, recent footnote to the mystery of Solomon, Makeda and Menelik, is the intriguing archaeological discovery in autumn 2004 of an ancient ship dating from their days. Found near Hof Dor, on the eastern Mediterranean coast, it possessed a massive stone anchor nearly three metres long. The timbers were radiocarbon-dated to the time of David and Solomon and provide intriguing contemporary evidence that Hebrew vessels of that period almost certainly travelled extensively. Does that fact increase the likelihood of the link between Sheba, Solomon, and the son they may have had?

Chapter 10

WAS CHARLEMAGNE A PRE-TEMPLAR GUARDIAN?

It can be fairly argued that Charlemagne is a strong candidate for inclusion in the list of pre-Templar Guardians stretching back into the mists of time.

Born in Aachen, in what was then the kingdom of Austrasia (now part of modern Germany), on April 2, 742, his German title was Karl der Grosse. The French called him Charles le Grand, while in Latin he was Carolus Magnus. Some historians regard him as Charles I of the Holy Roman Empire, and as Charles I of France, and his achievements certainly came close to equalling the multiplicity of his titles. He died on January 28, 814, leaving his achievements to entertain academic historians for centuries.

Charlemagne was the elder son of Pepin the Short, known formally as Pepin III. Between them, Pepin and his brother, Carloman, ran things as mayors of the palace to the mysterious Merovingian Dynasty, which they would eventually replace. Their dynasty, to be called Carolingian in honour of Charlemagne, was to enjoy cultural as well as political and military success.

Carloman and Pepin the Short were the sons of the mighty Charles Martel, who made sure that his boys took control over what the politically and militarily enfeebled Merovingians didn't seem able to handle.

The Vatican undoubtedly holds many strange and ancient secrets — including what went on between the papacy and the new Carolingian Dynasty. Popes Zacharias and Stephen II were both glad of Carolingian help and support. Charles was barely twelve years old — an impressionable age, perhaps? — when he went with his father to welcome Pope Zacharias. He also accompanied his father on numerous campaigns to subdue the Lombards and defend the papacy. This meant that, during his formative years, the young, future Charlemagne learned a great many pragmatic things about medieval military and political life. He became single-minded in his ambitions, determined to rule alone and unhindered by relatives who might be seen as rival claimants. After his brother, also named Carloman, died in 771 under circumstances that might have been suspicious, Carloman's sons (Charlemagne's nephews) also conveniently vanished from history.

(In balancing Charlemagne's achievements against suspicions that he gained power through ruthless and merciless means, it is helpful to remember the fate of the British princes in the Tower. There are three major theories about what might have happened to them. One accusing finger points to Richard III. Another school of thought blames Buckingham. Some historians favour Henry VII as a prime suspect. Simply because a particular death — or group of deaths — is politically advantageous to someone does not automatically imply that the most obvious benefactor is guilty.)

Charlemagne tackled the Lombards because they threatened the papacy; and when the Lombards were vanquished, he was the one who benefited most. Despite his promises to enlarge the Vatican's lands, the actual increase was nominal. He engaged the Saxons not only to acquire their territory, but to convert them to Christianity. They were not an easy people to conquer, convert or subdue: Charlemagne had nearly twenty battles with them before he regarded his victory as complete. In many of these campaigns he led the Carolingian army himself.

As is made clear in the "Song of Roland," which is explored in detail in Chapter Seven, when Charlemagne ventured into Spain he fared badly against the defences of Saragossa, and suffered rather worse damage when his rearguard, commanded by Roland (alias Hrodland) was ambushed by the Basques on the way back to Aachen — known in those days as Aix-la-Chapelle.

In 788, Charlemagne deposed his cousin Tassilo, who had until then been the Duke of Bavaria. This brought Thuringians, Saxons, Bavarians and Alemanni peoples together into a single political unit for the first time. Moving on into the former Avar kingdom, which once occupied Hungary and parts of Austria, Charlemagne found himself ruler of a huge territory. There are recognized methods and techniques for administering relative small tribal territories, but these differ vastly from the methods and techniques required to administer large kingdoms and empires. The differences are so great that they may be regarded as qualitative rather than merely quantitative.

Charlemagne's court consisted of scholars, academics and wise counsellors from a variety of backgrounds. Alcuin came from England, Theodulf was an Italian Goth, Leutrad was Norman French, and Agobard was a Spaniard. It was this cosmopolitan wisdom that enabled Charlemagne to function so effectively, and it must be asked how their presence in his court came about. It seems probable, rather than merely possible, that there were strong guiding hands, Guardians' hands, behind their appointments. There was a new dimension to thinking in Charlemagne's empire, and it is summed up succinctly in the words of the brilliant troubadour Richard de Fournival. This remarkable man, who lived between 1190 and 1260, was half-brother to the Bishop of Amiens, and chancellor of Amiens Cathedral in 1246. Although he was separated from Charlemagne's era by nearly four centuries, Richard could write in his *Bestiare d'Amour*, "The people who lived before we did understood certain things that those of us who are living now could not acquire today by virtue of our own unaided reasoning powers. Those things would not be known to our generation, if we had not acquired knowledge of them from those who lived before us."

Like the other Templars and Troubadours of his time, Richard de Fournival knew all too well that there were ancient and powerful secrets hidden in the distant past. What he was making clear — a factor that applied so relevantly to the qualitative cultural and academic changes that *began* during Charlemagne's reign — was that the ancient, classical natural science, mathematics, philosophy, law, logic and rhetoric had once been the unassailable fortresses of learning. Dark Age scholars had gone to learn from their ancient masters — but never to challenge them, nor develop their thought. It was already becoming clear to the great thinkers and counsellors of Charlemagne's court that they had to go beyond what the Greek and Roman writers had handed down to posterity.

Which raises the question of whether Charlemagne himself was one of the ancient pre-Templar Guardians — or whether he was manoeuvred by them into a position of political and military power so that they could flourish under his aegis in the persons of Alcuin the

Englishman, Theodulf the Italian Goth, Leutrad the Norman and Agobard the Spaniard.

There was another qualitatively different and distinctive dimension in the new thinking of Charlemagne's age. Wisdom and knowledge were not seen as having any intrinsic value of their own but were instead viewed as means to an end — and that end was salvation. Whether scholars were reading the Canon of Scripture, Plato, Aristotle or Church fathers like Augustine, their ultimate target was inevitably salvation. Wisdom, be it sacred or secular, was not valued for its own sake — it was seen as a tool, or instrument, by which Hell could be avoided and Heaven attained.

Was this attitude to classical wisdom something the Guardians were encouraging and reinforcing? Or was it something they were trying to persuade humanity to transcend?

Another important perspective on the relevance and importance of Charlemagne and his counsellors to the work of the pre-Templar Guardians can be seen in his relationship with Byzantium. Technically, in the later years of the eighth century, the Byzantine Empire claimed universal recognition. In a sense, therefore, the popes could be seen, constitutionally, as subjects of that Eastern Roman Empire. In terms of real power and dominion, however, Byzantium had long since lost its influence over Rome and was more or less limited to Sicily and a small area of southern Italy.

It was at about this time that Pope Adrian, hoping to establish some autonomous mini-principality in central Italy, produced a spurious-looking document entitled *The Donation of Constantine*. According to this highly dubious manuscript, the first great Christian emperor, Constantine (271–337), had donated territory to the papacy. Charlemagne aided and abetted the papal claims and, after a temporary rapprochement with Byzantium, invaded the territory in southern Italy that the Byzantines regarded as theirs.

In 799, Pope Leo III narrowly escaped death at the hands of his enemies and was sheltered and protected by Charlemagne, whose highly effective Frankish warriors escorted Leo safely home again. It was more or less in return for this kindness that the pope crowned and anointed Charlemagne when the people acclaimed him as their emperor.

Another clue as to whether Charlemagne was either one of the pre-Templar Guardians himself, or was one of their chosen hosts and protectors, is revealed when the cultural activities of his court are studied. He spent a great deal of time at Aix-la-Chapelle, where he established a relatively fine and comprehensive library — no mean feat in the eighth century. He read the Greek and Roman authors and the works of the Church fathers. He studied astronomy and mathematics — albeit at a fairly basic level. Under his aegis, and with his enthusiastic encouragement, an academy was initiated for the benefit of his young Frankish knights. With his family and courtiers around him — almost like precursors of the domestic Victorian Bible Reading and Prayers sessions, which servants and family members alike had to attend — he held sessions during which books were read aloud and learned discussions then ensued. Charlemagne himself seemed to find these sessions entertaining as well as educational and informative.

Education and culture spread from the emperor's court throughout his empire in what has been described by some historians as the Carolingian Renaissance — and this again suggests that the guiding hand of pre-Templar Guardians might well have been behind it. In Chapter Two, the moral precepts associated with some possible pre-Templar Guardians were examined in detail, and it was suggested that such moral precepts were an integral part of their secret organization — one of the "codes" by which they recognized one another. The culture that spread at Charlemagne's instigation and formed the backbone of the Carolingian Renaissance was a religious and moral one. His leaders and teachers travelled the empire, encouraging religious observance, church services, prayers, meditation and scripture reading. Morality and justice were also reinforced and encouraged. All of this had a great deal in common with the facts deduced from the analysis in Chapter Two.

Sometime in 784 or 785, the great English scholar Alcuin sent out *Epistula de Litteris Colendis* with Charlemagne's full authority. In fact, although Alcuin was almost certainly its real author, it went out under Charlemagne's name. The main theme of the work was that accurate linguistic expression was vital to all worthwhile religious and philosophical thought. Language was like the armour that protected a knight: the knight himself was the idea, the essential thought system; if the armour was less than perfect, the thoughts and beliefs themselves were vulnerable to the slings and arrows of dangerous heresies.

In 787 another publication went out in Charlemagne's name, although, again, Alcuin and the other scholars who drove the Carolingian Renaissance were almost certainly its real authors. This was *Libri Carolini*, an academic assault on the Council of Nicea for sanctioning the use of icons — a very hot potato for the medieval church both in Greece and Rome.

There was so much about Charlemagne that fitted the patterns of behaviour and belief associated with the later Knights Templar Order of Jerusalem. Like the order's nine founders, Charlemagne thought that what he was doing was in accord with the will of God — as he understood it. He was able to combine what he saw as personal piety with a lifestyle that left plenty of room for enjoying the good things of life. Despite their vows of poverty, the Templars lived well. Charlemagne managed to combine what he considered a sense of quest and mission with personal ambition and a love of power and conquest — the Templars did the same. They were undoubtedly a good and noble order with a very real sense of mission and purpose, but they were never averse to increasing their power, wealth and influence. Like Charlemagne, they were empire builders.

Charlemagne balanced that aspect of his nature that made him a rough and ready warrior with a desire for learning, knowledge and scholarship. The Templars combined the practical skills of warfare, undaunted courage, and great intellectual ability — as revealed by their knowledge of codes and ciphers and their superb contributions to architecture. In a very real sense, then, Charlemagne was a prototypical Templar.

Was he one of the ancient Guardians, or were the members who made up his court — the wellspring of the Carolingian Renaissance — simply using him as the shield for their activities?

Chapter 11

THE TEMPLARS AND THE ARTISTS' SECRET CODES

The history of art goes back a very long way indeed and this fact can be seen as a possible clue to the nature and origin of the ancient pre-Templar Guardians and their long-term purposes for humanity. The whole concept of artistic representation — communicating meaning by using shape, design and colour — opened up a limitless field of human cultural progress.

A few examples may serve to illustrate the point. By a curious coincidence of terminology, the Palaeolithic culture of the Dordogne area of France is referred to as Magdalenian, or Magdalénien, because of the historically important site at La Madelaine. This culture flourished between fifteen thousand and ten thousand years ago — an estimate arrived at through the radiocarbon-dating of the people's bone harpoons, in addition to which the Magdalenians also produced commendable flint tools. Besides their practical tools and engraved weapons, the Magdalenians also made bone and ivory figurines, and cave art was another important part of their remarkable cultural attainments.

Prehistoric pictures found in caves at Lascaux, near Montignac in the Dordogne, date back at least fifteen thousand years. They are mainly realistic images of large animals such as aurochs; the fossil evidence suggests that they lived there at the critical time.

The other common theme of these strange paintings is human handprints. Is it remotely possible to conjecture that these prints were intended for identification? Suppose, simply for argument's sake, that these hypothetical, ancient, pre-Templar Guardians really existed, and that they were teaching, training and helping our remote Palaeolithic ancestors in the Dordogne. What better way to identify their preliterate trainees than by using their handprints? They had no factory punch-card system to clock in by, no computerized record-keeping, no tutor's register to be marked, quite clearly no signing-in book: just put your hand in this nice wet pigment and press it on the wall.

If the ancient and mysterious pre-Templar Guardians *were* expressing something important in codes or symbols via the Palaeolithic cave paintings in Lascaux, how much more information would they have been able to express by way of what is generally referred to by art historians as medieval art?

This general term "medieval art" includes everything of recognizable artistic merit — including architecture — that was created between the fall of the Roman Empire in the fifth century and the dawning of the sixteenth century. Although medieval art and architecture are characteristically religious, it would be wrong to assume that the church was unique in employing artists, architects and sculptors at that time. Much of the art produced during those years was secular. Where did its central ideas originate? Did the pre-Templar Guardians influence it and use it to transmit coded messages and ciphers?

A great deal of medieval art depended upon what the Roman Empire had bequeathed to the Middle Ages and whatever artists had learned from the earliest days of Christianity. It must also be remembered that the old Roman and Christian sources were blended with the vigorous non-Roman and non-Christian artistic cultures of the north, creating an intoxicating and volatile mixture — an effervescent reservoir of talent and inspiration that the Guardians could use in a variety of ways to produce meaningful symbols and labyrinthine codes and ciphers.

Much of the religious art in the pre-Renaissance period was inspired by the work of Jacobus de Voragine, the Archbishop of Genoa, who lived from 1230 until 1298. He was a prolific writer who is especially remembered for *The Golden Legend*, an anthology of the legendary lives of the saints which was a very popular medieval work.

Jacobus was born at Varazza, a small Ligurian village near Genoa. He became a Dominican in 1244, while still a teenager, and he preached effectively all over Italy and taught in Dominican schools. Jacobus was a good, honest and industrious bishop who worked hard for peace in a world torn by internecine strife. His value was recognized in 1816 by Pope Pius VII when he beatified Jacobus.

But it is Jacobus's thirteenth-century work *The Golden Legend* which is of special significance when researching the Templar mysteries. Not content with the legendary lives of the less famous, more recent, saints, Jacobus included Adam, Noah, Abraham, Isaac, Esau and Jacob, Joseph and Moses in the first of his seven volumes. (That magical seven yet again!) His second volume discussed Joshua, David, and then, most significantly, Solomon and Sheba — turning the researcher yet again in the direction of the intriguing mysteries associated with the cult of the Black Madonna.

Jacobus also included Thomas the Apostle, who was thought to have preached the Gospel in India, Thomas Becket of Canterbury, and the mysterious St. Anthony. All three references have some considerable significance and help to draw together the threads of the Templar research. Becket has persistent, if semilegendary, connections with the activities of Templars and Crusaders in Palestine during the early part of the twelfth century.

The legend of Becket's birth records that his father, Gilbert, not only fought valiantly in Palestine for some years, but met and fell in love with a beautiful, spirited Saracen princess while he was there. She was equally devoted to him, and gave up everything to be with him. A cruel twist of fate took Becket's ship away from the harbour on an irresistible storm tide before she could get on board. The distraught princess was now isolated from her family and fellow Saracens. With tremendous courage and determination, she took the next boat for England, and reached there safely. All she could say in English was, "Becket — London," but miraculously this was enough to find him. The deliriously happy couple married, and Thomas — the future archbishop and martyr — was one of their children.

The less romantic version of Becket's birth suggests that his parents were of Norman stock: Gilbert came from Rouen and his mother, named either Roesa or Matilda, was from Caen. Their famous son was born in Cheapside in London, where Gilbert went on to become a prosperous merchant and, eventually, sheriff. Did Jacobus include Becket especially because of his father's possible connections with Palestine, the Templars and the Crusaders? Did Jacobus believe that Thomas Becket was really the son of a Saracen princess?

The St. Anthony reference seems to connect yet again with the Rennes-le-Château mystery in the Languedoc. Controversy continues to rage around the authenticity of the alleged "Priory of Sion" coded documents that were said to have been discovered in an altar pillar in Father Saunière's Church of St. Mary Magdalene in Rennes-le-Château in the late nineteenth century. *If* those manuscripts were genuine, and *if* the decoding was accurate, then Poussin and the Tenierses (father and son) were involved in some great, historic secret that was encoded in their pictures. Poussin's contribution to the mystery was said to have been embedded in his *Shepherds of Arcadia*. The Tenierses provided a picture of St. Anthony that coincided with the mysterious phrase "no temptation" in the supposed Priory of Sion coded manuscripts. The Tenierses depicted Anthony being tempted in the majority of their studies of him: demons, imps, evil spirits and similar tormentors and distractors were shown swarming around the pious and scholarly Anthony like so many large, obnoxious insects. In only one Teniers painting is Anthony shown with another saintly companion — both are looking tranquil.

Artist's impression of Teniers' painting of Saints Paul and Anthony. Is Rennes-le-Château on the hill to the right?

The Tenierses were Flemish, and did most of their work in and around Brussels and Antwerp during the seventeenth century. David the elder was born in 1582 and died in 1649. His son, David the younger, was born in 1610 and lived until 1690. It is highly significant that both Tenierses were contemporaries of Poussin (1594–1665), who was in his fifties when the elder Teniers died — and the younger Teniers was also in his fifties when Poussin died.

The elder David studied under Rubens in Antwerp, then under Elsheimer in Rome — which was also where Poussin worked. One of the senior Teniers' significantly symbolic pictures featured Vertumnus and Pomona from classical mythology. It was a theme that was very popular among other contemporary artists, including Jan Tengnagel (1584–1635) of Amsterdam. His version was painted in 1617.

Artist's impression of Vertumnus and Pomona by Tengnagel. Notice the mysterious griffoul.

Tengnagel was known to have visited Rome. Did he meet Poussin there? What strange secrets did the artists share, and were they encoded somehow in the Vertumnus and Pomona theme? It was some time after his visit to Rome that the enigmatic Tengnagel was promoted to the prestigious and influential post of deputy sheriff of Amsterdam, which he held until his death. Who was working behind the scenes to procure that position for him, and what tasks did he carry out for his patrons in return? Above all, what connection might the Vertumnus and Pomona myth have with the secrets of the ancient pre-Templar Guardians?

* * *

In the myth, Pomona was a hamadryad, or wood nymph. Abandoning the wild, she created a secure walled garden for herself, in which she concentrated on the cultivation of a superb apple orchard — she even diverted rivers to irrigate her apple trees. Devoted to cultivating her fruit, Pomona had no time for romance, although her beauty attracted gods and mortal men alike. Vertumnus, the god of the seasons, was greatly attracted to her and tried every conceivable approach — without success, until finally, having assumed the appearance of a very old woman, he entered the garden and told a number of stories that persuaded her that, without a loving partner, she was not fulfilling her life. He then resumed his normal appearance as a handsome young man, and they were married.

Meaningful symbols in the Tengnagel version include a spade, indicating that the treasure is hidden underground, and a broken pot, suggesting that at least part of the treasure is contained in an earthenware vessel — where Roman treasures were characteristically concealed when committed to the earth. Such jars were also used for cremated remains. The position of Vertumnus's fingers may suggest coded letters in the Ogham alphabet. The branches and tendrils over the head of Pomona are snakelike and may suggest the Eden serpent mythology, or may represent Arabic words or letters. The walled garden details are also reminiscent of the ruined château at Rennes-le-Château — or of some other fortification symbolizing medieval siege warfare.

Also of great significance is the fountain with the *griffoul* on the right-hand edge of the Tengnagel picture. This is exactly like the griffouls on the fountain in Couiza Montazels, where Bérenger Saunière was born. Who, or what, are these mysterious, intelligent-looking marine creatures, and why do they feature so prominently in the riddle?

What did the ancient pre-Templar Guardians know about them? Could they be identical to the enigmatic quinotaur, which was allegedly the joint father of Mérovée the Twice-Born?

Pomona's action in diverting rivers — in the legend, for no other purpose than innocent orchard irrigation — links curiously with the Visigothic custom of using river burials to protect the graves of its great leaders and chieftains. The Visigoths would divert a river, dig a tomb in the riverbed, seal it over, rake the sand and gravel back into place to camouflage it, remove the temporary dam and let the river resume its original course.

Taken together, all these points could suggest that the artists who produced the various versions of the Pomona and Vertumnus myth were actually preserving the secret that some great treasure — known to the pre-Templar Guardians and later to the Templars themselves — was hidden underground (or under the river) close to Rennes. The artists were also preserving important clues as to the nature and purpose of the strange, aquatic griffouls or quinotaurs.

It is particularly interesting to consider the relationship between Teniers, Tengnagel and Poussin in view of a letter that was written to Nicholas Fouquet in 1656. Nicholas was the all-powerful finance minister of France during the reign of the "Sun King," Louis XIV. Fouquet's younger brother acted for him as a seventeenth-century James Bond, and had been sent to Rome to visit Poussin. In his letter to Nicholas, the younger Fouquet wrote of Poussin:

> He and I have planned certain things of which in a little while I shall be able to inform you fully; things which will give you, through M. Poussin, advantages that kings would have great difficulty in obtaining from him and which, according to what he says, no one in the world will ever retrieve in the centuries to come; and, furthermore, it would be achieved without much expense and could even turn to profit, and they are matters so difficult to inquire into that nothing on earth at the present time could bring a greater fortune nor perhaps even its equal.

What were these amazing secrets? Had Poussin shared them with Teniers and Tengnagel? Were they concealed in some of the pictures that the three artists had painted — including the mysterious Pomona renderings?

* * *

The strange and enigmatic Nicholas Poussin deserves a great deal more research, if his part in the mystery is to be clarified. He was born in Les Andelys, in Normandy, in 1594, and his family was far from wealthy or privileged. In Paris in 1612, young Nicholas studied under a mannerist painter named Llalemald. This mannerist style of painting is not easy to define or categorize, and professional art historians are themselves divided about its use. One way to understand mannerism is to regard it as anything that differs from the High Renaissance style. Artistic quirks, humour and playfulness will get a painting into the mannerist camp; mannerist paintings experiment with perspectives and tend to distort objects in ways that allow the artist to express his emotions and personal ideas about the subject. Mannerism allows the painter to express himself as much as he interprets the people or objects which he is painting. It was his early mannerist training that almost certainly directed the young Poussin to express himself in his paintings and, later, to express the strange secrets to which he was party in his coded, symbolic, strangely geometric canvases.

Nicholas Poussin, 1594–1665: man of mystery.

Some of the deep, stressful mystery that surrounds Poussin's character is clearly evident in his face. This man knew something that troubled him greatly.

He moved to Venice in 1623, then to Rome, where he settled permanently except for a brief stay in Paris from 1640–1642. In 1629, Poussin married his landlord's daughter, and the paintings he undertook over the next few years had loving and harmonious themes. A decade later he turned to historical themes, and he was particularly interested in events with an ethical dimension. The political aspects of Poussin's life centred on his problems with the dominant and assertive King Louis XIV of France and that monarch's courtiers. Poussin returned to Paris only very reluctantly, and he was unable to contend with the jealousy and intrigue of rival court painters who envied his position as the man in charge of all the art in Louis's palaces. Through his combination of historical scenes and his studies based on classical mythology, Poussin bridged the gap between the gods and demigods of legend and the great Caesars, statesmen and generals of history. He also created a very interesting representation of the Golden Calf of the Exodus — with all the mysterious symbolism that that incorporated.

The combination of these distinct fields — the mythological and the historical — was almost certainly the result of Poussin's awareness of the existence of the Guardians, both in their ancient pre-Templar form and when they were later revealed as courageous and highly effective warrior-priests during the period of the Crusades.

* * *

The most significant line in all of Poussin's painted riddles is the phrase "*Et in Arcadia ego,*" which the shepherds are studying on the side of the tomb — one which bears an uncanny resemblance to the notorious tomb that once stood at Arques, very close to Rennes-le-Château. But where was the original Arcadia? One of the loveliest and most picturesque areas of the Greek Peloponnese, it is still very much part of the modern Greek mainland. The Arcadians are regarded as the most ancient of the indigenous people inhabiting the Peloponnese, and their history dates back millennia. Featuring high-peaked mountains, enchanting forests and verdant plant life, it is an area where time seems literally to have stood still. As well as its natural scenic landscapes, Arcadia offers a variety of ancient Frankish fortresses, cities half as old as time, historic settlements and picturesque Byzantine churches.

In romantic, poetic and artistic traditions, ancient Arcadia was a land of simple herdsmen and shepherds who lived peaceful, rustic lives in their idyllic, rural countryside. Arcadia was also the land associated with the god Pan and the almost hypnotic music of the syrinx, also called panpipes: seven hollow reeds of different lengths, capable of producing sweet and beautiful sounds. In a sense, Pan's musical ability made him a forerunner of the medieval minstrels and troubadours. Were there strange codes and symbolic messages concealed in *his* music, too? Who exactly was Pan, and how does he feature in the strange saga of the ancient pre-Templar Guardians and in later developments of the Templar mystery?

Pan, the Arcadian nature god.

Pan was traditionally a god of woods and fields, associated with flocks of sheep and their shepherdesses. His followers believed that Pan chose to live in woodland grottos; they imagined him wandering over mountains and strolling through peaceful valleys. To them, he was a god of fertility and sexual pleasure, and he was frequently thought of as dancing with nymphs and shepherdesses. Pan, like other gods and supernatural beings associated with woodlands, was also a source of fear, especially to those who had to travel through dark, sinister forests at night. The word "panic" is derived from his name; the lonely, nocturnal traveller giving way to sudden fear was said, literally, to be suffering from panic — the sudden, irrational fear induced by contact with Pan.

The subject of fear and dread links yet again with the mysterious church of Mary Magdalene at Rennes-le-Château. Above the door is inscribed *"Terribilis est locus iste"* — "This place is terrible." Just inside that door is a very curious statuary group that has been a source of disagreement and controversy among Rennes researchers for many years. One idea is that the main figure is Satan, or an artist's impression of the personification of evil, and that the angels above him making the sign of the cross are symbolically overcoming evil through the power of the cross. Other theorists regard this main figure as the demon Asmodeus, a traditional guardian of treasure in demonology. Yet another school of thought suggests that it is an earth spirit, like Pan. They consider that — including the salamanders, water and angels above the main horned and hoofed figure — the entire statuary group symbolizes the four elements of alchemy: earth, air, fire and water.

Traces of Pan are detectable in Tolkien's lovable but mysterious and powerful character, Tom Bombadil, in *Lord of the Rings*. Like Pan, he's a sort of eternal nature spirit with a great gift for magical songs and music. What hints is Tolkien dropping here? Like those of C.S. Lewis and the other Inklings, Tolkien's broad and brilliant academic mind encompassed and understood a great many of the strange mysteries and secrets of the past. Part of the unique power of their adventure fiction and heroic fantasy, set in Lewis's

The mysterious Pan-like statue just inside the church door at Rennes-le-Château.

Narnia and Tolkien's Middle Earth, is its clear reflection of Templar ideals and their ultimate ethic of good versus evil in the cosmos. Those same high moral codes and qualities can also be found in the heroic fantasy of their great predecessor George MacDonald; Lewis once said that he himself had never had one worthwhile idea that he hadn't encountered in MacDonald's work as well. How much did MacDonald, Lewis and Tolkien know of the ancient pre-Templar Guardians and their work? A close and detailed survey of their writings raises many fascinating questions.

Just as Pan's name is now a combining form meaning "all" or "completely," the god came to be considered a symbol of the universe and a personification of nature, and later still to be regarded as a representation of *all* the gods and demigods of paganism. Sylvanus and Faunus were parallel Latin divinities whose characteristics are so nearly the same as those of Pan that we may safely consider them as the same entity under different names.

The narrow, exclusively hostile attitude of the medieval church towards older, different religions transferred Pan's physical attributes — especially his horns and goat legs — to Satan and/or Lucifer. But far from being an epitome of evil and a personification of wickedness, the original Arcadian Pan was *good* — a friend of lovers and a kindly giver of pleasure and cultural gifts such as music. Was he more than a religious myth? If so, where had he come from? Was ancient Arcadia one of the significant locations of the ancient pre-Templar Guardians? Was that one of the strange meanings behind the enigmatic "*Et in Arcadia ego*" cipher in the mysterious coded canvases produced by Poussin and others? The riddle of *who* is in Arcadia is answered neither by Death nor by the body of the unknown man or woman in the sinister tomb: it is Pan and all that he stands for who is to be found in Arcadia.

Do the lonely mountains of Arcadia conceal something equivalent to a stargate, or an extradimensional doorway to infinity? Was this a portal through which the Guardians came and went?

* * *

Poussin, however, was by no means the only member of the secretive seventeenth-century art fraternity to use the Arcadian codes. Guercino (1591–1666) created a canvas with the title *Et in Arcadia Ego* sometime between 1618 and 1622. His nickname, Guercino, meant that he squinted. His full name was Giovanni Francesco Barbieri, and he was a member of the Bolognese School of painters.

Artist's impression of Guercino's Et in Arcadia Ego.

Although Guercino was almost entirely self-taught, he had a magnificent gift for painting, and he deservedly became one of the leading artists of his day. His achievements and widespread contemporary recognition were all the more remarkable because he spent much of his life in the little town of Cento, away from the bustle of seventeenth-century city life. It is particularly interesting to note that Pope Gregory XV called him to Rome in the early 1620s. What mysterious secret information did he exchange with Poussin while he was there? How much of that secret information related to the strange Arcadian mysteries?

Another painter of the time who is almost certainly connected with Guercino and Poussin and the mysterious Arcadian codes in their paintings is Bernardo Strozzi (1581–1644). Strozzi entered the Capuchin Order in 1597 or 1598, when he was a young man of sixteen or seventeen. He left the order having gained permission from his superiors to take care of his widowed mother, who had become ill.

His paintings were acclaimed in Genoa and Venice, and three in particular are worth very careful study and analysis in connection with the codes and ciphers. *David with the Head of Goliath* was painted in 1635, and it combines the Arcadian skull and shepherd theme — David was a shepherd boy when he killed the Philistine giant.

Strozzi also produced a very important picture of St. Veronica. Students of her legend generally regard her name as a distortion of the Latin phrase *icon veritas,* meaning the true, or real, image of Christ. It is significant that in Strozzi's canvas of her, Veronica is looking heavenward, as is the portrait she holds. Students of the secret geometry that many seventeenth-century painters used will notice immediately that Veronica's eyes, and the eyes of Christ

Artist's impression of Strozzi's David with Goliath's Head.

in the picture, can act as reference points for a quadrilateral. Veronica's outstretched hands and her one visible foot are significant reference points for a triangle. The cloth she holds, which bears Christ's image, is distinctly tasselled, and serious students of the Rennes-le-Château mystery will recall that when Bérenger Saunière died he was placed in a chair of state and dressed in a tasselled robe. His devoted villagers filed past his body and each plucked a tassel from his funeral robe.

The third of Strozzi's especially significant canvases is *The Lute Player*, painted at some point between 1630 and 1635. Just as in Poussin's intriguing coded canvases, the fingers are especially interesting. The musician is clearly manipulating the strings to produce the chords he wants, but the painter is almost certainly also using those complex finger positions to indicate letters in the old Ogham alphabet. The lute player of Strozzi's day has strong links with the troubadours and minstrels of an earlier period; Strozzi has probably chosen this subject to emphasize the importance of the coded musical messages the minstrels and troubadours almost certainly used during the thirteenth century. The book in front of the lute player is another symbolic clue to the probability that there are codes and ciphers here — is it the "Song of Roland" that this young musician is playing?

Artist's impression of Strozzi's St. Veronica.

Artist's impression of Strozzi's The Lute Player.

* * *

From the very earliest times, it seems probable that the ancient and mysterious pre-Templar Guardians were at work among our remote ancestors. Their influence continued into the classical period and the highly sophisticated Greek and Roman civilizations. When the Roman Empire faded, their mysterious influence almost certainly played a major part in the Merovingian era. Nine gallant, dedicated knights went to Jerusalem in the twelfth century at the instigation of the powerful Bernard of Clairvaux. Why did he send them? What were they searching for, and did their search involve the ancient cabalistic secrets kept securely by the wise leaders of the Jewish population of Septimania in southwestern France? The legend of Prester John provides another important link in the chain of mysteries. What was his connection with India and the church believed to have been established there by the apostle Thomas? Or was the Prester John nexus with the Templar enigma more to do with Ethiopia and the cult of the Black Madonnas — always assuming that Solomon and Sheba were the real founders of the ancient Ethiopian Dynasty via their son Menelik, whose name actually means "son of the wise man." How many of these Templar secrets were encoded and sung by the medieval troubadours and minstrels as they journeyed from castle to castle and from country to country? Their music and poetry was dominated to a great extent by the adventures, real and imagined, of Charlemagne and his doughty warriors such as Roland and Oliver. Just what vital Templar codes and ciphers were contained in the various lyrics which made up the different versions of the tantalizing "Song of Roland"?

If the troubadours and minstrels wrapped the great secrets in music and poems, and the artists concealed them in their enigmatic canvases, how much more effectively would the all round genius of Leonardo da Vinci have concealed them? A man of so many talents would have had access to an awesome selection of codes, ciphers and symbols.

Chapter 12

LEONARDO DA VINCI, MAN OF MYSTERY

Admirers of Leonardo da Vinci have described him as the greatest genius of all time, and not without justification.

Head of Leonardo da Vinci.

On April 15, 1452, Leonardo was born as the illegitimate son of a woman named Caterina, who was quaintly described in the class-conscious language of those days as a "peasant girl." His father, Ser Piero, was wealthy and in the legal profession. He raised Leonardo while Caterina went on to marry someone else. Between them, they produced nearly twenty children — though not with each other — and as a consequence Leonardo was provided with a large family of half-brothers and half-sisters. The Piero half of his family was wealthy enough to provide the young Leonardo with an excellent collection of books to stimulate his growing mind, and at the age of fifteen Leonardo was apprenticed to the painter Verrocchio.

In addition to his amazing mind, Leonardo possessed striking good looks, great physical strength and a fine voice — he sang almost as well as he painted. He reinforced his physical and mental health with a strict vegetarian diet, stimulated in part by his love of animals. On more than one occasion, he bought caged birds and freed them. His moral and ethical codes were as admirable as his music, his mind and his powerful, muscular body.

He stayed with Verrocchio until 1477, when he went into business on his own. Then, in 1482, Leonardo accepted a post with the Duke of Milan. He was there for nearly twenty years and did not leave until Duke Sforza fell from power, just before 1500. During those years, Leonardo was not only working as an artist, painter and sculptor but as a weapons designer, an architect, a naturalist, a mechanic, an anatomist and a canal designer. His problem, with which all inventors and researchers will deeply sympathize, was that he was too keenly interested in too many things. Consequently, not many of his projects were driven through to completion.

If only Leonardo had shared Ray Kroc's determination and ability to concentrate, he would have gone much further — albeit in fewer fields of activity. Kroc, co-founder of the McDonald's restaurant chain, died a contented multimillionaire. The philosophy of life that led Ray from mediocrity to global success and fame was simple: "Determination and persistence alone are omnipotent." Leonardo's fatal weakness was his inability to resist the seductive temptations of newer, different and more interesting problems — all demanding to be solved. His inquisitive genius could never resist the challenge of the strange and the unknown.

He shared his Renaissance world with some sinister and dangerous contemporaries. At one time he knew Machiavelli, whose name made its way into the dictionary as an eponym for unscrupulous dealing and the philosophy that, in politics, the end justifies the means. Leonardo also worked for the notorious Cesare Borgia. Perhaps as a result of what he'd observed in them, Leonardo — despite his previous generosity, goodness of character and high moral code — came off best in a family dispute over his late uncle's will. His multitudinous half-brothers and sisters had moved in greedily after Leonardo's father, Piero, died, and in so doing had deprived Leonardo of his share of that inheritance. Now, with the added help of his late uncle's wealth and land, Leonardo worked in Rome and undertook many projects for the Vatican.

In 1516 another of his important patrons, Giuliano de Medici, died, and Leonardo accepted an offer from the French king, Francis I, to become his premier architect, engineer and artist. It was a good move for da Vinci; he and the king were kindred spirits. When Leonardo died on May 2, 1519, at the age of sixty-seven, King Francis himself cradled the great man's head in his arms and nursed him tenderly until he breathed his last — a fitting tribute both to Leonardo's genius and his character.

Some of the more daringly imaginative theories that set out to explain his superlative genius suggest that Leonardo was not entirely human, and that nubile young Caterina — like Mérovée's mother, Basina — had acquired some additional genetic material from a quinotaur while swimming in the Mediterranean. Various other hypotheses see Leonardo as a man literally ahead of his time — or, perhaps, *behind* his real time.

Even the best and most avant-garde of our current scientists have never satisfactorily explained the metaphysical mysteries of time. Tesla, Einstein and Hawking have revealed more about the riddle of time than most researchers, but the essential nucleus of the enigma still remains hidden. The rules governing the curious nature and behaviour of time are not yet fully understood, but puzzling observations of what may be described as "time-slips" have been recorded. What if the man known to history as Leonardo da Vinci was a victim of one of these anomalies?

How would a man or woman from this twenty-first century have adjusted to life in the fifteenth?

Some theories concerning the subjective nature of time, exemplified in Shakespeare's famous lines about time running, walking and standing still for different people in different circumstances, suggest that if and when time travel occurs it might be a mental or psychic process rather than a physical one. This hypothesis suggests that the immaterial mind, spirit, astral body or consciousness of one person can, either temporarily or permanently, occupy the brain and body of someone else in a very different stream of time and space. So the mind of a twenty-first-century man — or woman — could have occupied Leonardo's fifteenth-century body. That amazing secret would have explained Mona Lisa's mysterious smile, not to mention the ambiguous gender of the disciple on Christ's right in Leonardo's controversial painting of the Last Supper.

In addition to quinotaur genetic material theories and time-travel speculations, hypotheses have been advanced that Leonardo was, variously, an extraterrestrial, a being from Atlantis or Lemuria, or a visitor from a parallel universe existing in another dimension. Just as the finest of our contemporary scientists have yet to solve the riddles of time, so they have yet to explain the enigma of the extra dimensions that are suspected to exist beyond the four we already know a little about. If there is a large number of unexplored dimensions out there somewhere, then there may be gateways connecting them. Might Leonardo have passed through such a portal into fifteenth-century Italy?

One thing about the strange Leonardo da Vinci is highly probable indeed: whoever he really was, and wherever he really came from, he was almost certainly one of the mysterious Society of Ancient Guardians.

* * *

So much for the man and his mysteries: but what of the codes, ciphers and symbols with which he recorded them for posterity?

Among Leonardo's other, lesser-known abilities was his apparent interest in prophecy, and some of his utterances made him at least the equal of Nostradamus, Mother Shipton and Coinneach Odhar, known as the Brahan Seer. Among Leonardo's utterances included among those listed as prophecies in Edward MacCurdy's excellent collected and edited version of da Vinci's notebooks, the following are especially interesting:

1. Something shall emerge from caverns and hollow places for which the nations of men shall strive desperately with heavy toil to gain its advantages. (Is Leonardo talking of precious metals and gemstones here, or does he mean oil?)

2. Destruction shall be seen in the sky with flames shooting downwards towards the earth. (Does he refer here to aerial warfare?)

3. Denizens of the water shall die when the water boils. (Is this some natural disaster, or is Leonardo prophesying some future nuclear cataclysm whereby atomic bombs or advanced laser weapons will heat the sea?)

4. People shall journey without moving; they shall speak and be heard when they are not there; they shall listen to those who do not talk. Those from the farthest places shall converse with one another as though they were together. (Could he possibly be prophesying journeys in airliners, satellite dishes, cable TV, video-conferencing, cell phones, e-mail, text messaging and the Internet?)

5. Invisible wealth will bring success to those who spend it. (Is Leonardo prophesying electronic bank transfers and credit cards?)

6. Those who feed them will be killed by them. (Could this be taken to refer to Creutzfeldt-Jacob disease, the human form of "mad cow" disease? Is the prophecy saying that people who have fed their livestock unwisely will die as a result of eating meat that is infected with bovine spongiform encephalopathy?)

7. People will live, eating and sleeping, among the trees in the countryside. (Is Leonardo referring to the tragedies of displaced people, refugees and asylum seekers?)

* * *

If Guercino, Poussin, Teniers, Strozzi and many other painters had learned to hide codes, ciphers and symbols in their canvases, had they learned it from da Vinci and his predecessors?

One of the greatest mysteries in all of da Vinci's superb paintings is the identity of the disciple to the right of Jesus in *The Last Supper*. Arguments rage back and forth as to whether the disciple that Leonardo depicted there is really a woman, and whether that woman is Mary Magdalene — and indeed, whether, as some claim, she was ever Christ's wife!

The key to the mystery may lie in some of the contents of a few of the Nag Hammadi Codices, some thirteen ancient volumes discovered in Upper Egypt in 1945. They include such gnostic teachings as the Gospel of Thomas, the Gospel of Philip and the Gospel of Truth. Among this Nag Hammadi library there are references to the apparent jealousy of the other disciples because of the loving attention that Jesus paid to Mary Magdalene, who may also have been the same woman as Mary of Bethany, sister of Martha and Lazarus.

In addition, there are interesting points made about Mary in a fragment of the Gospel of Peter, discovered in 1886 by the French Archaeological Mission based in Cairo. (They found it in a grave in an ancient cemetery at Akhmim in Upper Egypt.) Another fascinating discovery, referred to as the Gospel of Mary, consisted of an ancient papyrus book written in Coptic and apparently based on a first- or second-century Greek text. This was acquired in 1896 by a German academic, a Dr. Reinhardt of Berlin.

In the sixth century, Pope Gregory I (540–604), known as Gregory the Great, was responsible for the infamous Homily 33, which did much to damage Mary's reputation and reduce her former standing as a leading disciple. In the course of this homily, Gregory took it upon himself to declare that Mary Magdalene, Mary of Bethany and the "woman who was a sinner" (Luke 7:36–50) were one and the same person, and that the episode recounted in Luke's gospel indicated that she was a prostitute. In so disparaging her, Gregory was using his clerical and political astuteness to oppose any prominent leading role for women in the church that he led — to allow that one of the most favoured disciples was a woman would have set a precedent that the male-dominated priesthood would find threatening.

Is it possible to find evidence from *The Last Supper* that Leonardo intended Mary Magdalene to be the disciple on Christ's right, and that he believed her to be not only Christ's favourite disciple, but his bride as well?

Leonardo's *Last Supper* is in the refectory of the Convent of Santa Maria delle Grazie in Milan. It has been cleaned and restored many times since 1498. On top of those problems, it was damaged when bombs landed close to the convent during World War II. Allowance must therefore be made for all the changes and alterations to the picture since Leonardo put it there, two years before the fifteenth century drew to its close. Nevertheless, the face of this disciple is undeniably beautiful, sensitive and distinctly feminine. There is also the question of the body posture of Christ and this disciple. Leaning away from each other at symmetrical angles of approximately forty-five degrees, they form a letter M. Does that stand for Mary, for marriage, or for both?

The "royal" colours that Christ and the mystery disciple are wearing, reds and blues, suggest not only married partners but a royal dynasty as well. What else is Leonardo saying in the codes and ciphers in his picture? Reading from left to right, the very detailed hands — like the hands in Poussin's later canvases — spell out QQBBBNCHTQDHT in Ogham. Almost certainly initials, but in what language? Is it fifteenth-century Italian, or clerical Latin? It's reminiscent of the puzzling code on the Shepherd's Monument in the grounds of mysterious old Shugborough Hall in Staffordshire in England:

D O U O S V A V V M

This inscription has never been satisfactorily deciphered, but is almost certainly associated in some way with the Arcadian mysteries, with Nicolas Poussin's coded paintings and with the Templars of Rennes and the Languedoc. Admiral Anson, whose family owned Shugborough, was one of the pioneering circumnavigators. He returned to Britain with vast wealth. Did the adventurous admiral have access to some of the ancient

Templar secrets relating to the mysterious Arcadian treasure? And does the indecipherable Shepherd's Monument inscription refer to those secrets?

Returning to yet another sample of the secrets encoded in da Vinci's paintings, the *Madonna of the Rocks* is a particularly significant case in point. The angle of the woman's head, the blue of her dress, the way that her hair is falling and her exquisite face are all very similar to the ambivalent "beloved disciple" on Christ's right in *The Last Supper*. Ostensibly, *Madonna of the Rocks* depicts Mary, the wife of Joseph, with John the Baptist, the infant Christ and an angel — probably Uriel. The rocks and the cave are especially significant here. As noted in Chapter Three, Mary Magdalene is painted in a cave near Rennes-le-Château. Some researchers believe that, in *Madonna of the Rocks*, da Vinci is actually portraying Mary Magdalene in the French cave, protecting the three children she brought with her from Jerusalem — at least one of whom, it was said, eventually married into the noble ancestry of Mérovée.

Not far from the village of Rennes is a mysterious stone marked on the map as Roque Fumade — literally translated as "the smoking rock." One explanation of its name is that, in the days when mines were being worked in the area and ore was being smelted below ground, fumes issued from passages in this vicinity. Another theory is that the rock was seen as holy or sacred, and the smoke was the religious smoke of incense. The holiness came from the cave below the Roque Fumade in which Mary Magdalene was said to have taken refuge with her children.

Some religio-political theories suggest that Christ's enemies were well aware that he was a legitimate descendant of the royal house of David, and feared that he was planning to establish an earthly kingdom rather than a spiritual one. His triumphal entry into Jerusalem on Palm Sunday fits this theory. If Mary Magdalene was, in fact, his wife, and if they had children, then those who feared that Jesus had political ambitions would have been anxious to dispose of her and the children. Legend and tradition state that the ever loyal and helpful Joseph of Arimathea arranged for Mary Magdalene and the children to escape to France.

One of the major problems at this juncture is the apparent contradiction or paradox that the varying clues present. If Jesus was merely a mortal religious and political reformer who was judicially murdered by his enemies, and whose wife and children fled after his death to avoid a similar fate, then all of the spiritual aspects of Christianity appear to collapse. Jesus must be written off as just one more great and good teacher who suffered death at the hands of cruel, selfish, greedy and ambitious opponents in high places.

On the other hand, if the traditional religious view of him is historically accurate and the Gospel accounts of the crucifixion and resurrection are factual, Mary Magdalene is only one of many peripheral saved sinners who feature on the margins of the Christ narrative.

On the surface, then, the two versions are diametrically opposed and incompatible.

But there is a third way.

Escaping from the medieval church's prejudices about priestly celibacy on the one hand, and male domination of the church's hierarchy on the other — both of which are fallible human ideas, not divine principles — it is no longer impossible to reconcile both sets of facts. Jesus could very well have been the unique Son of God and the divinely ordained Messiah, as well as the loving husband of Mary Magdalene and the devoted father of their three children. In fact, whenever Jesus is called upon to bless children, he does so with delight — as in Luke 18:15, in which he sets a child in the middle of a group of his quarrelling disciples and tells them that unless they can become like that child, their chances of getting to Heaven are pretty slim. The more we contemplate Christ's teachings about children, and his deep love for them, the more likely it seems that he himself is a father in the ordinary sense. Furthermore: if, as Christians believe, Christ is both perfect and complete man, as well as perfect and complete God, his human completeness could not have been achieved without marriage and fatherhood.

Another clue to his marriage to Mary Magdalene is the curious incident (described in John 8:3) of the woman accused of adultery and dragged before Jesus by her accusers, who claim to have caught her in the act. The general interpretation of this episode suggests that its main purpose was to allow Christ's enemies to pose their trick question, "Is it lawful to stone her?" The ancient Law of Moses said that it was, but the occupying Romans now reserved the death penalty as their prerogative alone. Should Jesus instruct them not to stone her, his enemies — the narrowly hypocritical, puritanical scribes and Pharisees — would turn to the people and say: "This so-called leader is on the side of the hated Roman occupiers. He says we must obey them instead of Moses." If, on the other hand, Jesus had replied, "Moses gave us God's laws. Follow his teaching and stone her," his opponents would immediately run to inform the Romans that Jesus was illegally advocating the death penalty and was, therefore, a nationalistic troublemaker.

This episode becomes a thousand times more poignant and loaded against Jesus if the woman that his cunning opponents have dragged in front of him is his own wife, Mary Magdalene. Were they expecting an outburst of fury from an outraged husband who would, in his distress, shout, "Stone her!" Were they expecting that he would be overwhelmed by her behaviour and collapse with grief and shock? As John records in his Gospel, Jesus did neither. Unlike Shakespeare's tragic Othello, Jesus loves without limit and without anger or jealousy. He has perfect trust in Mary's love and loyalty, and immediately concludes — rightly — that this is yet one more foul trick dreamt up by his pernicious enemies. Perhaps John doesn't notice, or doesn't record, Jesus' gentle smile and the twinkle in his loving eyes as he tells her to go her way and sin no more — rather like the contemporary British farewell, issued lovingly to family members and close friends: "Be good! And if you can't be good, be careful!"

So, the Mary Magdalene paradox *can* be resolved without contradiction, dispute or rancour. Neither set of facts precludes the other. Jesus can be accepted as the unique Son of God; the pre-existent Word, or *Logos*, of the opening verses of John's gospel; the resurrected and ascended Saviour of the World, as outlined in the traditional Christian creeds. But he can also be the loving human husband of Mary Magdalene and the devoted father of their three children. Marriage and parenthood do not preclude his divinity — they enrich, reinforce and enhance it.

The da Vinci codes and ciphers did not say that Jesus was something limited and mortal *instead of* something divine. Leonardo's supreme genius recognized that Jesus had a human dimension *in addition to* his divinity — and Leonardo sought to share his insight with the world through his skill as an artist.

Chapter 13

TEMPLAR CODES AND SYMBOLS IN ROSLYN CHAPEL

As with all venerable sites and historic buildings, the spelling of Roslyn, or Rosslyn, varies from one set of records to another. This truly amazing building is crammed with codes, ciphers and symbols dating much further back than Templar times, although the building itself dates only from 1446 and is the work of Sir William St. Clair (or Sinclair), a member of the old and noble family who were princes, or *jarls*, of Orkney. William himself was known to have been a grand master of more than one important craft guild at the time, and there is evidence in Roslyn that its designers and builders knew a great many of the secrets of the pre-Templar Guardians. Sir William had intended it to be one of the Collegiate Chapels of Scotland — centres of learning as well as centres of faith.

This Roslyn carving of a Templar knight on horseback provides further evidence of the close connection between this mysterious old chapel and the Knights Templar.

The bold Sir William died in 1484, some thirty-eight years after he had set out to build Roslyn, and his mortal remains still lie in the chapel he never finished. Exploratory work well over a century ago revealed that the original foundations extended far beyond the present ground floor — clearly indicating that Sir William's original design had been for a much more extensive building.

Exterior of mysterious old Roslyn Chapel, near Edinburgh in Scotland.

Records indicate that quarrymen, smiths, carpenters, masons and their labourers were brought in from far and wide, and houses and land — as well as generous wages — were provided for the master craftsmen. Sir William had funded a provost, half a dozen prebendaries and a pair of choristers to run the establishment; later, his grandson would provide housing and land for them. When Sir William died, his son Oliver made sure that the building was well roofed, but didn't do much more, remaining content to preserve the work his father had begun rather than to expand upon or develop it further.

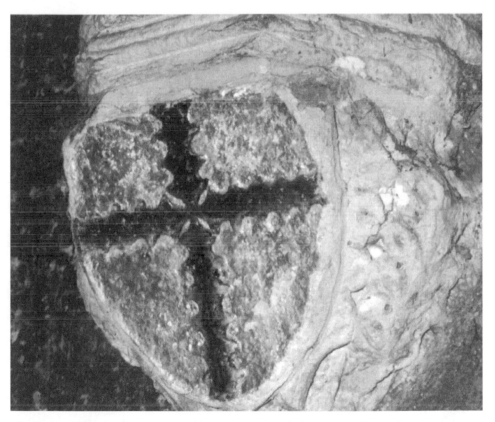

This engrailed Roslyn Chapel cross is a sign of the Sinclairs and is crafted in an undeniably Templar style.

There was trouble ahead because of religious intolerance. William Knox, brother of the famous John, was severely criticized in 1598 for daring to baptize the current Lord of Roslyn's baby in Roslyn Chapel. The furious Puritans preposterously described it as "a house of idolatry, not appointed for the teaching of the word or the ministration of the sacraments." In 1590, George Ramsay, then the minister of Lasswade, was forbidden to bury Lady Roslyn in the chapel, and in 1592 the altars were demolished and the chapel ceased to be a place of worship. Among the other vicissitudes that Roslyn suffered, General Monk arrived on Cromwell's behalf in 1650 and stabled his military horses in the chapel. A fanatical religious mob did further damage in 1688, shortly after the departure of Catholic James II and the arrival of Protestant William of Orange. The chapel then remained more or less derelict and abandoned until 1736, when James St. Clair put glass in the windows, improved the floor and repaired the roof. The boundary wall was also put into place.

In his *Religio Medici*, Sir Thomas Brown (1605–1682) described nature as the art of God. And Edward Young (1683–1765), in his long, sad poem *Night Thoughts*, wrote, "The course of Nature is the art of God." Those two powerfully inspired minds might well have been talking about the unique interior of Roslyn Chapel. The breathtakingly brilliant workmanship that is the hallmark of the entire structure gives the impression that those who designed, built and beautified it were doing their best to imitate in Roslyn what they had learned from the beauty of nature surrounding the chapel — and what they further believed to be the supreme power *behind* nature.

A stone Templar coffin from the thirteenth century, found in Roslyn Chapel.

In addition to the beauty of its workmanship and the secret codes, ciphers and symbols hidden there, Roslyn has a legend of hidden treasure associated with it. This legend is connected to the nearby Roslyn castle rather than the chapel itself, and the similarity to the Rennes-le-Château treasure legend is inescapable. There, too, the château and church are adjacent, and the central feature of the Rennes legend is the fabulous lost treasure — some of which, at least, appears to have been found and used by the mysterious Bérenger Saunière. The Rennes legend includes the riddle of Marie de Nègre, last of the Hautpoul family, who occupied the château. She is credited with knowing the secret and passing it to her chaplain, who in turn concealed it but left significant coded messages relating to it. Marie's gravestone also contained a vital cipher, which Saunière destroyed after having used it. In the Roslyn legend, a woman of noble birth, one of the Sinclairs from the remote past, was essential to the recovery of the treasure. As in the King Arthur returning-hero mythology, she has to be awakened from her sleep of centuries by the blast of a magical horn or trumpet.

Do the strange symbolic carvings inside the chapel provide clues to the legendary Roslyn treasure as well as to ancient secrets dating from the days of the pre-Templar Guardians?

One of the most remarkable carvings in Roslyn Chapel is the head of Hermes Trismegistus, creator of the Emerald Tablets and author of the Hermetic Texts. He was also known as Thoth, scribe of the gods of Egypt. Associating Hermes the Thrice-Blessed with the secrets of nature, and crediting him with a deep knowledge of the ultimate power beyond nature, has filled Roslyn Chapel with strange effigies of the Green Man — a mysterious pagan god — or nature spirit, like Pan.

* * *

What is the mysterious nexus between the pre-Templar Guardians, the activities of the medieval Templars and the myths and legends of the Green Man? Does the Arthurian romance of Sir Gawain and the Green Knight also find a niche here?

In this legend, Sir Gawain accepts the challenge from the Green Knight, who has arrived mysteriously at Arthur's Court, to allow any opponent to strike his neck with the huge axe that he's holding. Are there hints here that the Green Knight is being linked with Saxons, or Norsemen, who traditionally favoured axes rather than swords in their many bloody battles? Whoever accepts the challenge is honour bound to accept a blow from the Green Knight in return. The powerful Gawain, who was skilled in war — very much a prototypical Templar — beheads the Green Knight with a single blow. The witnesses are astounded when the decapitated green body retrieves its head, reminds Gawain of his agreement, and rides away as if nothing much had happened.

With honour to equal his strength and courage, Gawain duly keeps his appointment the following year. The mysterious Green Knight gives Gawain a very light, harmless wound, and allows him to return alive and well to King Arthur's court.

Although this particular story appears to date only from the thirteenth or fourteenth century, the Green Man tradition is very much older, and curious Templar and pre-Templar Guardian mysteries accumulate around it. One of the most intriguing aspects of the account is the detailed description of Gawain's armour and the device on his shield.

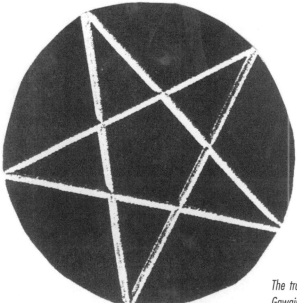

The traditional pentangle device, as featured on Gawain's shield.

The outside of the shield is a pentangle, or five-pointed star built around a geometrical, regular pentagon. The background is red — symbolic of blood and battle. This design has very powerful Templar connections. The *inside* of Gawain's shield, however, carried a picture of Mary — but was she meant to signify Mary, the wife of Joseph; Mary Magdalene; or the far older and more mysterious Black Madonna?

One interpretation of the pentangle device is that it represents the five senses — sight, hearing, touch, smell and taste — through which human beings relate to what they fondly regard as external reality. For such a chivalrous knight as Gawain, the message of the pentangle device is that he is determined to remain pure, true and honourable in every way, in every aspect of sensual life. Another meaning of the pentangle symbol for a Christian knight like Gawain would have been the five wounds of Christ — so that the red background symbolized Christ's blood. Is the story of the Green Knight meant, at one level, to symbolize the struggle between Christianity and paganism?

There are also traces of the Green Man mystery in the Robin Hood legends, where the mysterious and elusive outlaw of Sherwood Forest wears Lincoln green. If Robin is perhaps not entirely human, is he yet another aspect of the Green Man, a representation of a beneficent nature spirit who takes pity on the poor?

Another aspect of the Green Man appears in Robert Burns' poem about John Barleycorn:

> There was three kings into the east,
> Three kings both great and high,
> And they hae sworn a solemn oath
> John Barleycorn should die.
> They took a plough and plough'd him down,
> Put clods upon his head,
> And they hae sworn a solemn oath
> John Barleycorn was dead.
> But the cheerful Spring came kindly on,
> And show'rs began to fall;
> John Barleycorn got up again,
> And sore surpris'd them all.

How much did the incomparably brilliant, deeply sensitive and very human Scottish poet, Robert Burns, know of the mysterious Templar involvement with Roslyn Chapel and the numerous Green Man symbols it contains? Is his John Barleycorn another aspect of Sir Gawain's Green Knight? Very probably: Burns was deeply immersed in the ancient myths and legends of Scotland's bold and romantic history. He was a poet with wide and perceptive vision who saw deep truths and translated them in symbolic form. He was undoubtedly aware of Roslyn as a repository of secrets.

The Green Man appears so frequently in Roslyn because of his importance as a cipher. The numerous representations of him in the chapel are almost certainly reminding those who can read the codes that he is part of an ancient, ubiquitous, European folk culture, dating back to Pan in Arcadia — or even earlier.

Strange Pan-like representation of the Green Man in Roslyn Chapel.

There are many old European folk customs in which an actor dresses in foliage — perhaps a symbol of the leafy coverings adopted by Adam and Eve after they have eaten the forbidden fruit in the Eden story — and is then ceremonially "killed" to make the plants grow again next year, just as death came into the world after Adam and Eve ate the fruit.

During the Beltane festivals held on May 1, a character called "Jack-in-the-Green" is ceremonially "slaughtered" to ensure that spring is really arriving. There is a ceremony each year in the historic British coastal town of Hastings — immortalized by William the Conqueror's success there in 1066 — in which the Green Man is represented by a large framework of leaves and branches that a powerful actor carries in procession. In this ritual, the Green Man is accompanied by a mysterious female associate known as Black Sal. Could this possibly link the Green Man traditions with the cult of the Black Madonna? Was it an old European tradition from farther east — perhaps even as far away as Arcadia — that William had brought with him to Hastings?

In this Hastings ritual, does the Green Man represent the consort of the beautiful black Makeda, the delectable Queen of Sheba? Does he, as the spirit of nature who knows all about the natural order, represent Solomon's wisdom?

The other clear connection between Solomon and Roslyn Chapel is that Roslyn was originally envisioned, architecturally,

Is the creator of this beautiful statue from Walsingham in Norfolk, England, hinting that his Madonna is black? Does this statue represent Mary the Virgin with the young Jesus, or does it show the beautiful Makeda, Queen of Sheba, with young Menelik, son of King Solomon the Wise?

along the lines of the great Temple at Jerusalem — under which the nine original Templars were believed to have excavated so industriously.

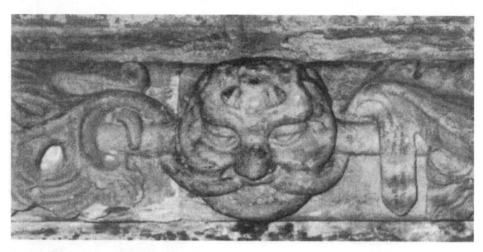

This benevolent and tranquil representation of the Green Man carved in Roslyn Chapel gives him an air of venerable wisdom, as well as the suggestion that he is a Pan-like nature spirit.

The brilliantly worked Apprentice Pillar in Roslyn Chapel. Notice the symbolic gate beside it. Is the architect hinting that those who can decode the pillar can open the gateway to the Roslyn mysteries?

* * *

Another of the Roslyn mysteries is the intricately carved Apprentice Pillar. According to the tradition, the mason responsible for it went abroad to study some similar masterwork there before completing it. In his absence, his highly skilled and talented apprentice finished it superbly. The master mason returned and, infuriated to realize that the boy was a better craftsman than he was, he killed his apprentice in a fit of uncontrollable rage. This story of the murdered apprentice carries overtones of the murder of Hiram Abif in Masonic history. Hiram was, traditionally, the brilliant master mason at the construction of Solomon's Temple in Jerusalem.

There may well be some accurate historic truth behind the story of the murdered apprentice. The Reverend Thompson, who was at one time a minister at Roslyn, maintained that the Bishop of St. Andrew's was in Rome visiting the pope as Roslyn neared its completion. In Thompson's account, the Bishop returned with the pope's authority to "reconcile" Roslyn Chapel. Reconciliation, as used here, was a sacerdotal term for a ceremony that was to be performed when it was felt that a sacred building had been "contaminated" or "polluted" in some way: a murder would certainly count as contamination in this theological sense. Was it the murder of the brilliantly skillful apprentice that made the reconciliation ceremony necessary?

In 1677, Thomas Kirk wrote an informative account of his travels in Scotland; in it he referred to his visit to Roslyn Chapel, which he rendered as Roslen Chapel. Kirk tells the tale of the murdered apprentice, and adds that one of the carvings shows a head with a wound corresponding to the fatal injury inflicted on the boy by the insanely jealous master mason's mallet.

Before the noble Sinclairs, who were descended from the *jarls* of Orkney, became Sinclairs, their proud Norse name was Mørs. Part of the legend of the murdered apprentice holds that the boy himself was also from the Orkneys, and that he would have been familiar with the Norse myths and legends of the Yggdrasil, the supernatural ash tree that unites Heaven, Earth and the nether regions. Every aspect of this mysterious, supernatural tree can be found in the Apprentice Pillar: its crown is the twelve-part zodiac, while the twisting branches are meant to represent the planets in their harmonious orbits. However, there is far more to the tree's mysterious root symbolism than the old tale of the dragons of Neifelheim (the hell of Norse mythology), who are supposed to be attacking the root of Yggdrasil. Close examination of the carvings at the foot of the Apprentice Pillar suggests an alternative explanation. Are these strange representations dragons, or are they the mysterious aquatic griffouls from the fountain at Couiza Montazels — *the same griffouls who are really the quinotaurs from the Merovingian legends?*

The mysteries of the Apprentice Pillar with its tree-like symbolism do not end there. Taken alongside the strange Roslyn carvings that represent scenes from the Garden of Eden, the question changes its direction: is the Apprentice Pillar the tree of life, or the tree of the knowledge of good and evil? The curves that spiral around the pillar, then, are not the planets in their orbits, but the serpent of Eden, tempting Eve.

This Roslyn carving of Adam and Eve with the serpent coiled around the tree of knowledge might be the clue to understanding the mysterious Apprentice Pillar. Are Adam and Eve black in this representation? Is this yet another pointer to Solomon and Sheba and the cult of the Black Madonna?

The southeast corner of the chapel contains the stairs that lead down to the crypt. Years of wear are still visible on them, which implies that, for at least a century prior to the chapel's problems during the Reformation, pilgrims were making sacred journeys down these steps. Why did they do it? It seems reasonable to assume that some special, holy object must once have been protected and venerated in this crypt — what could it have been? What did the nine original Templar Knights retrieve from under the Dome of the Rock? Did they find — or *think* they'd found — an ancient Black Madonna predating the Christian era? The Emerald Tablets of Hermes Trismegistus? The Ark of the Covenant? The Holy Grail? Was this artifact then preserved by their successors in the noble order after 1307, and did some Templar heroes reach sanctuary in the Orkneys, where they were welcomed and guarded by the Sinclairs, who later brought the object to the mysterious Roslyn crypt? Of equal significance is the question of whether the treasure is *still there.*

An interesting scholarly article appeared in *The Independent* on January 6, 2003. In it, Paul Kelbie, the newspaper's correspondent for Scotland, described how ultrasound and thermal imaging technology were being used to carry out noninvasive research into the labyrinth of vaults believed to exist below Roslyn Chapel. Part of Kelbie's well-researched article contains suggestions made to him by knowledge-able, high-ranking Scottish Templars that there is a possibility that some very important sacred artifact — perhaps even the Holy Grail — may actually be concealed inside the mysterious Apprentice Pillar, rather than in the secret vaults in the tombs below the chapel. Most tellingly, these same well-informed sources described Roslyn to Kelbie as "a book in stone."

Another interesting conjecture is linked with the age of the site that Roslyn Chapel now occupies. It is *said* to be a place renowned for its holiness and magical properties in ancient pagan times, long before the Christian era. Is that another reason for the hundred or more representations of the mysterious Green Man within the chapel? According to the very readable and meticulously accurate *Illustrated Guide Book to Rosslyn Chapel* written by Dr. Tim Wallace-Murphy in 1993, investigations have revealed that there are bodies in the sealed vaults below the crypt.

* * *

Near the north wall is a seventeenth-century stone, believed to be a Guild Stone, which makes reference to the King of Terrors. This has a curious link with Nostradamus, who lived from 1506 until 1566.

Just as the brilliant mind and artistic talents of Leonardo da Vinci make him a highly probable candidate for membership in one of the secret Guardian/Templar orders, so does the uncanny wisdom of Nostradamus. Co-author Lionel presented Roger Bolton's highly acclaimed TV documentary *The Real Nostradamus*, which was broadcast in July 1999. This was a highly significant date for followers of the Nostradamus prophecies because of one quatrain:

> *L'an mil neuf cens nonante neuf sept mois*
> *Du ciel viendra grand Roy d'effrayeur*
> *Resusciter le grand Roy d'Angoumois.*
> *Avant après Mars régner par bonheur.*

A broad translation of this reads:

> In the year 1999 seven months
> From the sky will come a great King of Terror
> To [resurrect/restore/resuscitate] the great King of
>   the Mongols;
> Before and after Mars reigns by good fortune.

A Nostradamus expert we consulted and interviewed for the documentary produced a very early version of this quatrain in which the apostrophe in the second line was missing, so that the phrase read simply *Roy deffrayeur* instead of *Roy d'effrayeur*. This has a completely different meaning in sixteenth-century French. To defray expenses is simply to pay them on behalf of someone else, so the king from the sky is a benevolent and generous monarch who will help the poor by defraying their expenses for them — he is not a source of terror, but a wealthy benefactor. A Christian interpretation might even see some Christlike qualities there: the concept of a divine redeemer paying our human debts. So why is there a reference to a King of Terrors on a stone in the crypt of Roslyn chapel, which is approximately contemporary with Nostradamus?

One very curious episode occurred while co-author Lionel was filming in the side chapel of the Church of St. Laurent in Salon (in

Provence, France), where the mortal remains of Nostradamus are interred in the wall behind a large, white, memorial grave slab. As the camera crew entered this chapel, a spotlight that was supposed to come on automatically to illuminate the slab began to flicker stroboscopically, making filming impossible. An expert, professional cameraman could easily compensate for the light being on or off consistently — but little could be done, even by the best cameraman, in this case. There were no church staff available to help our film team, so we tried every switch and plug we could find in that side chapel in an attempt to persuade the light to go out and stay out. Nothing worked!

As a last resort, one of the team suddenly remembered that Lionel was an ordained Anglican priest as well as a professional writer, Equity member, actor and broadcaster.

"You don't think it's Nostradamus messing us about because he doesn't want us to film his tomb?" he asked.

Common sense dictated that supernatural interference was an extremely low probability, but the production team had now reached the point where anything and everything was worth a try. This mischievous strobe light was costing a lot of money! Lionel duly said a short prayer for the repose of the spirit of Nostradamus and blessed the tomb. Precisely as he said "amen," the errant light obligingly went out and stayed out. The vital scene in St. Laurent's Church was duly and satisfactorily filmed.

* * *

Another curious mystery with a close connection to the noble Sinclairs of Orkney and Roslyn is the identity of Glooscap of Nova Scotia.

One of the greatest and best of the very creditable Sinclairs was Henry the Navigator. Henry was born in 1345, the son of Isabel and, through her, the grandson of Malise, the Earl of Straithearn, Caithness and Orkney. The man who looked after his loyal subjects on the Orkney Islands would have to sail to administer his lands and tend to his people, and in the process he would become expert at it — a real son of the sea. Such a man did Henry Sinclair become.

When Philip le Bel's treachery and spite drove the Templars to seek refuge away from his authority, there is a great deal of evidence to the effect that they were warmly welcomed in Scotland, and especially in the Orkneys. Their prowess at sea was of the same quality as their military and architectural ability on land. Sailors and navigators of their quality would be welcomed by the sailing fraternity of the Orkneys. In addition to his Templar friends, young Henry Sinclair was well known to the Zeno brothers, who were expert navigators from Venice and were descended from Zeno of Alexandria, the classical mathematician who had constructed the famous paradox of the mythical race between Achilles and the tortoise. Carlo Zeno was a leading Venetian statesman at the close of the fourteenth century, and it was his brothers Nicolò and Antonio who went up to meet with Henry Sinclair in the Orkneys.

This raises a huge question mark. What was their motive?

Christian Crusaders, Templars, Hospitallers, and pilgrims in general had more or less accepted that Jerusalem and the Holy Land were now controlled by the Muslim kingdoms of the Middle East, and would remain so for the foreseeable future. The old dream of a Christian kingdom of Jerusalem was fading, and Prester John's invincible — but legendary — forces had never made their longed-for appearance to revive it. A new dream was being born instead. The idealism of warrior-priests like the Templars was seeking out a New Jerusalem, a Promised Land far to the west, across the Atlantic. Shadowy legends of such lands already existed — the story of lost Atlantis among them — and tended to grow in the telling. So there were powerful motives that drew strong, able men together: the Sinclairs were ready for exploration and adventure; the surviving Templars and their young recruits were keen to find new lands across the Atlantic where holy treasures and worldly wealth could be safely stored away from greedy and unscrupulous monarchs like Philip; the Venetian Zeno family were good businessmen — and Venice survived on her trade. New countries across the Atlantic would be potential trading partners for their beloved Venice.

There is evidence that Henry Sinclair, the Zeno brothers and a small group of dauntless Templars crossed the Atlantic safely and landed in Nova Scotia, where they seem to have stayed for about a year. The local indigenous people, the Micmac, were friendly, intelligent, cultured and hospitable.

It was around this period that the important Micmac traditions about their Hiawatha-style hero, Glooscap, came into being. According to Micmac history, Glooscap was a wise and benign teacher who helped them in many ways during his visit to Nova Scotia. According to the legends, he taught them how to make fishing nets, which greatly improved their catches — previously, they had fished only with spears. There is archaeological evidence that the Micmac diet improved dramatically at this time, when they were able to take more fish protein on board.

Glooscap taught more than fishing skills, and this ties in with the moral, ethical and philosophical teachings associated with the ancient pre-Templar Guardians, and the high morality of the Templars themselves. In Chapter Two, the moral teachings of Alexander the Great, the ancient Egyptian ethical teachings, and the precepts of Hermes Trismegistus were discussed. Solomon's wisdom is also proverbial, and he, of all men, would have been one of the ancient, pre-Templar Guardians. Glooscap — very probably Henry Sinclair — also left important moral, ethical and philosophical teachings that the Micmac nation still treasures as part of its cultural heritage. He taught them such aphorisms as:

- The heart of the law is to concern yourself with controlling your own life. Never interfere with the lives and happiness of others.
- Listen carefully and think hard about all that is said to you.
- Control your temper.
- Never speak in your own praise.

All who met Glooscap made warm and favourable comments about him. They said he was "sober, grave and good," and that they felt he could look into the hearts and minds of men and understand what they were thinking.

Micmac accounts of Glooscap describe him as a great king or prince in his own country. He was an experienced and skillful sailor who said that his home was on an island far away and that he had reached their land via Newfoundland. The Micmac had met him for the first time at

Pictou, where later Scottish immigrants landed in 1773. Pictou is, therefore, rightly known as "The Birthplace of New Scotland." Today it is a fine, historic town that welcomes visitors to the full-sized replica of the good ship *Hector*.

Glooscap told his Micmac friends that he was the father of three daughters, which interested the local chiefs who were looking for suitable marriage partners for their sons. Henry Sinclair had three daughters: Elizabeth, Mary and Jean. Glooscap told the Micmac that he would definitely come back and visit them again, but he never did. Sinclair of Orkney was a man of truth and honour, whose word was his bond. If Glooscap *was* Henry the Navigator, why didn't he return as promised?

In 1400, Henry IV of England invaded Scotland, and some of his fleet attacked the Orkneys. As soon as this news reached Henry Sinclair, he rushed to attack the English invaders, even though it would have been far wiser to wait in his sturdy castle at Roslyn and let the English break ineffectually against his stalwart defences. Had Sinclair acquired this military style from his dashing and impetuous Templar friends? Did a dauntless band of Templars go down with him? Their motto was always, "First to attack — last to retreat!" Given the overwhelming odds against him, the intrepid hero Sinclair was defeated and killed. Thus, the original Glooscap never returned to visit his Micmac friends again.

But perhaps the Templars did.

Chapter 14

TEMPLAR MYSTERIES IN CANADA AND THE UNITED STATES

Much as the work of Christopher Columbus is rightly acknowledged and appreciated, there is a vast reservoir of evidence to suggest that he was by no means the first European or Mediterranean traveller to cross the Atlantic successfully.

One such piece of evidence is the mysterious Old Stone Mill in Newport, Rhode Island. It stands in Touro Park, off Bellevue Avenue, and its ancient stones are at the centre of many controversial theories. Its architectural style has been described by some experts in the field as medieval Scandinavian: its basic shape is cylindrical, and it stands on eight columns with arches between them — and it was there before Newport was founded in 1639. It could just as well have been Templar as Norse.

Research carried out by Dr. Youssef Mroueh suggests that Muslims reached the Americas before Columbus. He cites an episode that took place during the reign of Caliph Abdul-Rahman III at the end of the tenth century; it was claimed that African Muslims sailed fearlessly into what was referred to then as "the sea of fog and darkness" and returned with treasure from what they described as "a curious land." The Muslim historian and geographer Al-Masudi (871–957) gave an account of Ibn Aswad's earlier voyage to some huge unknown land mass across the Atlantic during the reign of Caliph Ibn-Mohammad, who ruled Spain from 888 to 912. Ibn Aswad came back loaded with treasure. Another historian, Al-Gutiyya, recorded how a navigator named Ibn Farrukh, who came from Granada, visited the Canary Islands during the reign of the Spanish Caliph Hisham II (between 976 and 1009). The renowned Harvard historian Leo Weiner, author of *Africa and the Discovery of America*, gave his opinion that Muslims from West Africa had reached Canada and North America, where they were not only trading with the Iroquois and Algonquin nations, but intermarrying with them. Another weighty reference comes from Al-Idrisi's work dating from the eleventh century. He records how an expedition sailed from North Africa into the Atlantic and eventually reached an island that was well cultivated by its people, who soon provided an Arabic interpreter to converse with the sailors! Al-Mazandarani set out from Morocco and reached one of the Caribbean islands towards the end of the thirteenth century.

Not all Templar interactions with Muslims in the Middle East were hostile, military ones. The Templars and other medieval Europeans learned considerable amounts of medicine, science, mathematics, geography, navigation and astronomy from their contacts with wise and cultured Arabians. There can be little doubt that part of the Templars' knowledge, and some Templar secrets, came from their contact with cultured and educated Arabians. Was it from these early Muslim navigators that the Templars acquired their knowledge of what lay beyond the "sea of fog and darkness," so that when their fleet escaped from Philip le Bel they had a serviceable idea of where to go and how to navigate their way across the Atlantic? Did they pass some of that important information on to Henry Sinclair the Navigator and his friends the Zeno brothers from Venice?

There is also evidence that Columbus was informed by the residents of Haiti that black navigators had already visited their island. The Haitians showed Columbus spears that these earlier visitors had left with them: these were tipped with a metal referred to by the Haitians as "guanine," which was a mixture of gold, silver and copper and was thought to be an alloy of the type made by craftsmen in their workshops in Bata, Mbini and Mongomo in Equatorial Guinea on the west coast of Africa.

* * *

There are also hints of pre-Columbian voyages by the Mandinka people of West Africa, who were made internationally famous by the widely acclaimed TV series *Roots*, which traced the origins of its hero, Kunta Kinte, to his Mandinkan origins in the village of Juffreh in Gambia, West Africa. What is especially interesting about the Mandinka is that they became an independent nation and then started to expand their empire and culture — during the thirteenth century. Did Mandinkan explorers and navigators make contact with the Templar fleet? Did they share their knowledge?

The Mandinkan navigators are believed to have ventured as far as America, and to have explored much of the interior via rivers and waterways, all before Columbus. The Four Corners, a unique area where the borders of Utah, Colorado, New Mexico and Arizona all converge, is home to some of the most spectacular and interesting ruins in the world. Well over a thousand years old, they are thought to be mainly the work of the Ancestral Puebloan people, but when knowledge of the early Mandinka navigators and explorers is added to what the Four Corners ruins reveal, the story becomes more complex. There are symbols carved in a cave at the Four Corners that can be translated, according to ancient Muslim records, as meaning "the elephants are unwell and behaving badly." If a Mandinkan Atlantic expedition staged a thousand years ago was massive enough to transport elephants, it would have been of some serious historical consequence.

Professor Howard Barraclough "Barry" Fell was one of the outstanding — if controversial — geniuses of the twentieth century, ranking in intellectual power alongside Einstein, Tesla and Hawking. Born in Sussex, England, in 1917, Barry Fell had a very distinguished academic career, ending with a professorship at Harvard. He also served with gallantry and distinction during the Second World War.

In his book *Saga America*, Professor Fell provided evidence, based on various old American texts, diagrams and charts, which suggested that schools had existed there in pre-Columbian times, and that those schools had taught in the old Kufic scripts of North African Arabic. Traces of them were found at Mesa Verde, Colorado, and at Mimbres Valley in New Mexico. According to Fell's research, these ancient schools taught mathematics, astronomy, geography and navigation.

* * *

Another interesting pointer to a pre-Columbian visit to America is the Knight's Carving in Westford, Massachusetts. Who is the knight commemorated by this strange old stone? Many expert historians, archaeologists and researchers think that he was Sir James Gunn, who was believed to have been a Templar and a close friend of Henry Sinclair. Gunn was one of the party travelling inland from the New England coast to investigate smoke they had seen in the distance. He died on the journey, and was buried on the spot. To remember a noble, loyal and gallant comrade, his friends carved the Knight's Stone in his honour and worked the Gunn family coat of arms into his shield. The sword has a break in it, which symbolizes the death of a knight. The Westford library contains a stone that dates from roughly the same period and shows a fourteenth-century ship, the number 184 and an arrow. Was it meant to tell other members of the Sinclair-Zeno expedition which way the explorers had gone, or to advise them of the location of the campsite?

Then there are the challenging discoveries of Roman, Berber, Phoenician and Egyptian artifacts in the Canary Islands, which provide evidence of trade between Europe and Africa and the Canaries from roughly 500 BC to AD 500. If maritime traders from Europe and Africa were in the Canaries, the probability that one or more of their ships went from the Canaries to the Americas — either by design or accident — is high. Another stubborn little piece of evidence from this period is the famous Roman terra-cotta head with features that don't seem to be typically Amerindian. It can be seen by researchers today in Mexico City, where it is displayed in the National Museum of Archaeology's Ceramics Hall.

The three-centimetre head was discovered in the Toluca Valley, near Tecaxic-Calixtlahuaca. It seems to have been some sort of interment offering that was placed in the tomb, or grave, during the twelfth or thirteenth century. Found with the little Roman head were seashells. Did they indicate that it had been brought in from over the sea? The style, design and facial features all strongly suggest that the head is Roman and may date to the second century AD.

* * *

Returning to Nova Scotia, the authors visited the Yarmouth Museum and made a close and careful inspection of the so-called Yarmouth Stone, otherwise known to scholars and historians as the Runic

Stone, or the Fletcher Stone, after the Dr. Fletcher who claimed to have discovered it in 1812.

Co-author Patricia with museum curator Eric J. Ruff and the Yarmouth Stone, Nova Scotia.

Fletcher's family averred that he was a highly intelligent man, but that he owned a mischievous sense of humour to match his intellect. The possibility of a hoax, therefore, must be taken into consideration. On the other hand, the stone weighs in the region of two hundred kilograms and was found in a place where Norse maritime adventurers might well have decided to leave a record of their visit for posterity. Runic experts have been divided on the subject for nearly two centuries. One said that the runes meant, "The son of Harko spoke to the men." Another experienced runist translated it as, "Leif to Eric raises this monument." Does this indicate that the Viking hero Leif Eriksson visited Yarmouth, Nova Scotia? Other experts, including Professor Magnus Oleson of Oslo, have expressed the opinion that the marks are not a genuine runic inscription at all, and have no meaning as such. The most intriguing possibility of all is that they are not runes but secret Masons' marks of the kind that would be understood by members of the craft, and which can be seen, discreetly placed, in Roslyn

Chapel.

Yet another possibility is that whoever carved the mysterious Yarmouth Stone was familiar with the strange Glozel alphabet, discovered near Vichy in central France in 1924. Despite the accusations of fraud and hoax levelled against the Fradin family who discovered the curious Glozel Tablets, the tablets and artifacts found with them stood up well to thermoluminescent dating tests: the youngest of them was at least five hundred years old, while some date back for several millennia.

Details of inscription on the Yarmouth Stone.

Could the enigmatic underground chamber at Glozel, where the tablets were found, have been the hiding place of a group of refugee Templars some time after 1307? Did some or all of that medieval Templar group from Glozel ultimately join up with Henry Sinclair, or with a vessel belonging to the lost Templar fleet, and so make their way across the Atlantic? If the letters on the Yarmouth Stone are a message in the cryptic Glozel alphabet, were they intended for later Templar expeditions?

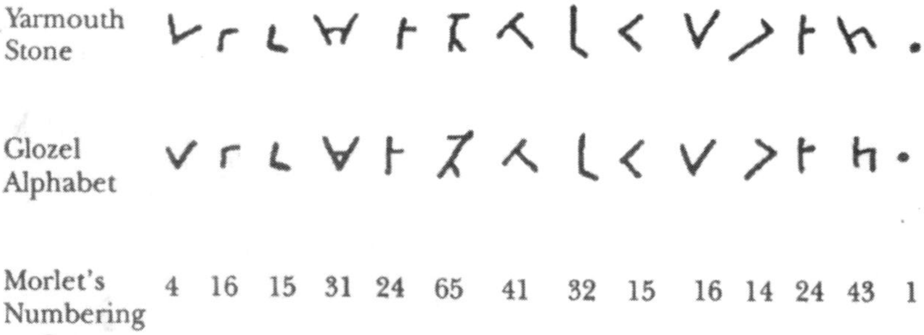
Yarmouth Stone
Glozel Alphabet
Morlet's Numbering
4 16 15 31 24 65 41 32 15 16 14 24 43 1

In 1955, Dr. Morlet wrote Origines de l'Ecriture, *in which he identified and numbered the Glozel alphabet. In this table the authors compare Morlet's work with their identifications of the Yarmouth Stone alphabet.*

Is it remotely possible that they were intended to indicate that the main party was busy on Oak Island in Mahone Bay, Nova Scotia, creating the artificial beach, the great coffer dam that made their work possible, and their death-trap flood tunnels designed to protect whatever mysterious treasure they concealed in the Money Pit (which will be discussed in Chapter Fifteen)?

Widespread as it is, the evidence is still not conclusive, but there are mysterious ruins, strange monuments, curious inscribed stones, and other odd, ancient artifacts throughout the Americas which, taken together, give credence to the possibility that not only the Norse adventurers, but Henry Sinclair, the Zeno brothers, the Templars, Ibn Aswad and the early Mandinkan mariners also crossed the Atlantic long before Columbus. What if all these heroic voyages were not random or haphazard, but were part of some grand design of the ancient pre-Templar Guardians? Is it possible that, one way or another, these Guardians were trying to establish something extremely important, or to hide something extremely important, on the western side of the Atlantic Ocean — for them, the ill-famed "sea of fog and darkness"?

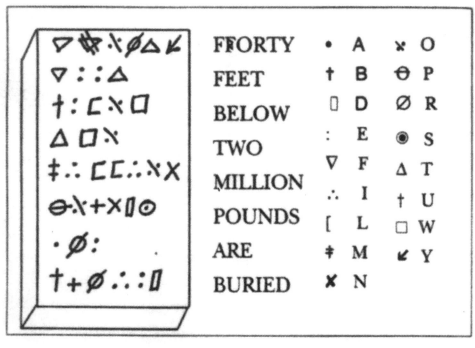

One possible interpretation of the inscribed stone found in the Oak Island Money Pit.

Chapter 15

THE TEMPLARS ON OAK ISLAND

In 1795, three young men still in their teens visited uninhabited Oak Island in Mahone Bay, not far from the little fishing village of Chester, Nova Scotia. As they explored the island they came upon a clearing, at the centre of which there was a curious depression in the earth — as though something fairly substantial had been dug there and filled in again. Beside this depression stood a sturdy old oak tree with one branch, more or less over the centre of the sunken earth, lopped off short. From a point near the end of this branch hung an old ship's block and tackle, almost falling apart from years of exposure to the weather.

To the three youngsters — Anthony Vaughan, Daniel McGinnis and John Smith — these clues meant only one thing: *pirate treasure!*

Life in Nova Scotia in the eighteenth century was not easy. You could grow up to be a farmer, a fisherman or a lumberjack — all of which involved hard, dangerous and demanding work. To find buried treasure would give you the key to freedom. The trio of teenagers began to dig furiously. It is greatly to their credit that they got to a depth of nearly twenty feet before sheer human exhaustion took the edge off their enthusiasm and they realized that the undertaking was beyond what three men could handle.

Their digging, however, had revealed certain vital clues. Less than a metre down, they had encountered a layer of flat stones, almost like paving stones, which were not like the native rock of Oak Island. They were, in fact, more like the stone found in the vicinity of Gold River, just a short distance up the coast of the mainland. This was a curiosity: why had someone gone to the trouble of bringing stones to Oak Island and laying a sort of floor across the top of their shaft?

The three young burrowers had spotted another important clue as they dug: the walls of their shaft were of brick-hard, impermeable clay, still etched with the marks made by the picks and shovels of the original diggers; but the backfill that Smith, Vaughan and McGinnis were lifting out was soft and friable — almost like brown sugar. This made it absolutely certain that the shaft they were excavating was manmade — not some freak of nature.

Their next clues were the platforms of oak logs that the original excavators had let into the brick-hard clay of the shaft's sides. The young diggers hit one at the ten-foot level, and a second at the twenty-foot level. Again they were puzzled: who would put such sturdy platforms into the tunnel — and why?

It must have occurred to the young men that the sturdy oak platforms, fastened so securely into the hard clay, were intended to take the weight of limited amounts of back-fill so that the whole mass of it didn't crush whatever the shaft was protecting lower down.

They knew that the shaft was definitely manmade, and they guessed that it was concealing and protecting something of great value, but it was far from easy to organize an expedition big enough get to the bottom of it — literally and metaphorically.

By 1802 John Smith was married, and his young wife was expecting a baby. Kindly Dr. Simeon Lynds from Truro had come to help, and while they waited for the baby to arrive, John told him all about his adventures on Oak Island with his friends. Lynds was very interested and managed to organize a group of friends to invest a little money to finance a small expedition. He had contacts in Onslow as well as Truro, and when it reached Oak Island in 1803, the Onslow Company included Sheriff Tom Harris and Colonel Archibald, who was a justice of the peace as well as the town clerk. Delving far deeper than the three young explorers had done in 1795, the Onslow men cut their way lower and lower into the shaft. They came across more platforms of oak logs at ten-foot intervals, as well as layers of putty, charcoal and coconut fibre. Were they triggering some kind of booby-trap when they took out the putty? Had it been instrumental in holding air and water pressure in balance?

The most significant discovery they made, however, was an inscribed stone, close to the thirty-metre level.

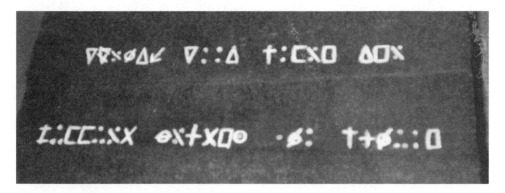

Replica of the inscribed stone found more than thirty metres down in the Money Pit.

The Onslow men had no success in deciphering the stone, but later cryptographers have suggested the meaning shown on page 174: a clear reference to treasure. The erudite Professor Barry Fell, whose opinions are always worthy of careful consideration, believed that it was a religious text and that the carefully protected secret at the foot of the Money Pit was probably a well-defended grave. He thought that the symbols carved onto the stone were the alphabet of an old Coptic dialect and were a religious text warning the people that disobedience to the holy law would bring disaster upon them.

The stone found its way into John Smith's fireplace, and then into the shop window of a Halifax bookbindery. Unfortunately, its present location is unknown. What is interesting, however, is that the Onslow Company's discovery of the stone occurred just a few years before Dr. Fletcher of Yarmouth discovered his rune stone there. It is more than likely that Fletcher knew Dr. Lynds. Did they discuss any similarities between the Oak Island stone and the Yarmouth stone?

Apart from the curious, controversial inscription, the nature of the stone itself raises more questions. Those who had seen and examined the Oak Island stone maintained that it was unlike any rock in the area, but was very hard and fine-grained, resembling porphyry. The best kind of porphyry in the ancient world was known as *porfido rosso antico*; it was used for many of the Egyptian monuments, and substantial deposits of it were to be found along the west coast of the Red Sea. How had a slab of porphyry from the Middle East found its way to the bottom of the Money Pit on Oak Island?

Having removed the interesting old coded stone, the Onslow men were dismayed by the amount of water that was now making its way into the base of their excavations. They probed down through the soggy earth below their feet with long iron rods, hoping that the stone was an indication that the treasure was not far below them. Three metres below them, their probes struck something impenetrably hard that extended all the way across the shaft. Darkness and the ever-increasing water problem prompted them to abandon work for the night and come back at first light. It turned out to be a life-saving decision: when they came back at dawn, the Money Pit was flooded to a depth of some twenty metres and the water seemed to be rising and falling with the tide.

Draining the shaft proved impossible; the Onslow Company very reluctantly gave up.

For the next two centuries — armed with ever-improving technology — one expedition after another has failed to solve the riddle of the Money Pit. More and more evidence has come to light with every group of explorers, and as a result of their cumulative work, seven theories as to what the Money Pit contains can be considered.

1. The pit was constructed by British army engineers during the War of Independence in the eighteenth century. It was intended to protect a British army payroll.
2. It was built by Sir Francis Drake and his men in the sixteenth century and was filled with gold they had captured from the Spaniards.
3. It was dug by William Kidd, or some other pirate, during the seventeenth century.
4. It was constructed as the tomb of an *arif*, or holy man, who had led a party of religious refugees over the Atlantic to escape persecution in the Old World.
5. It was built in the sixteenth or seventeenth century to house precious manuscripts — perhaps even texts proving that the brilliant and mysterious Francis Bacon was the real author of the plays attributed to Shakespeare.

6. It was constructed by Celtic or Norse sea rovers to provide a protected burial place for a great chief.

7. It was constructed by the Templars to protect whatever priceless, secret treasures they had uncovered below the Dome of the Rock in Jerusalem.

However, when the authors consulted the renowned American psychic Terry Ross for his opinions about the Oak Island Money Pit, he came up with some extremely interesting ideas. Most significant of all, in light of theories regarding the existence of ancient pre-Templar Guardians, was Ross's comment that the Oak Island mystery was connected with something "that went right back through the corridors of time — almost to the Garden of Eden." Terry was interested in the inscribed porphyry slab, and said that he felt it was central to the mystery. He also felt that it was connected with the other mysterious standing stone structures that had been erected throughout New England by unknown people at unknown times. He suggested a date in the region of 2000 BC. These stones — and the Oak Island Money Pit — gave Terry a strong impression that they were connected with ancient Mediterranean peoples. He also got the impression that their "mindset" was totally different from ours today: they were friends of the Earth; they nurtured the Earth and were in turn nurtured by it.

Terry also connected the Oak Island mystery with some archaeological investigations he had been making in Ohio. The mounds studied in Ohio, which were similar to Silbury Hill in Wiltshire, England, had seven distinct levels — not unlike the juxtaposition of different chemicals in an electrical battery. One of the layers of material in the mysterious Ohio mound had been brought all the way from Iowa — just as the stones of Stonehenge had been transported all the way from the Preseli Hills in Wales.

* * *

Stonehenge is constructed mostly of sarsens, but there are also dolerites, rhyolites and at least one example of micaceous sandstone — the famous "altar stone" itself. Most archaeologists believe that the stones had a deep religious significance for their builders.

Another interesting Welsh connection with the mystery of how Stonehenge was built concerns a Stone Age grave found near the monument, containing what are believed to be early Welshmen who were presumed to have been among the builders. Were they also among the hardy pioneers who transported the stones from Preseli?

Stonehenge could be connected with the work of the ancient pre-Templar Guardians, and they — or their descendants and successors — may well be as active today as they were when Stonehenge was constructed. Was it built under their direction, and were they connected with ancient Welsh druidism? Do the roots of their early wisdom go back much further than is generally realized, and to what extent is it manifested now?

In 1979 it was reported that a man calling himself R.C. Christian turned up at the Elberton Granite Finishing Company in Elberton, Georgia, and ordered what have since come to be known as the Georgia Guidestones. These consist of four very large upright stones that between them hold up a great capstone — in some ways they form a miniature of Stonehenge. The stones are engraved in eight different languages and carry ten distinct messages.

A book by Christian (if that was his real name) was found in the Elberton library. It was written in praise of Thomas Paine (1737–1809) and his philosophy, and the inscriptions on the Georgia Guidestones seem to be based on at least some of Paine's ideas. "When opinions are free, either in matters of government or religion," wrote Paine, "truth will finally and powerfully prevail."

A summary of the words on the Georgia Guidestones follows:

1. Aim for a sustainable global population of no more than half a billion in harmony with Nature.
2. Reproduce wisely.
3. One language for all the Earth.
4. Let reason — not emotion — rule all things.
5. Let there be fair laws for everyone within a just legal system.

6. Every nation should rule itself, but should refer international disputes to a World Court.
7. Let us do away with all petty, unnecessary rules and regulations and so be rid of useless bureaucrats.
8. Strike a balance between the rights of an individual and his, or her, social obligations.
9. Value the eternal verities of Truth, Beauty and Love.
10. Let not humanity usurp the Earth: always leave space for Nature.

It's also interesting to note that a hole was drilled in the centre stone so that observations of the stars could be made through it.

⋇ ⋇ ⋇

The Georgia Guidestones are a relatively modern mystery, but there are elements in the inscription they carry that date back far beyond Thomas Paine. The precepts on the Georgia stones have much in common with the moral and ethical teachings of Alexander the Great (as described in Chapter Two).

Many of these philosophical ideas link up again with what Terry Ross, the psychic, had to say about the Oak Island mystery. Ross emphasized that whoever had constructed the elaborate underground workings on Oak Island had possessed an entirely different motivation from that of contemporary humanity. In consequence, he felt that a different approach to the problem was needed. When the authors asked him just how different those original builders had been, and what impressions he had of them, Ross said that he had a distinct feeling that there was a connection with something very unusual. He sensed that there was an interchange, a "back and forth," of instructions and information. He thought that the Money Pit contained some kind of "implant" that was necessary for future developments, something connected with what he described as "Earth changes to be."

Our final question to Terry concerned the work that Fred Nolan, a qualified surveyor, had carried out on Oak Island over many years. Fred and his colleague, William S. Crooker, were of the opinion that they had probably uncovered the marker stones of a huge Templar cross on Oak Island. This consisted of a headstone where the upright and crossbar intersected, and five other marker stones, two of which were at the left and right ends of the crossbar, and the other three of which marked out the upright above and below the headstone.

To the Money Pit

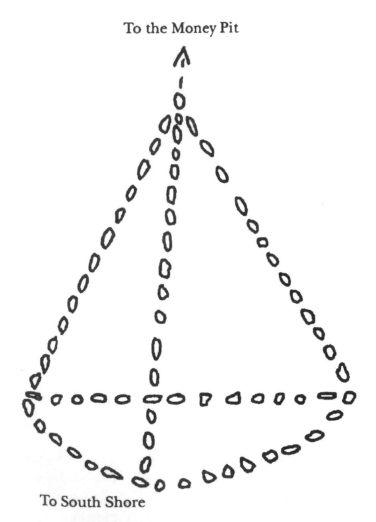

To South Shore

The mysterious stone triangle on Oak Island once pointed to the Money Pit. Does the cross inside this notorious triangle indicate that the Templars constructed it?

Those marker stones are the strongest evidence yet that the Templars reached Oak Island and buried something of immense value there.

Aside from its proximity to Gold River, on the Atlantic side of the main Nova Scotian peninsula, a curious fact about Oak Island is the one-time existence of *another* Oak Island on the Bay of Fundy side — close to which, there is *another* Gold River! Do these geographical anomalies suggest that Oak Island and Gold River were markers, or important signs, for medieval navigators with limited techniques for assessing their latitude and longitude? Suppose that winds, currents and positional uncertainties had driven a medieval mariner off course: instead of hitting the Atlantic seaboard of Nova Scotia in the vicinity of the famous Oak Island, the vessel had entered the Bay of Fundy. By sailing up the coast, the ship would encounter the *other* Oak Island and the *other* Gold River. Sailing up either Gold River would bring the mariners to the centre of the Nova Scotian peninsula and the mysterious medieval settlement that was believed to have been there long ago. Many historians regard the existence of this hypothetical, medieval, mid-peninsular settlement as problematical, but far from impossible.

The gifted author and researcher Michael Bradley has also examined the possibilities of such a settlement at length and in depth, and is of the opinion that it may well have existed.

We visited New Ross, and met Alva Pye, the owner of some controversial ruins. Alva was very hospitable and helpful, and he showed us around the ruins in detail.

Alva Pye of New Ross, Nova Scotia, with the mysterious mid-peninsular ruins.

The authors' great Nova Scotian friend, the gifted George Young — a Canadian naval war hero, scholar, surveyor, researcher and author, now sadly deceased — made many vitally important contributions to our research into the history of Oak Island and its Templar connections. One of his most fascinating pieces of work concerned the mysterious Mount Hanley stone. This ancient inscribed stone was discovered by Edward Hare on his Mount Hanley property in 1983, and George spent years deciphering and translating its ancient Ogham (also spelled Ogam) inscription. In George's opinion, which has the weight of his high intelligence and profound scholarship behind it, the Mount Hanley stone commemorates very early Irish colonists who reached Newfoundland and Nova Scotia at some time between 300 BC and AD 600.

As most languages do, versions of Ogham differed over the centuries, and the later form, which had additional vowels, was not the same as what was inscribed on the Mount Hanley stone. Strong historic connections link Ireland, Scotland and the Sinclairs' kingdom of the Orkneys. These demonstrate one possible route by which the refugee Templars (whom the Sinclairs protected after 1307) might have learned of the Ogham-using colonists in the New World. Other theories, and alternative scenarios, also connect the Templars with the Oak Island Money Pit mystery. Once again, we are deeply indebted to George Young's extensive knowledge of Nova Scotia, and his naval officer's professional understanding of tides, currents and sea-level changes.

As an historian, George was convinced that that there was a strong likelihood the Phoenicians and Carthaginians of the Mediterranean coasts had traded across the Atlantic with the indigenous Canadian and American peoples. Passing what they would have called the Pillars of Hercules (Gibraltar), these early mercantile mariners would have sailed north along the Iberian coast, around the Bay of Biscay and then westward along the English Channel until they were in sight of Cornwall and the Land's End peninsula. Keeping Ireland well to their starboard side, they would then head for the land known to them as Ogygia, which we know today as Iceland. From there, George calculated, their best course would be past the southern tip of Greenland and on past Cape Race in Newfoundland. Turning southwest would bring them to Nova Scotia, and they would then have sailed south — perhaps even as far as Florida.

George worked out an alternative course that would have taken them southwest of the Pillars of Hercules and down to the Canaries — already the site of the intriguing accounts by the historian Al-Gutiyya, who told how the fearless navigator Ibn Farrukh had been there during the reign of Caliph Hisham II (976–1009), as described in more detail in Chapter Fourteen. After reaching the Canaries, the Phoenician vessels would have had the advantage of westerly currents that would have helped them reach Cuba, then Florida — and northwards from there up the American and Canadian coasts.

Getting these maritime merchants safely back to the Mediterranean was an important component of George's well-reasoned navigational theories, and he calculated that from Cape Hatteras (in what is today's North Carolina) they would have been able to ride the easterly currents towards the Iberian Peninsula and the Pillars of Hercules. Once past Gibraltar again, they would have been more or less in their own familiar home waters.

The crusading Templars would certainly have encountered descendants of the Phoenicians and Carthaginians, and medieval navigators in charge of sections of the Templar fleet would have been only too pleased to learn whatever they could of the seafaring wisdom of those whose ancestors had sailed westward many centuries ago.

* * *

Tracing the arguments back once more to their beginnings, it seems reasonable to suppose that ancient and mysterious pre-Templar Guardians — like Hermes Trismegistus, Gilgamesh, Melchizedek and Abraham — were in possession of powerful, secret knowledge that could have originated extraterrestrially, from the lost civilizations of Atlantis or Lemuria, from another dimension, or from a strange parallel universe. These benign Guardians may well have passed on their plans to outstanding successors such as King Solomon of Israel, Alexander of Macedon, Mérovée the Twice born, Charlemagne, Bernard of Clairvaux and the Templar heroes he sent to Jerusalem in the twelfth century.

This raises enormous philosophical and theological problems. Continual wars, plagues, earthquakes, hurricanes, floods, volcanic eruptions and other major tragedies of nature and history tend to suggest to some thinkers that there may be "powers" of evil and chaos working against "powers" of goodness and order, like some cosmic version of the Royal Game of Ur (see Chapter One). Some of these supposed "malign powers" may exist only in human minds, and consist of negative characteristics such as greed, jealousy, selfishness and an obsessive desire to control others.

The obscure, tangential hints about gnostic dualism that percolate their way through the Dead Sea Scrolls and the Nag Hammadi library may be no more than symbolic attempts by early thinkers to come to terms with the major problem of reconciling the infinite love, omnipotence and omniscience of God with the recurring, appalling spectacles of misery, suffering and death.

There are some who might argue that if the pre-Templar Guardians and their successors throughout the centuries are the agents and instruments of health, happiness, goodness and human progress, they could well have antagonists and opponents who are pulling as hard as they can in the other direction. Certainly, the Manichaeans, Paulicians, Bogomils and Cathars of the Languedoc appear to have embraced these dualistic theories to some extent. Their simplistic approach to the riddle of God and human suffering, however, makes only a minor contribution to one of many possible answers. Nevertheless, it may shed a little light on the causes of the conflict between those who seek to do good and those who seek to do harm — a conflict that has percolated down the centuries.

It may perhaps be allowed, for the sake of argument, that the conflict between good and evil is undeniably real and tangible, even though its philosophical and theological origins and explanations remain obscure and unresolved. It can nevertheless be personified and dramatically symbolized by the romantic, heroic figures of the Knights of the Round Table, Templars, Rosicrucians, Illuminati and Freemasons. The question of whether the Templars actually reached Oak Island, Nova Scotia, and hid something of great significance there in the Money Pit is of major importance. What had they found under the Dome of the Rock? What had the Cathars given them for safekeeping? Was it knowledge? Was it an artifact? Was it both an artifact *and* the knowledge that empowered it? How could the Money Pit protect whatever it was the Templars had concealed there?

Discoveries made on Oak Island over the last two centuries indicate that the enigmatic shaft originally went much deeper than forty metres, and that there is some sort of labyrinth and a series of caverns below it in the limestone that lies below the clay. Whoever built it in the first place may have constructed the entire labyrinth, or adapted some natural caverns and passageways through the rock. Various attempts have been made by treasure hunters over the past two hundred years to construct coffer dams across Smith's Cove. None of those dams lasted long enough to be of any practical use to the expeditions that built them. Remains of huge, ancient, dam-building timbers numbered with Roman figures were found in Smith's Cove, so at some time in the distant past a totally successful coffer dam *was* built across Smith's Cove, and it lasted long enough for the unknown builders to create an artificial beach that would prevent the protective flood tunnels from silting up.

These tunnels were another major work, leading all the way from the artificial, silt-resisting beach all the way down to the depths of the Money Pit. The putty and charcoal layers that augmented the platforms of oak logs at their regular three-metre intervals may have served as some sort of trigger to allow the deadly flood tunnels to operate once the air seal provided by the putty had been broken.

One of the strange and deadly secrets that could have been shared by the ancient pre-Templar Guardians was that our modern investigators are looking at the Oak Island Money Pit from entirely the wrong direction: maybe it wasn't built to keep anything out — *but was built to keep something terrible in!* What if the Guardians were all too well aware of the existence of dangerously intelligent, extraterrestrial amphibians — things like griffouls and quinotaurs that were aiming to dominate the planet and enslave human beings. What if Ea or Oannes was not a mythological water deity but something powerful and dangerous, something that had plans for our ancestors other than their development into an advanced technological culture? What if the ancient Guardians and their twelfth-century Templar successors had the unenviable task of trying to confine and contain one or another of these hazardous amphibians? Killing it — or them — was safer, cheaper and permanent, but perhaps it had knowledge, skills or information that even the Guardians didn't possess.

Maybe the situation led to a traditional "Mexican standoff": it's too dangerous to let the being live — but you can't kill it, or you lose the vital information you know that it possesses. Alternatively, it might not be *possible* to kill it. What if Ea's mythological reputation as something divine, or semi-divine, was built on his apparent invulnerability and great longevity? If some sort of force field, like those found in science fiction, surrounded the creature, it might have been beyond even the Guardians' power to destroy it — but they could, perhaps, have imprisoned it. The nearest modern parallel might be the question of what is to be done with radioactive waste. It can't just be left lying around, and it has to be kept out of the wrong hands at all costs. So a metaphorical Money Pit is built to contain it.

In order to understand more about what the medieval Templars might have taken to Oak Island for safekeeping, it is necessary to know more about the men themselves: where they went, what they did, and how they fought.

Chapter 16

THE INDOMITABLE TEMPLAR WARRIOR-PRIESTS AND THE CRUSADES

There is far more to the Knights Templar than their straightforward, conventional history, but it is helpful to use that conventional history as a jumping-off point from which to examine the myths, legends and secret history that may aid us in painting a very different picture.

The best way to examine the simple, straightforward, conventional history of the Templars is to think of them as a monastic military order that came into being after the First Crusade. Ostensibly, their duties were focused on guarding and assisting pilgrims who made their way along the hazardous routes to Jerusalem and other sacred sites in the Middle East. They had the distinction of fighting alongside King Richard I (the Lionheart), and were the allies of other distinguished Crusader warriors.

As warriors, they were second to none: bold and fearless to the point of being rash and impetuous, they lived and died by their maxim, "First to attack and last to retreat."

Their prowess in battle made them greatly feared as well as greatly admired, and lesser men envied their peerless reputation for courage and skill in times of war.

They began in poverty, but their financial acumen and architectural skills were of the same high calibre as their military achievements, which makes it highly likely that they were the creators of the Oak Island Money Pit and the mysterious labyrinth below it.

Their financial power and the vast influence it gave them also caused widespread fear, resentment and jealousy throughout the courts of Europe and farther afield. Although usury was technically forbidden under church laws, there were subtle ways around that dilemma, and the Templars employed them. Indeed, some commentators have credited them with inventing banking as our financial markets know it today. Ironically, it was the mountain of debt that Philip le Bel of France had piled up with them that prompted him to attack them.

Returning to the earlier theories of ancient pre-Templar Guardians and their enemies, it hardly seems feasible that nine relatively poor twelfth-century knights could rise to such heights and achieve such power and influence unless someone very influential wanted them to do so. Bernard of Clairvaux backed them to the hilt, and he was an exceptionally able and powerful mentor. But could even Bernard have done it alone? If he was behind the Templars, the ancient Guardians were almost certainly behind him — indeed, it is highly likely that Bernard was one of them, or that he knew about them and thoroughly approved of their work for humanity.

Among the many things that Bernard did to support, encourage and reinforce the Templars was to draw up their rule. It has, however, been argued insistently for many years that there was, additionally, a highly significant Secret Templar Rule that Bernard may also have devised. He was not referred to as the "second pope" without good reason! Whoever devised it, this hypothetical Secret Rule has aroused controversy and speculation over the centuries.

The medieval Templars' secrets were well kept; what was not so well kept was the knowledge that they held secret meetings, practised secret ceremonies, and used codes, symbols and ciphers that were not understood outside their noble order. A secondary motive for the obnoxious Philip le Bel's move against the Templars in 1307 was that he was in desperate need of funds to finance his war against the powerful and ambitious Edward I of England.

The heresy charges made against the Templars by Philip's unprincipled henchmen allowed their avaricious master to take control of their lands, property and other assets. Following the usual medieval tortures, all sorts of ludicrous "confessions" were extorted from Templar victims. The validity of these admissions is an infinitesimally small distance from zero! Given a sufficiently painful inducement, the most transparently innocent prisoner will confess to anything from broomstick flying to turning an unsuspecting bishop into a toad.

Their reputation for wizardry was probably increased, rather than diminished, by the curse that Jacques de Molay — the last medieval grand master of the Templars — is alleged to have laid on King Philip and Pope Clement as he was being burned at the stake on

March 19, 1314. De Molay said that they would both join him within the year and answer to God for the cruel injustices done to him and his men. Clement lasted barely a month, while Philip died barely six months after Clement!

Tragically, the malicious propaganda instigated by Philip's minions — however obviously false it was — tended to stick to the Templars, and in the minds of some of their contemporaries their once deservedly glorious reputation was tarnished. As ridiculous and groundless as the charges were, the Templars were accused of sodomy, of trampling and spitting on the cross and of worshipping an idol called Baphomet.

Who or what, exactly, was this Baphomet? There are many possible answers. Some thought it was either a black cat — linked with all the medieval superstitions about witchcraft, imps and familiar spirits — or a severed head. Baphomet was also supposed to have been a satanic goatlike creature, an idol with a human face, a head with two faces like the god Janus, or something with the head of a goat, the body of a human being, wings and cloven feet. This weird multiplex idol was also thought to have had the head of a cockerel, a female upper body, and a candle perched on its head.

The Assassins of Alamut were a heretical Persian Islamic sect. The great medieval traveller Marco Polo (1254–1324) brought back strange tales about their activities after visiting the site of their castle in Iran shortly after the Mongols had destroyed it. Polo told of how recruits to the Sect of the Assassins were given hashish and introduced to what they were led to believe were the "Gardens of Paradise." Here, for a few days, they were given the best of food and allowed to experience the sensual delights of beautiful *houris*, the delectable maidens of Paradise who would be theirs for all eternity — provided, of course, that they died while loyally doing their duty for the Old Man of the Mountains.

Before Marco Polo's anecdotes reached Europe, however, stories of the Syrian branch of the Assassins were circulating via the accounts made by William of Tyre, historian of the Crusades. William was an able and reliable contemporary chronicler. Born in Jerusalem in 1128, he eventually rose to become Archbishop of Tyre. He was one of those relatively rare people, a child of the original European Crusaders who began his education in Jerusalem and then went on to study in Paris and

Bologna. Returning to the Middle East in 1168, he became a leading figure in Tyre Cathedral and was made an archdeacon in 1167. King Amalric entrusted him with an important diplomatic mission to Byzantium, and William was also sent to Rome in 1169. He was tutor to Amalric's son, who grew up to be King Baldwin IV and who, after his accession, made William the chancellor of Jerusalem. When the archbishopric of Tyre was added to this chancellorship, it meant that William controlled the most significant aspects of both church and state in the kingdom. He was, therefore, in a unique position to understand the society and culture, politics and religion of the twelfth century.

His knowledge extended to a rich understanding of the Assassins, and their almost unbelievable offer to support the king of Jerusalem and subsequently become Christians. They had already formed a fairly flexible alliance with some Frankish warriors who were busily engaged in fighting Saladin, and were glad of any support — no matter how dubious. Assassin support, however, consisted mainly of two or three unsuccessful attempts to kill Saladin, whose loyal and efficient guards provided a security service that the Assassins failed to penetrate. When Saladin took Jerusalem in 1187, the Assassins promptly changed sides and aided the Muslims against the Franks.

* * *

Conrad of Montferrat was a leading protagonist in the Third Crusade and was (very briefly) king of Jerusalem, until he was assassinated on April 28, 1192. Naturally, the Assassins were given credit for Conrad's death, but the circumstances may have been rather more convoluted.

Conrad had been an ally of Isaac II of Byzantium, and had married Isaac's daughter, Theodora. The native Byzantines, however, didn't like him, and in 1187 he escaped from his Byzantine foes by going to Syria. After taking Jerusalem, Saladin turned his attentions to Tyre, where Conrad put up a spirited defence, temporarily frustrating Saladin's plans. Conrad was also an effective naval strategist, and he savagely mauled the Egyptian fleet.

There was then some unpleasant internecine conflict between Guy de Lusignan, who had been king of Jerusalem, and Conrad — who no longer recognized Guy now that Jerusalem had fallen to Saladin. Guy stormed off in a huff and joined the Crusaders, who were attacking Acre. At this point, Guy's wife, Sibylla, through whom he had claimed the throne of Jerusalem, rather inconveniently died.

In the twelfth century, marriage, money and politics were more or less synonymous. Although still married to Theodora, Conrad promptly married Isabella, who was the late Sibylla's sister — thus creating for himself some sort of a claim to the throne of Jerusalem. Isabella's marriage to Humphrey IV of Toron in 1183, which had taken place when she was only thirteen, had to be annulled to enable her to marry Conrad. This annulment led to strong suspicions that Humphrey might have been responsible for sending some of his agents to annihilate Conrad, thus leaving Isabella as an eligible young widow whom he could remarry. Guy de Lusignan also had good reasons to dispose of Conrad, and Guy was technically a vassal of Richard the Lionheart of England. Great and noble warrior that he was, and a man with a deserved reputation for fairness and justice, Richard could also be ruthless.

King Richard I of England, known as the Lionheart.

Richard and Guy, therefore, both appear on the list of suspects who might have launched secret killers against Conrad — who was, after all, supported by Philip II of France and Leopold of Austria. The jealous rivalry between the various European kings was one of Saladin's best weapons!

Nor should Queen Isabella be above suspicion. It seems highly likely that, after spending most of her formative, teenaged years with Humphrey, she had grown deeply attached to him and neither of them wanted the enforced annulment. When the assassination took place, Conrad was away from home, more or less alone, in a singularly dangerous area.

The circumstances under which he came within range of the assassins' blades were a shade suspicious, to put it mildly. He had arrived home, hungry, to find that Isabella had no meal waiting for him. Instead of hurrying-up their servants to prepare his food immediately, she suggested that he should go and eat at the home of their neighbour, the Bishop of Beauvais. Conrad duly went. The bishop, however — possibly in league with with Isabella — told Conrad that, regrettably, he had already finished his meal; so Conrad, still hungry, set off for home again. It was on that short journey that the assassins struck from the shadows.

Of course, they could simply have been opportunist members of the Assassins' brotherhood — but other candidates seem equally strong.

Before the year was out, Queen Isabella was married again — not to the forlorn Humphrey, but to Henry II of Champagne. This union produced two daughters before there was a mysterious "accident" — Henry fell from a tower window in 1197. In view of Conrad's convenient death, it is tempting to wonder whether Henry's fatal descent from that high window resulted from something other than clumsiness and gravity.

Isabella's fourth and final marriage was to Amalric II, brother of Guy of Lusignan. He died in 1205, shortly before Isabella herself passed away. Was he her last victim? And might she then have died of something other than natural causes? She was, after all, only thirty-five years old. There are reasonable grounds for suspicion that she was, perhaps, another Livia of Rome, or Lady Macbeth, and that someone who feared he might be her next victim made a pre-emptive strike.

* * *

Whether the Assassins disposed of Conrad of Montferrat in 1192 — with or without Isabella's assistance — fear of them spread and increased throughout the Holy Land. Even after the destruction of their citadel at Alamut by the Mongols, the Assassins were far from finished. There is a legend that they reappeared in India, where they were thought by some historians to be strongly connected with the Kojas. Is this another possible link with the Indian Christian traditions of Thomas the Apostle, and with the earlier links connecting Abraham and Sarah with ancient Indian gods? Where do the ancient pre-Templar Guardians fit into this strange, recurring pattern? How many of the Assassins' strange secrets reached the medieval Templars, and what mysterious links might connect the Assassins to the mysteries of Baphomet?

As has already been noted several times, the Templars' dealings with Muslims were not always hostile. Some theorists have suggested that they were well acquainted with "the Old Man of the Mountains" and his Sect of Assassins, and that, etymologically, the word "Baphomet" had Islamic origins.

If Baphomet was indeed a severed, mummified head in the Templars' keeping, it would fit in with the Assassin tradition. Part of their recruitment technique was to bring prospects before a man whose body was concealed in a secret space below the floor, his neck encased in a tight-fitting basin/collar filled with chicken blood. This gave the impression that, although he had recently been beheaded, he was still able to chat happily about the joys of the Assassins' *houri*-filled Paradise — attainable after death in the service of the Old Man of the Mountains.

Having served his propaganda purposes, the recruiting officer in his chicken-blood collar would be genuinely decapitated. His head was then placed on top of a pole to convince the recruits that they had indeed been talking to a severed head. The genuine decapitation also prevented the dead man from giving away the secret of the hole in the floor. Safely on the pole, of course, he became much more taciturn.

Did one such grisly trophy make its way back to Jerusalem, and then on to Europe, among the souvenirs of a returning Templar? Did it eventually find its way into the vaults below the London Temple? Were strange, exaggerated tales told about it over the years?

Descriptions of Baphomet that suggested it was a head of some type varied from a fierce, glittering-eyed, heavily bearded one to a mere bony skull. Some accounts declared that it was made of wood. Others said it was metal. Different stories maintained that it was painted in black and white, while further descriptions gave it four feet. One Baphomet kept in Paris was alleged to have been a silver construction with two faces and a beard, while some others supposedly had three faces. Some evidence given against the medieval Templars in England was that they had four such Baphomets in the United Kingdom, the major one being kept in their Temple in London.

Medieval Temple Church, London. Was there a Baphomet here long ago?

The Temple Church is dedicated to St. Mary, but was it secretly connected with the mysteries of Mary Magdalene, the Black Madonna, Solomon and Sheba? Hugues de Payns himself established the London Temple Church before returning to his duties in Palestine. The church was consecrated on February 10, 1185, by Heraclius, the patriarch of Jerusalem. King Henry II was present at the consecration.

Co-author Lionel beside an ancient tomb adjacent to the Temple Church. Who or what lies buried in these mysterious, medieval vaults? Is it one of the Baphomets?

* * *

Light from another strange source was thrown on the Templar Baphomet mystery by an intriguing nineteenth-century occultist, Alphonse Louis Constant — better known to researchers of the unexplained as Eliphas Lévi. Born in 1810, Alphonse began training for the Catholic priesthood, but he parted company with the church for some years. One version says that he was expelled for "heretical views" — if so, what exactly were they? Was he, perhaps, involved with the cult of the Black Madonna? With gnosticism, Manichaeanism, the Cathar doctrines, Baphomet, or other ancient and mysterious Templar secret?

One thing, however, is certain: Lévi became an expert on the enigma of Baphomet. In his opinion it symbolized the Absolute, and was said by some experts who had studied Lévi's life and work in depth to be based on a strange gargoyle that Eliphas had studied at the Templar Commandery of St. Bris le Vineux, not far from Auxerre in France. According to Lévi, the Baphomet represented life's dualism and the female and male aspects of all creation. One arm is male, the other female, and there are additional symbols of both genders. The arms point in different directions: one indicates the sky and stars, the other points down to the Earth. These arm symbols link up with the hermetic wisdom, "As above, so below."

There are also white and black crescent moons. Did Eliphas intend these to symbolize the dualistic nature of Good and Evil that he believed in, or are they simply representations of the natural phases of the moon? Did he perhaps intend them to signify what he thought of as the power and importance of the moon goddess Selene, also known to the Romans as Luna?

Selene was the daughter of Hyperion, the Titan, who was the mythological bringer of light. Her mother was Theia, sister of Helios — the young Greek sun god. Selene herself is seen in the mythological representations as a beautiful young woman with a very white face. She travels on a silver chariot drawn by two pale horses, although she is also depicted riding on a bull — which would tie in again with the strange Cretan bull legends and the worship of the golden calf in the Book of Exodus. The crescent moon can also be represented as bull's horns. Selene is additionally tied in with Pan of Arcadia, who gave her a herd of white oxen.

By a curious coincidence, the chemical element selenium is named after her, via the Greek word *selene*, meaning "moon." Crystalline monoclinic selenium has a deep red colour reminiscent of blood, whereas the stable hexagonal form of the element is a lustrous, metallic grey — not unlike the surface of the moon! Does this connect with the red and white emblems of the Templars?

Medieval metallurgists were well aware of the properties of copper — it had been known for at least seven thousand years, dating right back to the dawn of the pre-Templar Guardians. The ancient Chaldeans were making things from copper almost five thousand years before the Christian era. Intriguingly, selenium today is frequently extracted as a byproduct of copper refining. Were those in the know doing it too, in the earliest days of copper working? The deep red form would have symbolized blood, while the silvery type would have been associated with their lunar goddess. How much of this might have been known to perceptive Eliphas Lévi in the nineteenth century? How much of that ancient, secret knowledge about the goddess Selene would have been encoded in his version of the Baphomet?

It is also known that Lévi undertook part of his early religious training at St. Sulpice, in Paris, which has a close connection with the riddle of Father Bérenger Saunière and the mystery of what was possibly Templar treasure at Rennes-le-Château. Although there are numerous controversial and contradictory accounts of the circumstances under which Saunière became wealthy, many of them focus on mysterious codes — very possibly Templar codes. There is some evidence, albeit hotly disputed, that Saunière took some mysterious coded parchments (whatever they really were, and wherever they really originated) to the expert cryptographers at St. Sulpice, who then deciphered and translated them for him. It is alleged that the information the St. Sulpice experts provided enabled Saunière to recover the Rennes treasure. Could that Rennes treasure possibly have included a medieval Templar Baphomet richly adorned with gold, silver and gemstones?

Lévi died in 1875. It was only a short while after Eliphas's death that Saunière was said to have made his fateful visit to St. Sulpice. What secrets might Lévi have left with the scholarly experts at St. Sulpice? Did his secret — if heretical — knowledge enable them, a few years later, to help Saunière to find the treasure of Rennes-le-Château?

* * *

The mysterious Church of St. Sulpice in Paris, which is connected with Bérenger Saunière and Eliphas Lévi.

More Templar codes, ciphers and symbols existed in the order's arms and armour and the accoutrements of their warhorses. The official orders and instructions included what a Templar could or could not use on his warhorse. Warhorses were seen as functional; to the medieval soldier's mind they were the equivalent of our twenty-first-century tanks and gun carriers. Templars were forbidden to attach gold or silver ornaments to spurs, stirrups or bridle. There were, for example, special Templar rules about war saddles, which were used only when on active service. If a knight joined the order and brought a jewelled saddle with him, he needed special permission to use it. Other Templar rules concerning their warhorses listed items that were not to be lent or borrowed. There were, additionally, special methods of making a saddle extra secure because of the exigencies of battle.

There is also a Saracen description of a Frankish cavalryman — possibly a Frankish Templar — whose horse carried a chain-mail coat that covered its entire body and descended as far as its hooves. But what did the various items signify? Since the earliest days of chivalry and knightly combat, the winning of spurs was a great honour, almost a rite of passage, for a knight, and each of the remaining pieces of armour was specifically important.

It cannot be emphasized too strongly that armour was difficult to make in the twelfth and thirteenth centuries — and very expensive indeed to buy. The process required great skill and painstaking effort on the part of the armourer. To make chain mail, for example, every link had to be connected to four others and held in place with tiny rivets. There could literally be thousands of rings in one suit of chain mail.

Traditionally, the heavy lance, held under the warrior's arm, extended well beyond the horse's head. It had many advantages in mounted, medieval combat, enabling the mass impact of an entire body of cavalry to be delivered more or less simultaneously — with a devastating effect on the enemy. This immensely powerful, simultaneous impact needed long days of rigorous training, during which co-operation was an essential ingredient. The Templars, who were masters of the technique, had both the discipline and wholehearted co-operation that was needed.

The lance served an additional purpose: as it became the traditional weapon of the mounted knight, or high-ranking cavalry soldier, so it served as a symbol of his social rank and prestige. Horses, armour and weaponry were not cheap. The dominance of heavy cavalry in the battles of the medieval Middle East can be analyzed as being inseparably inter-related with social status and financial power: money paid for horses and armour, while horses and armour meant victory, plunder and more wealth. The value of the couched lance as a cavalry weapon depended to a great extent on the courage and skill of the horses as well as the courage and skill of their riders.

Much information about the use of the lance comes from the auto-biography of Usamah Ibn Munqidh, who lived from 1095 until 1188 and wrote circa 1175. He was a good and honourable soldier and courtier in the service of Saladin, who not only fought valiantly against the Crusaders but actually helped and befriended them during the brief interludes of peace. His writings contain many references to the noble part that horses played during the Crusades, and his attitude is summed up in the aphorism, "What else is there to do other than fighting and hunting on horseback?" He is also credited with asking the rhetorical question, "Why should I ride a horse unless I am going into battle astride it?"

His anecdotes immortalizing the courage and spirit of the twelfth-century warhorses include an account of his battle with a Frankish warrior on a huge black horse. Usamah overtook the tiring black; his mare charged and his heavy lance apparently penetrated two layers of armour and jutted out of the front. The impact was so great that Usamah was forced back over his own cantle. Miraculously, the Frank was only slightly wounded. Another of Usamah's anecdotes tells of a mortally wounded horse, dying from heavy, arterial blood loss, which deter-minedly galloped until its rider was out of danger before collapsing dead.

The use of the lance, as Usamah described it, was by no means the only technique open to medieval warriors after the invention of the stirrup. This discovery, according to theorists like David Black, Heinrich Brunner, Rupert Furneaux and Lynn White, changed the face of medieval cavalry encounters. It now became possible for a mounted soldier to stand up in the stirrups and use mace, sword, axe or battle-hammer with devastating effect. If the lance failed, or broke, a cavalry-man with strong, reliable stirrups could rise up in the saddle and use a lethal, handheld weapon.

Templar warhorses, and other mounts, were allocated according to rank. Knight commanders had four, knights had three, and sergeants had one. There were also a number of reserve horses in case an animal was ill or injured in battle. In emergencies, and arguably because of poverty in the early days of the order, it was traditional to see two Templars on one horse. This ancient and honourable Templar tradition is remembered on the column of the Templar Monument beside the Temple Church in London.

Two Templars sharing a horse on the column outside the Temple Church, London.

* * *

Paul's epistle to the Ephesians would have been well known to warrior-priests like the Templars, and in Chapter 6, Verses 10–18, the various pieces of armour are equated with particular spiritual powers and attributes. The first reference is to the "whole armour God," and a girdle of truth and a breastplate of righteousness follow this. The Christian warrior's feet are protected by "the preparation of the gospel of peace," while the rest of the body is protected by the shield of faith. The final items listed are the helmet of salvation and the sword of the spirit.

In Templar symbolism, the idea of the whole armour stands for totality and completeness. You could not belong to the order without absolute commitment to it: you might be only a humble lay groom, or farrier, but you were just as involved with the Templar Crusades as if you were the grand master himself. The girdle of truth symbolized integrity. When Jacques de Molay made his final statement and recanted the false confession that had been wrung from him by unendurable torture, he said proudly: "The only wrong that my brothers and I ever did was to make false confessions because of overwhelming pain. They were all lies. We are totally innocent." The breastplate of righteousness symbolized the goodness, honour, kindness and chivalry of the Templars. As their honesty and goodness protected them like a breastplate, so they protected others and helped poor pilgrims to reach their sacred destinations. Protecting the feet was very important for a fighting man in the Middle East in the twelfth and thirteenth centuries. The word "gospel" in the Epistle to the Ephesians means "good news" — and good news about peace, about victory against all odds, about the end of the war, about the securing of Jerusalem, about the arrival of loyal Crusader allies — all of these gave psychological speed and strength to the feet of those who brought such news. The helmet of salvation covered and protected the mind and the thoughts within it, just as the soldier's iron helmet physically protected the head and the brain.

Morale has always been vitally important during warfare. The warrior whose mind is set on victory or death, the fearless soldier to whom retreat is not an option, will often emerge bloody but victorious against all odds. The fearful and the afraid who doubt and hesitate, the pessimistic and the overanxious who see defeat and disaster around every corner, are far less likely to survive, let alone to achieve a great victory.

Although the theme is controversial and has been open to challenge over the years, there is some evidence that not all the medieval crusading warriors were male. Imad ad-Din, a Muslim chronicler, recounts that there were women fighting alongside the Christian male knights, but that their Saracen enemies did not realize they were women until they had been killed and their armour was looted. Were these female warriors an integral part of the medieval Templar secrets? It seems that few, if any, Christian historians referred to them because it was considered unthinkable for a woman to take up arms and be as effective as her male comrades in battle. Arabian historians of the period, however, refer to wealthy female warriors leading the charge of male knights whose services the woman's wealth had subsidized. There are also references by Muslim historians to Christian women archers standing alongside their men and firing accurately and effectively into the Saracen ranks until killed in the fighting.

* * *

Assuming that the Muslim historians were reliable contemporary witnesses, just how many Crusades did these male and female Christian warriors participate in between the end of the eleventh century and the end of the thirteenth? The origin of the First Crusade can be traced to the Byzantine Emperor Alexius I, who called for help to protect his empire from the Seljuk Turks. Consequently, Pope Urban II sent out a call to all Christians to fight the Turks, and promised that doing so would count as complete and perfect penance. Not surprisingly, in view of the simplistic, medieval concepts of Hell and Purgatory, and an equally simplistic belief in the effectiveness of penance, Crusaders marched to Jerusalem conquering and sacking various cities en route. In 1099 they took Jerusalem itself, killed most of its Muslim inhabitants, and triumphantly occupied the city. A number of miniature Crusader states were then established, the kingdom of Jerusalem being the most significant one historically. There followed a period of comparative peace, during which the Templars would have had many opportunities to meet with wise Muslim scholars and learn some of the strange secrets of the Middle East.

The Second Crusade came about in 1147, three years after the Turks led by Zengi of Mosul stormed Edessa. Pope Eugenius III's appeal for Crusaders did not elicit an enthusiastic response, but once Bernard of Clairvaux threw his powerful oratory into the fray, things began to happen — especially when Bernard reminded his noble audience that taking part in a Crusade was a surefire shortcut to absolution and the consequent avoidance of Purgatory and Hell. German and French armies were finally mustered, accomplished very little, and returned in 1149.

The Third Crusade was triggered by Saladin's recapture of Jerusalem in 1187. Pope Gregory VIII persuaded several influential European rulers, including Richard I of England, Philip II of France and the Holy Roman Emperor Frederick I, to recover Jerusalem for Christendom. In 1190, Frederick was drowned in Cilicia, and the English and French were not enthusiastic allies. The Templars, however, were prominent in the capture of Acre from the Muslims, and they remained there until it fell in 1291. With Acre safely in Christian hands, Philip went home to France. Richard the Lionheart stayed on to establish a truce with Saladin, then left.

The Fourth Crusade in 1202 has often been regarded as a tragedy of political and commercial rivalry between the Byzantines and the Venetians. Pope Innocent III's original intentions were to attack the Holy Land via Egypt. The Venetians, who were prominent in this Crusade, turned it into an attack on Constantinople, together with an attempt to usurp the legitimate emperor by placing a Byzantine exile of their choosing on the ancient throne. Constantinople was sacked in 1204. There is a very real sense in which historians regard this Fourth Crusade as the last real one; five more followed, but they were sad and lacklustre affairs, tainted with political chicanery and Machiavellian plotting. There seems to have been a chronic desire on the part of the papacy to divert the military energies of the European powers against Syria during these centuries.

The misdirected and downright evil Crusade against the Cathars, also known as Albigensians, was ostensibly an attack on what the church called the Cathars' heretical doctrines. The Cathars were, in fact, the gentlest, kindest and most charitable of all the medieval Christians. Cathars healed the sick, fed the hungry and cared for the poor. Known to the people of their native Languedoc as *les bonhommes* — literally "the good men" — because of their unstinting helpfulness, much of the venom levelled against them was motivated by greed. Those who fought and destroyed them, as detailed in Chapter Four, were out to acquire their lands and wealth, which many of their enemies believed also included some ancient, powerful and mysterious secrets.

There were very close connections between the Templars and the Cathars, and it seems highly likely that sympathetic and humane Templars were party to some, if not all, of the Cathars' mysterious secrets.

The old walled city of Carcassonne, Languedoc, France, where large numbers of Cathars were persecuted and killed during the Albigensian Crusade.

The so-called Children's Crusade was another of history's unspeakable tragedies. None of the young hopefuls ever reached the Holy Land — many were sold into slavery on the way, while the remainder died of hunger and disease. There are historians, folklorists and students of the connections between myths, legends and historical facts who claim to trace parallels between the Pied Piper legends and the Children's Crusade.

The Fifth Crusade was noted for the capture of Damietta in Egypt in 1219, but there were no lasting achievements. The Templars were particularly prominent and heroic during this campaign. What strange old Egyptian secrets might they have learned?

In 1228, despite his quarrels with the pope and a sentence of excommunication that he had the good sense to ignore and even laugh at, Emperor Frederick II sailed from Brindisi to Syria on the Sixth Crusade. More by negotiation than by military might and manpower, Jerusalem, Nazareth and Bethlehem were ceded to Christendom for ten years.

Sadly, the Templars themselves, pursuing papal policies at Rome's behest, were largely the cause of a quarrel with Egypt in 1243, and this led to the Seventh Crusade and the loss of Jerusalem yet again. As a famous British prime minister once said, "A week is a long time in politics." European political attitudes had certainly changed since 1187, when the fall of Jerusalem had created a tidal wave of anger and indignation among Christian monarchs and their people. Louis IX of France made a halfhearted, and poorly supported, effort to make war on the Egyptians between 1248 and 1254. Predictably, it was a dismal failure, and Louis spent most of his time as a semi-refugee, rather than as a charismatic military commander, in the Crusader kingdom of Acre, where the Templars were very prominent.

The Eighth Crusade in 1270 was Louis's swan song. He set out for Syria to relieve and help the Christians there, accompanied by the future Edward I of England. The expedition was diverted to Tunis — where, unfortunately, Louis died two months later.

In the absence of Louis IX, the Ninth (and last!) Crusade was led by Prince Edward of England in 1271. It would take a powerful microscope to detect his achievements — he negotiated a truce and withdrew after barely a year.

After the Ninth Crusade, the Christian kingdoms in the Middle East withered and fell: Antioch went down in 1268, Tripoli succumbed in 1289 and Acre — the great Templar stronghold — fell in 1291.

After the fall of Acre, Cyprus became the Templars' most important holding. It was there that their last grand master, Jacques de Molay, made his home until the cowardly and evil treachery of Philip le Bel brought down the great and noble order in 1307.

The last vestige of the connection between Cyprus and the Templars was severed in 1571, when the Ottoman Turks captured the island and destroyed the priceless Templar archives. How many of their precious secrets vanished during that fateful year?

Counting the founder, Huguens de Payns (1118–1136), there were twenty-two grand masters before Jacques died in 1314. The most important as far as the mysterious treasure of Rennes-le-Château and the Arcadian enigma is concerned is Bertrand de Blanchefort, who ruled the order from 1156 until 1169. He was closely connected with Château Blanchefort close to Rennes-le-Château, so the Templar chain with Rennes-le-Château encircles the mystery once again.

Chapter 17

TEMPLAR CODES, CIPHERS, SYMBOLS AND THE MEANING OF MEANING

Our basic theories concerning the mysteries of the Templars and their strange codes and symbols begin with the idea that, long ago, there were mysterious and powerful ancient Guardians, forerunners of the organization known as the Knights Templar that came to prominence as the medieval group of warrior priests in Jerusalem in the eleventh, twelfth and thirteenth centuries. The basic suppositions include the idea that there are still those today who have highly confidential knowledge of them, and that part of that knowledge is enshrined in Templar codes, ciphers and symbols.

With no limits on free and fair speculation, it seems possible that if, for argument's sake, we allow the existence of such a group of Guardians in the first place, they could have originated anywhere at all: another galaxy, another dimension of space-time, or a lost civilization such as Atlantis or Lemuria. They might equally well have been angelic beings in the paranormal or supernatural sense. Evidence of their handiwork appears in many ancient, sacred and religious writings where they are credited with numerous superhuman powers including flight, teleportation, telekinesis and terrifying weaponry beyond our understanding — even with the advantages of our twenty-first-century technology.

Following the thread of the argument, it seems possible that such beings were known to, and were the power behind, outstanding historical human figures such as Alexander the Great, Mérovée and the Merovingian Dynasty, and Bernard of Clairvaux and the medieval Templars whom he supported.

The existence of the mysterious kingdom of Septimania in the Languedoc, between the Pyrenees and the Ardennes, provides another rich source of secret information that might have come originally from the ancient Guardians.

The theories next encompass the strange medieval legends of Prester John and his "hidden" Christian kingdom, from which the Crusaders hoped that powerful reinforcements would arrive to supplement their efforts in the turbulent Middle East. If Prester John and his kingdom *did* exist, was he himself one of the mysterious ancient Guardians, or was he being used by them like a piece in the ancient Royal Game of Ur? Prester John might have been an Ethiopian monarch of the Solomonic Dynasty, a descendant of Menelik (Son of the Wise Man). There is some challenging evidence that the beautiful and nubile Makeda, the biblical queen of Sheba, bore Solomon's child after her visit to Jerusalem. Did that child grow up to rule her kingdom? And did his royal father later acknowledge him and bestow priceless treasures on him — treasures that are still preserved at Axum in Ethiopia?

Research then took in the medieval minstrels and troubadours — widely travelled men of great intelligence and ability. Were some of the Templar secrets concealed in their carefully written and rigorously metrical poems and songs? These performers would have been ideal emissaries and undercover agents.

The next vast and complex mystery of which the Templars were almost certainly aware links the hypotheses yet again with Solomon and the lovely Makeda. Why did the secret cult of the Black Madonna flourish for so long? And is it still in existence? Do these mysterious, symbolic effigies conceal clues to Solomon, Makeda and their son, Menelik, rather than portray the traditional Holy Family of Joseph, Mary and Jesus? These very puzzling and enigmatic depictions may date back as far as Isis, Artemis, Venus-Aphrodite, Diana — or even all the way back to Gaia, the Earth Mother, herself. The figures of Eve and Adam in Eden, carved in Roslyn Chapel, are both black; is the sculptor hinting that Eve is the Black Madonna? How much mysterious truth lies beneath the creation legends of Eden? Is the story of Adam's rib, for example, just a simplified account of human cloning carried out with the supertechnology of the ancient Guardians?

The hypotheses then take a detailed look at the enigmatic figure of Charlemagne — mainly a good and honourable man with very great ability, but with a few shadowy corners in his life as well. His many great abilities, together with a happy coincidence of favourable circumstances, might have been enough by themselves to complete his amazing conquests — but there could equally well have been some far greater power behind him. Was that power in the hands of the ancient pre-Templar Guardians?

Our next field of research was the secret of the codes and ciphers used by the great artists and sculptors of the Renaissance — especially Leonardo da Vinci, Strozzi and Poussin. Poussin in particular was known to be deeply involved with the old Arcadian mysteries — including Pan, the strange and mysterious nature god. Could Pan have been identical to the Arthurian Green Knight and the many curious carvings of Green Men in Roslyn Chapel?

The "*Et in Arcadia ego*" theme, which intrigued Poussin so much, has never been definitively decoded or understood to the satisfaction of all researchers. Undoubtedly, the artists themselves had their private, professional codes and ciphers by means of which they exchanged important, secret information. Da Vinci, the most talented and scholarly of them all, is a very powerful candidate for the role of a Guardian. Was he a full member of that ancient and ultrasecret fraternity? Or was he simply very much aware of their existence and willing to work alongside them?

The research was then directed specifically to mysterious Roslyn Chapel: a veritable Aladdin's Cave of codes, ciphers and symbols. The medieval Templar influence in this astonishing building is very strong indeed, and it has a great deal of arcane knowledge to impart on those who can comprehend even a few of its enigmatic riddles.

The secrets of the Templars, and the ancient Guardians before them, are by no means confined to Europe, Asia and the Middle East. Our research took us across the Atlantic to Canada and the United States — especially to the mysteries of the Oak Island Money Pit and the Newport Tower. Many significant clues pointed decisively to pre-Columbian visits to the New World, some of which may have dated all the way back to Phoenician adventurers.

The hypotheses then took in the crusading adventures of the Templars, and the strange symbolic meanings that lay behind these heroic men, their armour, their weaponry and their warhorses.

In general terms, the codes, ciphers and symbols that they used so effectively need to be considered in conjunction with the sad death in

October 2004 of Jacques Derrida, who contributed so much to our twenty-first-century comprehension of *meaning* itself. There is little point in investigating codes, ciphers and symbols without first looking into what philosophers like Derrida refer to as "the meaning of meaning." No one knew this better than Derrida himself. He was deeply concerned with hermeneutics, the area of philosophy that deals with human thinking, human comprehension and the way we interpret written texts. Interestingly, the word "hermeneutics" is based on the name of the Greek god Hermes, who, in Greek mythology, was the patron of communication and comprehension. As long ago as 1440, Lorenzo Valla, working in Italy, successfully used his pioneering forerunner of modern hermeneutics to argue that the famous *Donation of Constantine* could not possibly have been written by the Emperor Constantine.

Wilhelm Dilthey, working in the nineteenth century, stood metaphorically on the shoulders of Lorenzo Valla. Dilthey developed "methodological hermeneutics," which set out to produce scientific, systematic interpretations of what had been written by trying to place every text firmly within the context in which it was created. Dilthey believed that in order to understand any text at a reasonable and sensible level, it was essential to know when, where, why and how it was created.

Derrida is usually classified as a deconstructionist. His deconstructionism is a technique not only for analyzing literature and linguistics, but such disciplines as architecture, law and philosophy as well. In essence, Derrida challenged the traditional way of reading. He said that traditional reading contains the false premise that language can express an idea without altering it. Derrida maintained that a text does not necessarily have an unchanging, unified meaning. He went on to assert that a writer's intentions are not necessarily unconditionally acceptable. If this is so, he argued, a text could be interpreted quite legitimately in a great many different ways. His deconstructionism, therefore, attempts to illustrate that there are several strata of meaning in a language — which is, in any case, in a constant state of flux.

What are the consequences of Derrida's deconstructionism for code-breaking, decipherment, and the interpretation of symbols? Is there, in his hypothesis, any real, steadfast and unequivocal meaning waiting to be revealed within a text — or are all texts open to negotiation and interpretation? To what extent was deconstructionism the ultimate secret camouflage behind all codes, ciphers and symbols?

Reverting to the Jesus and Mary Magdalene theories referred to in detail earlier provides a clear Derridan example of the different strata of meanings within language and the messages that the text attempts to convey. If the well-known version of the story as contained in the New Testament is taken at face value, Mary Magdalene is a rather unimportant, peripheral character — just one more repentant sinner. If the Nag Hammadi documents and certain other variant traditions are followed, Mary was married to Jesus, was his most dearly loved disciple and was the mother of his children. Further controversial evidence points to Leonardo da Vinci's secret belief that this was the case, and to his apparent inclusion of this scenario in his painting of *The Last Supper*.

The disciple on Christ's right in the picture could very well be a woman, and the angles of their shoulders could be meant to represent the letter M — standing both for *Mary* and for *marriage*. If no account is taken of Derridan deconstructionism, there are only two conclusions: the gospel accounts are correct, *or* Jesus is married to Mary — with all that that implies for traditional Christian doctrine. However, by allowing that there are *many* possible shades of meaning — and room for many interpretations — within texts and the languages that are intended to convey messages, it is perfectly possible to accept a number of alternatives and to resolve an apparent paradox. Both scenarios can be simultaneously true. Jesus *is* the unique Son of God of the traditional gospel; he has genuinely divine powers; he has a special mission to the human race; he is crucified, dead, buried and resurrected — but none of this negates his equally full and genuine humanity. He is *also* the husband of his beloved Mary Magdalene and the loving father of their children. Derridan deconstructionism allows the reconciliation and harmonization of the two apparently mutually exclusive scenarios. There is no need for the established, traditional church to shout "Heresy!" when historians suggest that Jesus was married to Mary. There is no need for the open-minded, scientific, materialist historian to retaliate by ridiculing orthodox Christian faith as deluded, childish, pathetic and simplistic. A miraculous Messiah can also be a happily married Messiah; neither state of being excludes the other.

* * *

From the general to the particular: what can a study of codes, ciphers and symbols reveal about Templarism and the ancient pre-Templar Guardians? Although the words "code" and "cipher" are more or less interchangeable in ordinary conversation, there is a subtle difference. Cryptographers distinguish between codes and ciphers. Technically, a code can represent a whole word, a phrase, or even a sentence, by using a symbol, a single letter or number, or an arbitrary group of letters and numbers. For example:

> A1 could mean, "Proceed along the normal route";
> A2 could mean, "Return to HQ"; and
> A3 could mean, "Join the convoy at our normal
> rendezvous point."

Books containing these various meanings would be held by those using the code.

A cipher, on the other hand, uses letters, numbers or symbols for each letter of the message. For example:

A= ✔
B= 🚲
C= ☐
D= ♥
E= 🎁
F= 🚌
G= ■
H= ⌨
I= ①
J= ⚓
K= ✷
L= ✦
M= ❗
N= ●

O=⬎
P=🚐
Q=()
R=✕
S=?
T=📪
U=😑
V=🚍
W= ۲
X=⊘
Y=⊖
Z=⊛

Using this cipher, which simply replaces the normal font with the Webdings font on any word processor, we can reproduce the authors' names as: ✢ⓘ⬎●ﬔ✢ ✔●♡ 🚍✔📪✕ⓘ☐ⓘ✔ 🚍✔● 📪♊⬎✕🚍ﬔ. Simple substitution ciphers like this example can be broken with relative ease because of the frequency with which certain letters occur in different languages. *E* is the most frequently occurring letter in English, so the appearance of ﬔ in Lionﬔl and again at the end of Fanthorpﬔ can help us decipher the message. The larger the sample of enciphered letters, the easier it becomes to use letter frequency to solve the cipher.

Another simple cipher is referred to as a substitution cipher; in this one, the next letter of the alphabet is used as a replacement — i.e., *A* is written as *B*, *B* as *C*, and so on. The authors' names would then appear as:

MJPOFM BOE QBUSJDJB GBOUIPSQF.

Another frequently used cipher is created by splitting a word over two lines, and putting alternating letters on alternate lines. The authors' names then become:

L	O	E		A	D		P	T	I	I		F	N	H	R	E
I	N	L		N			A	R	C	A		A	T	O	P	

We can assemble those letters thus:

LOEINL ADN PTIIARCA FNHREATOP

Yet a third frequently used method is the Hebrew Atbash Cipher, which would have been well known in the mysterious old kingdom of Septimania in the Languedoc, and also known to the Templars and troubadours of that area. This cipher consists of putting the last letter of the alphabet against the first, the penultimate letter against the second, and so on. It can be demonstrated visually by folding the alphabet between its two central letters:

A B C D E F G H I J K L M (FOLD HERE)
Z Y X W V U T S RQ P O N

N O P Q R S T U V W X Y Z
M L K J I HG F E D C B A

Using this cipher on the authors' names yields: ORLMVO ZMW KZGIRXRZ UZMGSLIKV.

To appreciate the Atbash Cipher in full, it helps to have access to the Hebrew alphabet. The following table shows from which object each letter was evolved, the sounds associated with the letters, the names of the letters and finally the letters themselves.

OBJECT	SOUND	NAME OF LETTER	HEBREW LETTER
An ox	Interrupted Breath	Aleph	א
Dwelling place	*v, bh* or *b*	Beth	ב
Camel	*gh* or *g*	Gimel	ג

OBJECT	SOUND	NAME OF LETTER	HEBREW LETTER
Portal or door	dh or d	Daleth	ד
Air hole	h	He	ה
Fishing Hook or Arrow	w	Waw	ו
Weapon, spear or sword	z	Zayin	ז
Fence, wall or hedge	Another form of h	Heth	ח
Scorpion, serpent or snake	Another form of t	Teth	ט
Human hand	y	Yodh	י
Curved Hand	kh or k	Kaph	ך כ
Goad for livestock	l	Lamedh	ל
Liquid or water	m	Mem	ם מ
Fish or aquatic creature	n	Nun	ן נ
Trestle, prop or support	s	Samekh	ס
An eye	A stonger breath than א, almost ה	Ayin	ע
A mouth	p or ph	Pe	ף פ
Another form of fishing hook	Soft c, or s	Cadhe	ץ צ

OBJECT	SOUND	NAME OF LETTER	HEBREW LETTER
A narrow gate; needle's eye or rear of a human skull	*kw* or *q*	Qoph	ק
A head	*r*	Resh	ר
A tooth	*s* or *sh*	Sin or Shin	שׁ
An indicator, a sign, a marker	*t* or *th*	Taw	ת

The Hebrew Atbash Cipher folds back on itself between the letters ך כ (Kaph) and ל (Lamedh), as shown:

א   Aleph becomes Taw   ת

ב   Beth becomes Sin, Shin   שׁ

ג   Gimel becomes Resh   ר

ד   Daleth becomes Qoph   ק

ה   He becomes Cadhe   ץ צ

ו   Waw becomes Pe   ף פ

ז   Zayin becomes Ayin   ע

ח   Heth becomes Samekh   ס

ט   Teth becomes Nun   ן נ

י   Yodh becomes Mem   ם מ

כ   Kaph becomes Lamedh   ל

In the late 1960s, co-author Lionel was the Further Education Tutor at Gamlingay Village College in Cambridgeshire, responsible for organizing several series of academic lectures there. One of the celebrity lecturers who accepted the college's invitation was the brilliant Dr. Hugh Schonfield, author of *Those Incredible Christians* and numerous other excellent scholarly works. Among Dr. Schonfield's discoveries was the Atbash Cipher, and it was a real privilege for the authors to discuss it with him in depth as we drove him home to London after his outstanding lecture. One of Dr. Schonfield's very interesting observations was that the Hebrew *hokhmah* translates into the Greek *sophia* — meaning *wisdom* in a very special, personified sense. Dr. Schonfield believed that by using the Atbash Cipher, the word *Baphomet* can actually indicate wisdom in this sense.

Another interesting concept discussed at that time was that the Latin phrase, *"Templi omnium hominum pacis abhas"* — meaning "the father of the Temple of universal human peace" — can be abbreviated as *tem-o-h-p-ab*. If it is then read from right to left, as is done in Hebrew, the result is *Baphomet*. *Baphe metios* can also convey the idea of "the baptism of wisdom." Symbols, codes and ciphers can often take researchers and cryptographers on long, convoluted and circuitous journeys!

Dr. Bacon, who used to teach New Testament Criticism at Yale, was a specialist in the philosophical and theological implications of *hokhmah* — the Divine Wisdom personified. He saw wisdom, as portrayed in the Wisdom literature, as the Divine Spirit — a manifestation of God's redeeming love. *Hokhmah* went out to seek and save the lost. If the Templars' Baphomet represented wisdom in this sense, then it explains the urgency with which they themselves went out to redeem and restore renegade knights and nobles who had lost their sense of chivalry and vocation somewhere among the hardships and temptations of the Middle East.

Far from dabbling with the delusions and follies of so-called "devil worship" and black magic, it seems probable that the medieval Templars had compounded the divine *logos* — the *word* in the opening of St. John's gospel — with *sophia*, the Divine Wisdom. The mysterious Book of Enoch, which also contains its fair share of codes, ciphers and symbols, has a lot to say on the subject of *hokhmah*: the tradition states that because of human rejection, Wisdom returned to Heaven, but it will eventually return to Earth to provide inspiration and strength for the faithful of the Messianic Age.

Another coding technique, known as steganography, was known in ancient Greece. The word is derived from *steganos*, meaning "covered up," and the verb *graphein*, meaning "to write." A message inscribed on a thin piece of wood would be sandwiched between (and concealed by) a pair of clear wax tablets. The recipient would then have to melt the wax off to read the steganographic message on the wood.

Several centuries BC, the Spartans devised a method known as the *scytale*. This consisted of a strip of leather (which could later be disguised as the messenger's belt) wound around a wooden cylinder. The message was written while the leather was wound, so that it became a meaningless jumble of letters when unwound. If the belt was worn so that the jumble of random letters was on the inside, the messenger's chance of getting past sentries and roadblocks was increased. Upon reaching the intended recipient, the belt was wound around an identical cylinder and the message was deciphered.

The ingenious idea of using something as flexible as a leather belt to create and conceal a code, or cipher, was not confined to ancient Sparta. Incan mysteries are so complex and diffuse that it would require several large volumes to do them even partial justice. Their *khipu* codes consisted of lengths of cord, from which hung other elaborately knotted threads and strands of varying colours and lengths. The twenty-six letters of the modern English alphabet could very easily be organized into such a system. If each vowel was a short white string, then *a* could be a plain string like this: ————; *e* would have one knot: ————* ; *i* would contain two knots: ——*—*; *o* would have three: ——*—*—*; and *u* would have four: —*—*—*—*. A longer string, or a string of a different colour, could represent the labial consonants *p* and *b*, with one knot for *b* and two knots for *p*. There could also be doubled or entwined threads for dental consonants like *t* and *d*; for example, *t* could be a red and white string, while *d* might be a red and white string with one knot added. As far back as the 1920s, a science historian named Leland Locke proved that the *khipu* were not only decorative, but they also acted as simple calculators — along the lines of beads on an abacus. And

Professor Gary Urton of Harvard has recently produced an excellent book on the subject, *Signs of the Inca Khipu*. Locke's pioneering work accounted for a number of *khipu* as numerical records, but many were not susceptible to numerical interpretation. It seems reasonable, therefore, to assume that these were messages of some type — possibly a language, but also possibly a non-linguistic code.

Contemporary road signs giving advice or instructions to drivers are a modern example of non-linguistic codes. We may automatically translate them into words when we drive by them, but their actual message can short-circuit verbal thinking and produce the required reaction without using word-thoughts like "turn right," "oncoming traffic has the priority," "roundabout," or "two-way traffic" as intermediaries.

Some researchers into the *khipu* once thought that they were mnemonic codes, and would therefore defy translation forever unless someone who knew the facts that they were designed to prompt in the memory still survived to explain them. Modern research has demonstrated that they are almost certainly a form of binary coding, not merely simple mnemonics.

So how do the *khipu* connect with the ancient secrets of the pre-Templar Guardians, and with the medieval Templars of Jerusalem?

The Inquisition made out a list of ridiculous false accusations against the Templars in August 1308. These accusations focused mainly on their Baphomets, but among the risible anti-Templar propaganda there was one very curious fact: the Templars were accused of touching the Baphomet with lengths of string, or cord, of different types, that they then wore around themselves under their armour. Their commanders apparently distributed these cords to members of the noble order, just as Incan chiefs would have given *khipu* to their messengers.

It is now necessary to examine the situation in Spain and Portugal prior to Columbus's voyage to the Americas in 1492 — bearing in mind that it is extremely unlikely that he was the first European to make the crossing. The five centuries of war between Spain and the Muslim Empire of Cordoba and Granada had ended. Warrior-priests from Alcantara, Calatrava and Santiago had been among the heroes of these battles, and their techniques and military skills owed much to the influence of the Templars. After 1307, many of the Templars in Spain transferred to other noble orders such as the Knights of the Cross and the Order of Montesa in Aragon. The castle of Calatrava, for example, passed into Templar hands in 1147 before becoming the headquarters of the Order of Calatrava. A similar group, the Order of Alcántara, was recognized by the pope in 1177, and the Order of Santiago was formalized by Fernando II of León in 1161. Typically, the Order of Montesa was founded by King Jaime II of Aragon, with the express purpose of creating a safe and honourable environment for Templars after the tragedy of 1307. It was originally known as *Nuestra Señora de Montesa* and was recognized by Pope John XXII in 1317. The order had the special duty of defending the coast of Valencia against Moorish pirates and slave traders. The Moorish seamen would very probably have had access to ancient navigational knowledge and old maps. Did they know about the transatlantic routes beyond the Pillars of Hercules, and the exciting new lands on the other side of the Atlantic? How much of that knowledge found its way into the hands of the Templar-based Order of Montesa?

Many strange secrets still lurk in the depths of the old Spanish-Moorish castles and palaces.

Mysterious old Aljaferia Castle in Spain. How many Templar secrets lie below it?

Co-author Lionel explores the sinister dungeons below Aljaferia Castle in Spain.

Stark and forbidding Belmonte Castle in Spain: another possible hiding place of ancient Templar secrets.

Co-author Lionel, researching Belmonte Castle in Spain.

Although most generalizations are suspect, it is probably true to say that the Crusades in the Middle East, and the examples of courage and determination set by the Templars and the noble and valiant Spanish orders, were the springboard that launched Hernan Cortes and the conquistadores into the Americas. Just as, two centuries before, the Crusaders had headed for the Middle East, motivated by religion, lands and gold, so Cortes and his conquistadores headed west — driven by the same three powerful motives.

Cortes was born in Spain in 1485. At nineteen he sailed from Seville and landed in what was then Hispaniola (now the Dominican Republic), which Columbus had discovered in the Caribbean in 1492.

Fortune smiled on Cortes. The governor was a family friend who treated the young adventurer well. He was given land and slaves, and after his positive role in the successful invasion of Cuba he was rewarded again.

There were well-substantiated rumours of gold to be had in a land away to the west (modern Mexico). When Cortes was still in his early thirties, he led an expedition there: he had barely five hundred fighting men, fewer than twenty horses, and a hundred seamen who were also useful in a fight, but only eleven ships. His inadequate little cannons were loaded with spherical stones rather than proper cannonballs or chain shot, and he and his men had swords, pikes and muskets, plus a few crossbows. Apart from the same kind of courage and determination that was characteristic of the Templars, Cortes had two great allies in his conquest of the huge Aztec Empire with its thousands of warriors. The first of these was the Aztec religion: Montezuma, their ruler, believed that the god they called Quetzalcoatl was due to return to them. He thought for a while that Cortes was Quetzalcoatl, and by the time he had realized his error, time was up for the Aztec Empire!

Even more important to the success of the conquistadores was a beautiful girl named Marina. Her real-life story is stranger than fiction. Her parents were Aztec nobility, and her father was a chieftain. When he died, her mother promptly found another husband, by whom she had a son. It was then decided that Marina was now surplus to requirements, and she was promptly handed over to some passing slave traders. The story almost parallels the biblical account of Joseph and his coat of many colours. Marina found herself enslaved to the Cacique of Tabasco, who was a military leader.

It was this transfer of ownership that enabled Marina to become an expert linguist and interpreter. She still understood her own Aztec language, but she now knew the Mayan dialects and subdialects that were spoken in the Yucatán. The Cacique, seeking to curry favour with Cortes, gave him twenty attractive young slave girls — Marina was one of them. Despite having had no choice in the matter, she became the most loyal, courageous and faithful companion that Cortes might have wished for. It is no exaggeration to say that without her skills as an interpreter, the conquistadores might have failed. It is much in Cortes's favour that he treated her with the greatest of respect, and reciprocated her love and loyalty. When Cortes finally had to return to his wife in Spain, he made sure that Marina was safely and securely married to his worthy friend, Don Juan Xamarillo. Also known as *La Milanche*, meaning "the commander's lady," Marina was also given estates in her own right.

The great question of the American Inca *khipu* codes and the strange cords used in the Baphomet ceremonies and then worn by the Templars remains unanswered. However, the tenuous links are there. The Templars and other crusading orders fought in the Middle East in the eleventh, twelfth, thirteenth and fourteenth centuries. Some sort of cord message system seems to have existed among the Templars. Did any other noble orders have one too? Following the loss of their Middle Eastern strongholds, the spiritual descendants of the Templars struck out westward across the Atlantic in search of the New World — where the highly intelligent Inca nation (and almost certainly the Aztecs as well) employed a sophisticated cord message system, the *khipu*. What if early Phoenician traders had made contact with the Incas, Aztecs, Mayans and other highly cultured and civilized indigenous Americans? What if they had learned of the *khipu* and brought that secret knowledge back to the Middle East? Remember that Leland Locke unravelled the secret of some *khipu* as being numerical: could some of them have been bills of lading, or merchants' accounts of transactions? What more natural way might a Phoenician transatlantic merchant sailor come to understand the way that his American trading partners reckoned the values and quantities of goods bought and sold?

Having considered two of the great advantages that won the war for Cortes — the beautiful and brilliantly intelligent Marina, and the errors over Quetzalcoatl — was there a third? Did Cortes or any of his men know about the *khipu* codes because a Phoenician sailor had once brought back examples from a trading voyage?

* * *

Our research moves on from the complexities of the *khipu* knotted-thread codes to the equally intricate problems of the Knight's Tour on a chessboard of sixty-four squares. The Templars enjoyed depicting themselves as chess knights, and many of their codes — including the Rennes-le-Château codes, if they're genuine and not interpolated forgeries — consisted of laying out letters on a chessboard, then deciphering the message by writing the letters in the order of a Knight's Tour.

However, chess has a venerable ancestor in the form of the Royal Game of Ur. Found in a royal tomb in Ur, the game dates from about 2500 BC. Rules relating to it were found on cuneiform tablets that were millennia younger than the board and pieces found in Ur, but as the boards were identical, it seems reasonable to suppose that the same, or very similar, rules would apply. The boards all contain squares marked with five rosettes — which may give Rosicrucianism a far longer pedigree than is usually assigned to it! Did some of the strange, secret knowledge of the ancient pre-Templar Guardians find its way into Rosicrucianism?

Some experts believe that the path that the counters take around the board — not unlike a simple forerunner of the Knight's Tour — begins in the left-hand corner when the board is in the position indicated in the diagram below. Controversy about the rosettes includes the theory that they may be squares that the players try to avoid because landing on one returns the counter to its starting position. Another theory is that they are refuge squares, where a player is safe from his opponent. Was this ancient game known to the pre-Templar Guardians?

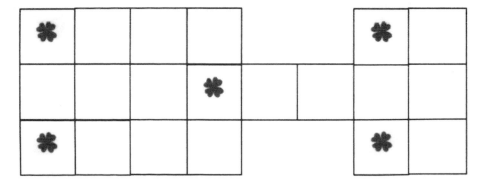

In a sense, the game corresponds to Manichaean ideas and gnostic dualism: two opposing forces wrestling for cosmic supremacy. What would the medieval Templars of Jerusalem have made of it? It would certainly be an ideal form on which to lay out the letters or symbols comprising a cipher. It is also interesting to note that, from the central rosette, each of the others can be reached by a move very similar to that of a knight on a chess board — except that on this Royal Game of Ur board, the move has to be two forward and then one diagonal, instead of one forward and one diagonal. It can also be thought of as three forward and then one after a ninety-degree turn in either direction on the Ur board, whereas the knight's move on a chess board can be visualized as two straight and then one after a ninety-degree turn in either direction.

The knight's tour on an ordinary eight-by-eight, sixty-four-square chessboard consists of making a *closed* tour in which, after touching each square once only, the knight returns to his starting place — or an *open* tour, in which the knight touches each square once only, but is unable to reach his starting square after making his sixth-fourth move.

The first diagram shows a closed tour that enables the knight to reach his starting square 🐴 from the square that he reached at the end of his sixty-third move.

35	40	47	44	61	8	15	12
46	43	36	41	14	11	62	9
39	34	45	48	7	60	13	16
50	55	42	37	22	17	10	63
33	38	49	54	59	6	23	18
56	51	28	31	26	21	🐴	3
29	32	53	58	5	2	19	24
52	57	30	27	20	25	4	1

One of many possible variations of the closed Knight's Tour.

1 Start	48	31	50	33	16	63	18
30	51	46	3	62	19	14	35
47	2	49	32	15	34	17	64 Finish
52	29	4	45	20	61	36	13
5	44	25	56	9	40	21	60
28	53	8	41	24	57	12	37
43	6	55	26	39	10	59	22
54	27	42	7	58	23	38	11

Leonhard Euler's Open Knight's Tour: a "magic square" in which each row and column adds up to 260.

Leonhard Euler's father, Paul, had studied under the great Professor Jacob Bernoulli at the University of Basle in Switzerland, and Leonhard made the most of that family connection when he, too, studied under Bernoulli. Starting his university career at the age of fourteen, Leonhard's great mathematical gifts were soon discovered by Bernoulli, who helped the boy make the most of his outstanding talents in that field. Mathematics can be thought of as a singularly elegant and expressive language, and this linguistic aspect of the discipline aligns closely with the special skills needed by code-makers and code-breakers. Leonhard either discovered the Knight's Tour, with its unusual "magic square" properties of adding up to 260 vertically and horizontally, or it was secretly revealed to him by one of the cognoscenti who were aware of at least some of the Templar codes, symbols and ciphers. If da Vinci, Poussin, Teniers and other leading members of the art fraternity had access to both codes and secrets, then mathematicians like Bernoulli and Euler were likely to have enjoyed similar privileges. The mysterious secret threads woven by the ancient pre-Templar Guardians were as available to gifted mathematicians as they were to gifted artists. This suggests that the ancient Guardians' objectives included encouraging and developing the arts and sciences for the benefit of their human flock.

Because there are a great many possible tours for the chessboard knight (using the orthodox move of one straight followed by one diagonal square), Templar cipher makers and readers needed to know which particular tour was employed. It seems likely that the "magic square" tour would have been selected frequently, largely because of its symbolic numerology — whether Euler created it, or the Guardians passed it down to him.

The combination of the Knight's Tour and the Vigenère cipher together create almost unbreakable message protection.

Born in 1523, Blaise de Vigenère received an excellent education — as if he had been a member of the sixteenth-century French nobility, which he wasn't. That fact alone is enough to suggest that there could well have been benign Watchers, Guardians or Mentors taking care of him and his family with long-term plans in mind. Blaise went into the French Diplomatic Service and was secretary to the Duc de Nevers. These were very turbulent times as far as the Catholics and Protestants were concerned. The Duc was a Nicodemite who, rather ironically, died fighting for Catholicism in the Battle of Dreux in 1562.

A large group at this time in Reformation Europe was referred to as Nicodemites, after the reference to Nicodemus in John's gospel (Chapter 3, Verse 1). Nicodemus was a leading Pharisee and Jewish ruler — a member of the Sanhedrin who was nevertheless convinced that Jesus had been sent by God. Nicodemus visited him secretly by night because he was afraid that open identification with Jesus and his cause would jeopardize his authority and position in the community.

There were numerous prestigious Catholics in the sixteenth century who felt much the same about the reformers' cause, but decided that it was prudent to do nothing to support it openly. Consequently they earned the name Nicodemites.

In 1562, Charles, Cardinal of Lorraine presented documents to the privy council expressing his liberal Catholic views and trying hard to bring about a reconciliation with the reformers. Charles was an honourable and openhearted peacemaker who might well have succeeded; it is one of the tragedies of religious history that he did not. Significant numbers of Protestants were very much afraid that his open-minded liberalism and willingness to talk to those with different religious ideas might persuade at least some of the reformers to join him. Stuart Carroll's excellent, detailed paper on the subject was published in *The Journal of Ecclesiastical History*.

There seem to have been wheels within wheels in these particularly bitter and brutal religious wars of sixteenth-century Europe, and the involvement of mysterious hidden forces using human soldiers and politicians like chess pieces cannot be ruled out. If many of the ancient Watchers and Guardians were positive and progressive on behalf of their human flock, there also seem to have been sinister, negative forces in the equation. Blaise de Vigenère may have had excellent reasons for creating what he believed to be an undecipherable cipher.

When his employer, the Duc, died, de Vigenère was sent on a diplomatic mission to Rome, where he was involved in lengthy and detailed discussions of a work on cryptography by Giovanni Baptista Porta, a doctor as well as a mathematician — yet another link, perhaps, with later mathematical code-sharers like Leonhard Euler. Once de Vigenère was safely back in Paris he wrote a book entitled *A Treatise on Secret Writing*, in which he explained and demonstrated what cryptographers have known ever since as the *Vigenère Tableau*. Porta's method had been effective, but it was almost inoperable in practice: senders and receivers had to carry tables with them — not a sensible thing for a secret agent to be caught with! The technique Blaise developed needed only a word or phrase that was easy enough to remember. His system depended on a square of twenty-six alphabets, and a vital keyword that directed the users to the correct alphabets in the proper sequence.

A	B	C	D	E	F	G	H	I	J	K	L	M	N	O	P	Q	R	S	T	U	V	W	X	Y	Z
B	C	D	E	F	G	H	I	J	K	L	M	N	O	P	Q	R	S	T	U	V	W	X	Y	Z	A
C	D	E	F	G	H	I	J	K	L	M	N	O	P	Q	R	S	T	U	V	W	X	Y	Z	A	B
D	E	F	G	H	I	J	K	L	M	N	O	P	Q	R	S	T	U	V	W	X	Y	Z	A	B	C
E	F	G	H	I	J	K	L	M	N	O	P	Q	R	S	T	U	V	W	X	Y	Z	A	B	C	D
F	G	H	I	J	K	L	M	N	O	P	Q	R	S	T	U	V	W	X	Y	Z	A	B	C	D	E
G	H	I	J	K	L	M	N	O	P	Q	R	S	T	U	V	W	X	Y	Z	A	B	C	D	E	F
H	I	J	K	L	M	N	O	P	Q	R	S	T	U	V	W	X	Y	Z	A	B	C	D	E	F	G
I	J	K	L	M	N	O	P	Q	R	S	T	U	V	W	X	Y	Z	A	B	C	D	E	F	G	H
J	K	L	M	N	O	P	Q	R	S	T	U	V	W	X	Y	Z	A	B	C	D	E	F	G	H	I
K	L	M	N	O	P	Q	R	S	T	U	V	W	X	Y	Z	A	B	C	D	E	F	G	H	I	J
L	M	N	O	P	Q	R	S	T	U	V	W	X	Y	Z	A	B	C	D	E	F	G	H	I	J	K
M	N	O	P	Q	R	S	T	U	V	W	X	Y	Z	A	B	C	D	E	F	G	H	I	J	K	L
N	O	P	Q	R	S	T	U	V	W	X	Y	Z	A	B	C	D	E	F	G	H	I	J	K	L	M
O	P	Q	R	S	T	U	V	W	X	Y	Z	A	B	C	D	E	F	G	H	I	J	K	L	M	N
P	Q	R	S	T	U	V	W	X	Y	Z	A	B	C	D	E	F	G	H	I	J	K	L	M	N	O
Q	R	S	T	U	V	W	X	Y	Z	A	B	C	D	E	F	G	H	I	J	K	L	M	N	O	P
R	S	T	U	V	W	X	Y	Z	A	B	C	D	E	F	G	H	I	J	K	L	M	N	O	P	Q
S	T	U	V	W	X	Y	Z	A	B	C	D	E	F	G	H	I	J	K	L	M	N	O	P	Q	R
T	U	V	W	X	Y	Z	A	B	C	D	E	F	G	H	I	J	K	L	M	N	O	P	Q	R	S
U	V	W	X	Y	Z	A	B	C	D	E	F	G	H	I	J	K	L	M	N	O	P	Q	R	S	T
V	W	X	Y	Z	A	B	C	D	E	F	G	H	I	J	K	L	M	N	O	P	Q	R	S	T	U
W	X	Y	Z	A	B	C	D	E	F	G	H	I	J	K	L	M	N	O	P	Q	R	S	T	U	V
X	Y	Z	A	B	C	D	E	F	G	H	I	J	K	L	M	N	O	P	Q	R	S	T	U	V	W
Y	Z	A	B	C	D	E	F	G	H	I	J	K	L	M	N	O	P	Q	R	S	T	U	V	W	X
Z	A	B	C	D	E	F	G	H	I	J	K	L	M	N	O	P	Q	R	S	T	U	V	W	X	Y

Table devised by Blaise de Vigenère, 1562.

Now suppose that the keyword is *templars,* and the message is once again the authors' names, *Lionel and Patricia Fanthorpe.* To cipher the message, we write the keyword above it as often as is necessary:

T E M P L A R S T E M P L A R S T E M P L A R S T E

L I O N E L A N D P A T R I C I A F A N T H O R P E

The next step is to select the row beginning with *T,* the first letter in the keyword *templars.* Trace that alphabet along as far as *L,* the first letter in *Lionel,* then follow that column upwards until the top line is reached. In this case, the top letter is an *S.* This starts the encryption. Returning to the keyword, we see that the second letter must be taken from the row starting with an *E.* Follow this row to the *I* — the second letter in *Lionel.* Trace that column upwards to find *E* on the top line. So, the first two characters in the encrypted message are *SE.* Repeating this method for the rest of the name *Lionel* yields *SECVTL.*

Decoding the message is predicated on knowing the keyword, *templars.* We begin by repeating the keyword above the characters in the ciphered message.

T E M P L A R S...

S E C V T L...

Go to *S* on the top line, and follow the column down to row *T*. The square where column *S* and row *T* intersect contains the initial *L* of *Lionel*. Next, find E on the top line and descend to row *E*: the result is *I*. *C* on the top line translates into *O* on the horizontal *M* alphabet ... and so the process continues.

The above example is a simple one, intended only to indicate the rudiments of the Vigenère technique. Just how complex and elaborate a combination of the Vigenère Tableau and any one of the Templars' Knight's Tours can become is demonstrated by the decipherment carried out at Rennes-le-Château, using the inscription from the defaced tombstone of Marie de Nègre of Hautpoul to find the keyword. Certain letters on that damaged stone (said to have been very conveniently copied by an antiquarian before Bérenger Saunière defaced it) were misplaced or in the wrong case. These letters formed the words *mort épée*, meaning "sword death." A slight rearrangement, however, created the word *emprunté*, meaning "false," "borrowed" or "pretended." Was that a secondary clue advising researchers and cryptographers not to take the stone too seriously? Was it all false, just a curious red herring? Had the supposed message been borrowed from somewhere else? Was it not all that it pretended to be? The Vigenère work is a little different here, too, because the French alphabet has no letter *w*: there are only twenty-five alphabets in the square — not twenty-six, as in the English version. But when all the work *has* been done — including guiding a knight over *two* chessboards — what emerges is a message that is almost as strange as the alleged inscription from Marie de Nègre's mysterious obliterated tombstone:

BERGERE PAS DE TENTATION QUE POUSSIN
TENIERS GARDENT LA CLEF PAX DCLXXXI
PAR LA CROIX AT CE CHEVAL DE DIEU
J'ACHEVE CE DAEMON DE GARDIEN A
MIDI POMMES BLEUES.

This translates more or less literally as, "Shepherdess no temptation to which Poussin and Teniers possess [or guard] the key peace 681 with the cross and this horse of God I reach [or overcome?] the demon guardian at mid-day [or in the Midi?] blue apples."

Since our own investigations on site at Rennes-le-Château first began in 1975, numerous investigators and researchers have put forward interesting and wide-ranging suggestions about the alleged coded manuscripts and tombstone inscriptions. Were they genuine, and if they were, who put them there and what do they mean?

The *Shepherdess* reference is probably to Poussin's painting of the *Shepherds of Arcadia* — so artists from da Vinci downwards may well be deeply involved. The strange old Tomb of Arques is also in the running, as it features so prominently in Poussin's famous canvas. The Teniers were also members of the art circle and would have known something about its secret codes, symbols and ciphers. The word *peace* may symbolize several things. The old code-makers were fond of word play and often linked chains of meanings. Peace suggests a symbolic dove. Noah sent out a dove from the Ark in the old flood story — in both its Babylonian and biblical versions. The nautical Ark may well be intended to hint at the mysterious Ark of the Covenant and its hiding place. Is it in Axum? Did the nine medieval Templars unearth it below the Dome of the Rock in Jerusalem? Where did it go from there? Does the number 681 refer to a significant date, or are the numbers vital directional clues — like the numbers used on traditional treasure maps? The *cross* may have religious significance, or it may refer to a technique necessary for untangling a Templar version of an alphabet code similar to — but older than — the Vigenère Tableau. The *horse* probably refers to the chessboard knight on his bewildering tour, but who is the *demon guardian*? Did Saunière think it was literally some evil, paranormal force? Was that why he erected the mysterious statuary inside his Church of Mary Magdalene? *Midi* may suggest that when the sun is in the right place at midday on the appropriate day of the year in the Rennes-le-Château latitudes, something strange will be revealed via its light inside the ancient church. *Midi* can also be an area of France. Poussin's canvas entitled *L'Automne, ou La Grappe de la Terre Promise* (Autumn, or the Grapes of the Promised Land) was painted between 1660 and 1664. It shows two men carrying a huge bunch of grapes on their shoulders. Each grape is as big as an apple, and is blue. As in many of Poussin's other enigmatic pictures, the background scenery may be intended to furnish a clue to the secret location of some ancient and mysterious treasure.

It is certainly possible for today's researchers and investigators to go on discovering more intriguing clues and pointers to the enigmatic riddles that seem to have been the hallmark of the ancient pre-Templar Guardians and of the medieval Knights Templar of Jerusalem. Almost certainly the inner enclaves of early mathematicians, self-styled magicians, minstrels, musicians and artists had access to at least some of those amazing secrets. One clue above all is worth pursuing: all these codes, symbols and ciphers tell us that important and powerful Templar secrets are still hidden somewhere.

The famous Glastonbury Thorn.

THE FIVE GREAT TEMPLAR MYSTERIES

Vitally important ancient mysteries are camouflaged and disguised not only by codes and ciphers but also by the passage of time and the changing of cultural myths and legends. Sand dunes cover forgotten ancient cities. Oceans erode vulnerable coastlines. Vegetation covers abandoned settlements of the past. Hidden by confusing changes of name, time and place, five great mysteries remain: the emerald tablets of Hermes Trismegistus; the Grail; the Spear of Destiny; the Ark of the Covenant; and a mysterious cloak, robe or fleece that gives its wearer the power of flight or invisibility — or both — and occasionally conveys other strange gifts as well. These five basic riddles await the unwrapping of layers of legend in order to give them a close and careful analysis and evaluation.

There are some very curious stones (perhaps emeralds, perhaps something else that is green and crystalline) that are credited with being the storage place of vast knowledge — the kind of knowledge that really *is* power. They first appear in close association with the character known to some as Thoth, scribe to the Egyptian pantheon and archivist of all their powerful magic — their superior technology.

There is a very interesting old Hebrew legend in which Sarah, the wife of Abraham, finds Thoth (Hermes Trismegistus) motionless in a cave. He is either in a very deep natural sleep or in a state of suspended animation. Beside him are the glittering Emerald Tablets. Drawn by natural curiosity, Sarah picks one or two of them up. As she does so, Thoth begins to stir. She flees.

Did she carry the tablets with her? Did they eventually become the mysterious Urim and Thummim, the precious stones used by the Jewish high priests to ascertain the will of God?

If the Urim and Thummim came via Sarah from Hermes Trismegistus, where did *he* come from? For that matter, where did the whole Egyptian pantheon (whom he apparently served as both archivist and librarian) come from? Were they supertechnologists from Atlantis or Lemuria, survivors of the aquatic cataclysm that somehow destroyed their great achievements? Were they visitors from beyond the stars — or from the future? Were they transdimensional travellers from other probability tracks — the tantalizing worlds of If?

If the mysterious Emerald Tablets were indeed artifacts capable of storing and categorizing data, they were a vital link in the chain of power. Without adequate data, sorted into usable and accessible formats, there can be little or no scientific and technological progress. The first great, ancient mystery is the data store and processing power described in myth and legend as the Emerald Tablets.

* * *

If those Emerald Tablets really are a vast store of carefully arranged and processed, networked knowledge, what is the Grail — or Graal? Clues to its true identity may exist in the Poussin, Teniers, Strozzi and da Vinci artists' codes, the Nag Hammadi documents, the supposed archives of the enigmatic Priory of Sion — or in the secret excavations that the medieval Templars made below Jerusalem's Dome of the Rock. Such clues as do exist point to something exceedingly old, challengingly mysterious and awesomely powerful.

The oldest and most persistent grail myths and legends point to it as being another amazing artifact — something at least as astounding as the Emerald Tablets, but very different in its purpose and modus operandi.

If the Tablets held the power of knowledge, the Grail seems to have been a source of productive, creative and transformative power. Einstein's mass-energy formula is $E = mc^2$, where E represents the amount of energy obtained when a unit of mass is converted into energy and c is the speed of light (186, 000 miles, or 300, 000 kilometres, per second) — and this has to be *squared* in the formula! In simple, pragmatic terms, there are gigantic amounts of energy to be released by converting one tiny unit of mass. And, conversely, enormous amounts of energy are required to create a minute amount of mass. Rearranging Einstein's equation and making mass (m) the subject gives us $m = E/c^2$, which implies that the amount of mass created will be equivalent to the energy expended in its creation, *divided by the speed of light squared*.

The suggestion is that the Grail could do just that! It was, according to this theory, a stupendous technological artifact that could actually create matter as the result of a colossal expenditure of energy. It was, therefore, a cornucopia — the legendary horn of plenty. It was the mythical purse from which, whenever a coin was extracted, another "grew" in its place. It was the magical mill that would grind out whatever you wanted it to grind out. It was Aladdin's wonderful lamp that would provide its owner with anything for which he or she wished. Seemingly, it either created or teleported matter — and perhaps both.

The much later, Christianized, versions of the legend represented an attempt to lend the Grail a totally different significance as a supernatural Christian chalice. These Christian versions overlaid and camouflaged the far older Cornucopia Grail traditions and eventually become conflated with them. In some versions, the Grail became the cup that Jesus had used when establishing the Mass, or Eucharist — the ceremonial and liturgical use of bread and wine to represent the body and blood of Christ — at the Last Supper. Supposedly brought to England by Joseph of Arimathea, this Christianized Holy Grail became associated with Glastonbury and King Arthur's Knights of the Round Table. In addition, Joseph of Arimathea's miraculous staff was said to have sprouted into the wonderful Glastonbury Thorn Bush that, in legend, blossoms at Christmas and Easter.

Variations of the same story maintain that the Christian Grail was the chalice that caught some of Christ's blood during the crucifixion, and that it was his blood that made the vessel holy and endowed it with its many miraculous powers.

In one of their earlier investigations, the authors examined the famous Nanteos Cup in Wales. This was an ancient wooden cup that was thought by its adherents to have been made by Christ himself when he worked as a carpenter in Nazareth prior to embarking on his preaching, teaching and healing mission. There are many well-authenticated miraculous healings associated with the Nanteos Cup and with water that has been blessed by first being placed within it. Legends associated with the Nanteos Cup maintain that it had originally been brought to Glastonbury by Joseph of Arimathea, and subsequently taken to Strata Florida in Wales for safety before Henry VIII's brutal henchmen went looting in Glastonbury. In Wales, it passed into the safekeeping of the noble and trustworthy Powell family of Nanteos, who guarded it well for four centuries.

Another Christianized version of the Grail (or Sangreal) legend alludes to Mary Magdalene's hypothetical marriage to Jesus. In this interpretation, she herself is a living, human Grail, carrying Christ's blood in the sense that she bore children who share their divine father's genes. Supporters of this hypothesis usually use the term *Sangreal,* meaning the *real,* the royal or ultra-special *sang,* or blood, of Christ.

As expounded in detail in an earlier chapter, the authors do not consider Christ's hypothetical marriage to Mary Magdalene beyond possibility. Neither is it beyond the bounds of reason that Jesus and Mary's children should have been raised in the Languedoc and eventually united in some way with the Merovingian Dynasty. The additional role of loving husband and father simply increases and fulfills Christ's humanity, making him perfect, complete and total man *as well as* perfect and complete God. It is only the anti-Christian implications of Christ's marriage to Mary, which is put forward by some other researchers from time to time, with which the authors vehemently disagree.

Some writers suggest that if Jesus *were* Mary's husband and the father of her children, he could not at the same time have been the unique Son of God and saviour of the world. But why on Earth not? Marriage and parenthood are good, wholesome and delightful things: they do not preclude Christ's divinity, they *reinforce* it. There is no reason at all why Jesus, as portrayed in the gospels as the uniquely divine, messianic saviour (who died on the cross, was miraculously resurrected and ultimately returned to the Heaven from whence he came) could not *also* be Mary Magdalene's husband and the loving father of her children.

Arguably, the greatest and most important message tied up in the mysterious codes — including the codes left by da Vinci and his fellow artists — is not that Jesus was Mary's husband *instead* of being the Son of God, but that Jesus was her husband *as well as* being the Son of God. While it is important to consider the possibility that some secret, coded references to the Christianized Grail could refer to Mary Magdalene as a living Grail, it is rather more likely that the medieval Templars and the ancient pre-Templar Guardians were party to the secret of the amazing artifact that could create material objects from pure energy.

What if the "talking head" or Baphomet, which their enemies seized on so avidly as part of their accusations against the Templars, was in fact an ancient artifact — perhaps an Atlantean or extraterrestrial one, roughly the same size and shape as a human head? What if this roughly spherical container was a cornucopia, a technological miracle that provided material objects by creating them from energy? What if the so-called "head" or "skull" was just a grisly, elaborate container for that miracle-sphere?

* * *

The third great, controversial Templar riddle — from earliest times — is the enigma of the Spear of Destiny, sometimes called the Lance of Longinus. The fivefold hypothesis continues to develop: the Emerald Tablets were presumably a powerful store of organized knowledge; the ancient, pre-Christian Grail was theoretically a source of material objects — a Templar version of Aladdin's lamp — and what it produced may have included part of the Templars' fabulous wealth. The third mystery, the awesome Spear of Destiny, was presumably a weapon that gave its bearers enormous advantages in battle.

Like the other two arcane riddles, the Spear was also appropriated and Christianized. The persistent idea of a staff, a wand, or a rod of power, dates back for millennia — but once the Christian era began it was necessary for the makers of myths and weavers of legends to give that very powerful staff a Christian context. The factual and historical gospel accounts of the crucifixion refer to it clearly: a lance, or spear, was thrust into the side of Christ to ensure that he was dead before he was taken down from the cross. Just as the legendary Holy Grail in one version was endowed with power because it had once held his blood, so his blood also empowered the legendary Spear of Destiny. It is even possible to suggest that the two legends were conflated — welded together at Glastonbury: Joseph of Arimathea's staff, which sprouted and became the miraculous flowering thorn had originally been the spear of Longinus.

There is a significant link here between the flowering staff of Glastonbury and an Old Testament reference to the staff of Aaron, the brother of Moses, which also sprouted miraculously. A further reference to a dried wooden staff that produced miraculous shoots is found in the Tannhauser legend.

Tannhauser, also known as Tanhuser, was a thirteenth-century German minnesinger and Crusader, as described in Chapter Seven. At one time he was in the service of Frederick II, Duke of Austria, and he later worked for Otto II, Duke of Bavaria. In the legends, Tannhauser finds himself inside the Hörselberg in the court of Frau Hulda, the irresistibly beautiful equivalent, in German folklore, to the classical love goddess Venus-Aphrodite. When Tannhauser finally leaves her and seeks forgiveness from the pope, he is told that there is a greater chance of the dried and polished papal staff of office sprouting new leaves than there is of Tannhauser's sins being forgiven. Subsequently, the papal staff duly sprouts! Papal messengers are sent to find Tannhauser, but they fail. He is never seen on Earth again.

Myth and legend say that he has had the good sense to remain within the mysterious palace deep in the Hörselberg, enjoying Frau Hulda's incomparably warm hospitality until Judgement Day finally arrives. And good luck to him!

The idea that the flowering staff of Joseph of Arimathea had once been a Roman lance would have appealed greatly to early Christian mythmakers, who would have seen the concept of a spear becoming a flowering bush as totally right and relevant to Christ's teachings of peace and love — a close parallel to the idea of "beating swords into ploughshares."

Medieval Templar involvement with the Lance of Longinus, or Spear of Destiny, came into sharp focus in 1097, when the strange, mystic monk Peter Bartholomew claimed to have had a vision that it was hidden under the floor of the ancient Church of St. Peter in Antioch. As described in detail in Chapter Four, Peter led Raymond IV, Count of Toulouse, to the exact spot — and the Crusaders duly recovered the Holy Lance.

Old Testament prophets like Elisha used their staffs to perform miracles, and Moses himself did the same while his people were crossing the wilderness. The ancient Egyptian "magicians" also had wizards' wands or staffs. The fairies and little people of legend often waved magic wands to grant wishes or cast spells. Tolkien's Middle Earth was inhabited by wizards like Gandalf and Saruman whose power was channelled through — and sometimes derived from — their vitally important magical staffs.

It may therefore be argued that the Spear of Destiny, in reality the far older Staff of Power, was in use long before it got transferred in legend to the hand of a Roman soldier named Longinus in the first Christian century. The ancient Templar secrets apparently included knowledge of some very powerful and mysterious weapon in the shape of a spear, a rod, a staff or a lance. Might it have owed its efficacy to technology rather than magic? Could it have been a ray gun (of the type favoured by early science-fiction authors) or, perhaps, some type of laser weapon?

* * *

After the Emerald Tablets, the Cornucopia/Grail and the Sacred Spear comes the communication power of the Ark of the Covenant. Part of the hypothesis that the authors put forward in their 1999 book, *Mysteries of the Bible*, was that the Ark might well have been some extremely ancient and powerful artifact that Moses brought with him when he led the Israelites out of Egypt. Pharaoh had already decided that enough was enough and that the Israelites could go free. Then, displaying what was little short of military insanity, he sent the pride of his Egyptian chariots after them across a soggy seabed that was likely to flood again at any minute when the Red Sea returned with a vengeance. Why did he do it? Our hypothesis in *Mysteries of the Bible* was that Pharaoh had just been informed that Moses had taken the most important and powerful artifact in Egypt — the mysterious Ark that was to feature so prominently in later Hebrew history.

Its loss would have been incalculable. In Pharaoh's mind, it must be recovered at any cost. Hundreds of Egyptian charioteers and their horses died in the catastrophe of the Red Sea's sudden return, as Moses and the triumphant Israelites went on their way with the Ark.

When the infant Samuel was at the Holy Sanctuary at Shiloh, assisting old Eli the priest and sleeping close to the Ark, a mysterious voice was heard calling Samuel by name. Some researchers have referred dramatically to the Ark as "a radio for talking to God"! Is there some strange truth beneath that melodramatic statement? If the Emerald Tablets store and sort knowledge, does the Ark communicate or broadcast that knowledge in some way?

Like the Spear of Destiny, however, the Ark seems to control — or to incorporate within itself — powerful weaponry of some awesome, unknown kind. It won numerous battles for the Hebrew army — it was with Joshua's soldiers when they destroyed Jericho. It was also capable of striking a man who touched it suddenly dead. It was thought to have brought disaster on the Philistine enemies who had captured it and taken it to Gath, where it was held responsible for an outbreak of disease. Consequently, the Philistines were glad to return it. When the Ark was captured by the Philistines and placed overnight in the Temple of their god Dagon in Ashdod, the statue of Dagon was found broken on the floor in the morning.

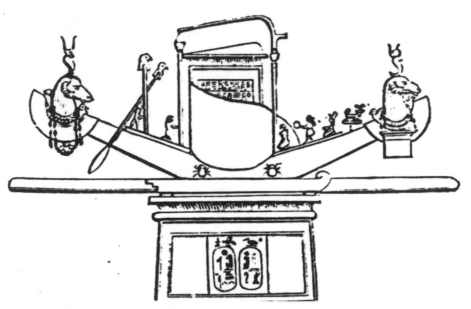

Ancient Egyptian Arks. Did Moses take one of these when the Israelites left Egypt? What enigmatic mysteries did it contain? What did its strange carvings symbolize?

Referring back to the mystery of Solomon and Sheba, did the Ark make its way to Axum in Ethiopia with their son, Menelik, and is it still there now in its secret sanctuary? There are other fascinating links with Ethiopia that go a great way further back than Solomon. In the Old Testament Book of Numbers (Chapter 12, Verse 1), there is a reference to

Moses having an Ethiopian wife, which for some reason upset his brother Aaron and his sister Miriam. In some translations, "Ethiopian" is rendered as "Cushite." The clearest biblical statement about Moses' wife is that she is Zipporah, a daughter of Jethro (also probably called Reuel and/or Hobab). The Exodus account calls Jethro a priest-ruler of Midian. There is some scholarly controversy over whether Cushites and Ethiopians might be one and the same in the minds of early Bible translators — in which case, Zipporah of the Exodus account and the Ethiopian woman from the Numbers account are the same girl. There is, however, an interesting case to be made for them being two quite separate and distinct people. One ingenious suggestion made by a commentator is that Jethro was an Ethiopian by birth who had gone to Midian and become its ruler: therefore Zipporah was ethnically Ethiopian, although Midianite by birth.

Aside from the biblical evidence, however, there are other ancient accounts that make the Ethiopian woman of Numbers 12 a very different person from Zipporah, daughter of Jethro, priest-ruler of Midian. These same accounts say a great deal more about Moses than the biblical records do. Manetho, an Egyptian priest and writer under the patronage of Ptolemy, gives the birthplace of Moses as Heliopolis at a time when the Egyptian oppression of the Hebrew slaves was at its worst. There is a Hebrew aphorism: "When the overseer's demand for bricks is doubled, God sends Moses." Heliopolis is a fascinating site for the Egyptologist because of its association with Tem, the god of sunset. The root word *tem* leads on to *temen*, meaning "to be complete," "to be finished." In ancient Egyptian art and sculpture, Tem is always shown in human form: was he one of the ancient pre-Templar Guardians? His children, Shu and Tefnut — simplistically, the god and goddess of dry air and moist air respectively — were produced from Tem's own body. The ancient Egyptian myths and legends of Heliopolis that are associated with their unusual origins may possibly have influenced the Mosaic story of his being drawn from the water.

In these old accounts, the Egyptian princess who rescued him is named as Thermuthis, which is the Greek equivalent of Taweret, the mysterious hippopotamus goddess who protected mothers and their infants. She is also referred to as Merrhis. In these old non-biblical versions, when the rescued infant Moses refused the milk offered by Egyptian nurses, Moses' elder sister Miriam, who was keeping faithful watch, ran to fetch her mother, Jochebed. According to old rabbinical records, Jochebed was also known as Shiphrah and worked as a midwife. She was a woman of strength and character who had the humanity and courage to disobey Pharaoh's cruel command to kill male Hebrew infants at birth.

Again according to the ancient, non-biblical traditions surrounding Moses' early years as an Egyptian prince, he was educated at Heliopolis and was trained there as a priest. His Egyptian name at this time was Osarsiph, although, naturally, his special name Moses was never forgotten nor abandoned. The Coptic word *mo* can be translated as "water." *Ushe* was Coptic for "saved." *Mosheh* in Hebrew is derived from *mashah*, a verb meaning to extract from, to draw out of. The priestly name Osarsiph that he was given in Heliopolis comes from an Egyptian root meaning "saved by Osiris."

According to these same old traditions, Moses was educated in Greek, Chaldean and Assyrian literature. It was during this educational phase of his life, and his priestly training as Osarsiph, that he almost certainly learned the strange secrets of the sacred and mysterious Egyptian Arks. This makes it increasingly likely that he took a singularly important and potent one with him when the Israelites left Egypt.

Some wildly exaggerated old accounts of his prowess and wisdom even have him teaching music to Orpheus! Far more likely to be factual are references in the ancient accounts to his skill as a boatbuilder, as a weapon designer, as a mathematician and as an expert in such diverse fields as hydraulics and hieroglyphics. What the old records are pointing towards is that Moses had a great deal in common with Leonardo da Vinci. Was Moses a pre-Templar Guardian, or was he just another great and powerful human leader who approved of what they were doing and supported them accordingly?

There can be little doubt that Moses, like da Vinci, was very powerful physically as well as mentally. In the biblical account of his anger with the Egyptian taskmaster who was mistreating a Hebrew slave, Moses seems to have killed the cruel overseer with one decisive blow. Further evidence appears when he arrives in Midian and rescues Jethro's daughters from the bullying shepherds who take the girls' turn at the well. There are several shepherds. Moses stands alone against them. This is the action of a powerful, skillful, experienced and confident warrior who knows that he can put away half a dozen shepherds with no trouble at all. They take one look at him and decide that to tangle with this muscular and well-armed Egyptian aristocrat would not be a sensible idea. Another non-biblical account says that when Pharaoh and his henchmen sent an assassin to kill Moses, the assassin met the same fate as the overseer! Moses is demonstrating the characteristics of Alexander and Charlemagne — as well as the characteristics of Leonardo.

His tactical and strategic military skills were also emphasized in these old non-biblical accounts. He led a highly successful military expedition against the Ethiopians and reached their capital, Saba, which he renamed Meroe in honour of his adopted mother, the Egyptian princess who had saved him from the Nile. Impressed by his military power, Tharbis, daughter of the king of Ethiopia, fell in love with Moses and returned with him to Egypt as his bride. Is she, then, the enigmatic Ethiopian woman of Numbers 12 of whom Miriam and Aaron disapproved?

It is also significant that Moses' father, Amram, and the reigning pharaoh both had strange dreams and visions to the effect that the child who was to be born to Jochebed would be a very significant person. He would bring Egypt low and be instrumental in benefiting the Israelites.

Moses and the Ark of the Covenant are inseparable riddles.

* * *

The fifth and final mysterious artifact associated with the pre-Templar Guardians — and with the mysteries behind the codes and ciphers of the medieval Templars — may have been the Cloak, Robe or Garment of Power. Whatever this ancient fabric might have been originally, it now features in two intriguing Christian legends: the Shroud of Turin (possibly, the same cloth referred to as the Mandylion and as St. Veronica's Handkerchief — or the Icon Veritas) and the history of Christ's seamless robe after the soldiers who carried out the crucifixion had diced for it.

The pre-Christian myths and legends of such a quasi-fabric include the mysterious Golden Fleece from the Greek legend of Jason and the Argonauts — and it is significant to remember that there is today an Order of the Golden Fleece that traces its origins back to medieval times and, most significantly, includes references to the

Habsburgs in its literature. One of the many theories about Rennes-le-Château and Bérenger Saunière is that Saunière found some priceless artifact that he passed over to the Habsburgs as notional Holy Roman Emperors, even though their official title had vanished in 1806. Was the "treasure" that Saunière may have discovered in Rennes-le-Château this mysterious quasi-fabric, this object of power?

Another aspect of the legend of Jason has a curious Templar connection. The head on the prow of the *Argo* could speak, and it gave the adventurers good advice when needed. How closely does that tie in with the "talking head" of the Templars?

The mythological origins of the Golden Fleece relate that another hero of Greek mythology, Phrixus, had escaped death on a magical ram that could fly. When his journey was complete, he sacrificed the magnificent golden beast to Zeus and hung its fleece in a grove. The fleece itself was said to have great powers, especially the power to heal — and in some Greek mythology, Jason is primarily a god of healing rather than a heroic adventurer.

Poseidon, or Neptune, the powerful god of the seas and oceans and brother of Zeus, was credited with making the cloak of invisibility that was given to Hades, god of the underworld. If the magical ram that saved Phrixus was able to fly, did its Golden Fleece retain those powers after the ram was sacrificed?

Flying cloaks, flying carpets and flying machines abound in old myths and legends. Was an ancient Chinese man-carrying kite, or hang-glider, regarded as a "flying cloak" (and described as such) when spectators watched a daring pilot leap off a cliff with it wrapped around his shoulders — and survive? The old Babylonian document called *Halkatha* says: "It is a great privilege to use a flying machine. The gods gave the knowledge of flying as a precious gift to save human lives." All of which reopens the question of the origins and identity of the ancient pre-Templar Guardians: were they technocrats from space, or from Atlantis or some other dimension? The Babylonian account of Etana's amazing flight is also intriguing. The detailed descriptions of what he saw read like an eye-witness account of someone who has actually flown at a great height. There is another very ancient Chaldean manuscript called *Sifr'ala* that seems to be a fairly technical account of how to construct a flying machine.

The Arabian Nights stories refer more than once to magical flying carpets, and Exhibit Number 6347 in the Cairo Museum of Antiquities' special register relates to an object that has every appearance of a model glider. As the ancient Egyptians tended to make models of real artifacts, it raises the question of whether they had succeeded in making gliders — if not a powered flying machine. Some experts who have examined Exhibit 6347 in detail have wondered whether it once had a propulsion unit.

As well as accounts of flying cloaks, kites and carpets, some of the ancient legends refer to cloaks that make their wearers invisible. Professor Susumu Tachi of Tokyo University has recently done some exciting modern work suggesting that "invisibility" may actually be technically possible. His work in optical camouflage has already produced some impressive results in which a subject, wearing one of the experimental fabrics being developed, gives the appearance of having become partially transparent.

* * *

The great Templar questions remain: did their secrets include these five mysteriously powerful artifacts — the Emerald Tablets of Hermes Trismegistus that later became Urim and Thummim; the Cornucopia that became the Grail; the Rod of Power that became the Lance of Longinus; the Ark that Moses brought from Egypt, which became the Ark of the Covenant; and the fabric that became the Mandylion, the robe and the Shroud of Turin?

The mighty mind of Leonardo da Vinci encompassed many of these areas of mysterious secret knowledge. How much did he say about what he knew in the tantalizing codes he left behind?

It has often been suspected that Bacon's Secret Society members used ingenious watermark codes such as these for their important messages. Could the letters RC stand for Rosicrucians? Do the letters CR stand for Christian Rosenkreuz? What does the jester's head signify? Does it indicate a connection with the medieval minstrels and troubadours? What do the Arabic letters on the shield tell us? Above all, was Bacon's Secret Society in touch with the ancient pre-Templar Guardians, or with Templar groups that had evaded the depredations of Philip le Bel?

Chapter 19

MYSTERIES OF THE TEMPLARS AND OTHER SECRET SOCIETIES

Assuming, for the sake of argument, that ancient pre-Templar Guardians actually existed and employed strange knowledge and superhuman powers, it seems probable that the Templars were not their only terrestrial instruments. Many contemporary secret societies and hidden, closed orders claim to have Templar connections and to share at least some of the arcane secrets that the ancient Guardians later entrusted to the medieval Templars. The Rosicrucians are prominent among these other secret societies.

Circa 1610, there appeared a strange pamphlet entitled *Farma Fraternitas RC*. The initials RC stood for *Rosae Crucis*. A number of similar pamphlets appeared shortly afterwards; the gist of what they had to say was that a Rosicrucian Brotherhood had been founded by a high-ranking German aristocrat named Christian Rosenkreuz, who had lived from 1378 until 1484. It was said that Rosenkreuz had at one time been a monk and that he had travelled extensively, including visits to Fez, Jerusalem and Damascus. During these journeys in the Middle East he had learned much from the Arabian friends he made there, and some of the secret knowledge he had acquired from them was described as "magic."

It was said that his early Rosicrucian teaching was opposed to formal Roman Catholicism and papal authority, and these seventeenth-century Rosicrucian pamphlets also apparently upheld a form of theosophy. Theosophy may be described as a body of belief contending that all religion worthy of the name represents humanity's various attempts to reach "the Divine" — whatever that ultimate mystery may eventually turn out to be.

The *Concise Oxford Dictionary* defines theosophy in part as "any of various philosophies professing to achieve a knowledge of God by spiritual ecstasy, [or] direct intuition." Modern theosophy, which is not a million light years from the ideas ascribed to Rosenkreuz, has seven main features. Its first principle is that consciousness is both universal and individual. Theosophists believe that nature and the entire natural order are directed and guided by laws and principles. Nothing is haphazard. Nothing happens by pure random chance. Theosophists also suggest that everything experiences consciousness.

Their second premise is that human beings are potentially immortal, but their eternal aspect is part of a "higher self." The individual personality and normal self-awareness, which we call the individual or the character, is unaware of the undying "higher self." Immortality, in theosophy, is dependent upon uniting the "lower" human self with the "higher" spiritual self.

Their third concept is reincarnation. They see it as something universal: a human being may once have been a rock, then an insect, a fish, an amphibian, and a mammal before attaining human form.

Karma is their fourth basic idea, but their version of karma seems to approach gnostic dualism of the kind known to the Cathars of the Languedoc (whose secrets almost certainly passed to the Templars during the thirteenth century). Spirit is seen as good, and matter is regarded as bad. One seems to turn into the other, then back again. This part of their teachings suggests that universal destiny consists of progressing through as many as seven distinct stages.

Fifthly, there is a belief in universal brotherhood and sisterhood, because everything — and everyone — came from the same divine source. The word *monad* is used in this context by theosophists, who believe that all things are really monads. A number of dictionaries define *monad* in its philosophical sense as "one of the simplest individual entities of which the universe is made up, according to Leibniz." In its Greek aspect of being an ultimate, indivisible unit, monad is derived from *monas*, or *monados*. The mysterious mathematical codes and ciphers of men like Euler and Bernoulli may well have contributed to the da Vinci Code and the enigmas it conceals. It is particularly significant at this stage to remember that Pythagoras — one of the earliest fathers of mathematics — also referred to the monad. In his view it was the unity from which all numbers and multiplicity flow. In his *Metaphysics*, Aristotle called the monad the principle (the Greek *arche*) of number. To him it was without quantity, and was unchangeable and indivisible.

The neo-Platonists used "monad" to signify what they called "the One"; the Christian Platonist writer Synesius of Cyrene, who lived from AD 370 until 414, described God as "the Monad of Monads." If Leibniz got it right in his struggle to bridge the intellectual chasm between Descartes's teaching that matter is inert and Spinoza's pantheistic monism, then Leibniz's monads may well provide useful insights into the real nature of the ancient pre-Templar Guardians. Other philosophers have certainly considered monads to be indivisible centres of force, but have not always gone along with Leibniz's wider view that such monads can also have the distinctive qualities of representation and perception.

The sixth principle of theosophy is often called evolution — but it is evolution seen from a particular and special perspective. Theosophical evolution incorporates progress in ethics and morality, goodness and concern for other people's welfare, philosophy, science, religion and the arts. Theosophists see this kind of evolution as helping humanity to approach the Divine.

Their seventh and final principle is numerological — the mathematical codes return! This final idea is known to theosophists as the Septenary: their universe is understandable in terms of the mysterious number seven. To summarize this theosophical Septenary concept, the monad is seen as having seven distinct bodies: physical, vital, desiring, mental, causal, intuitional and finally — ineffable.

Although it was alleged by the early-seventeenth-century Rosicrucians that the alchemical production of gold was a relatively simple and straightforward process, Rosenkreuz apparently aspired to go far beyond the advantages of mere material wealth. He wanted his followers and co-workers — sometimes referred to as the Invisibles — to concentrate on theological and philosophical principles and to study the deep secrets of nature in order to benefit humanity. That sounds remarkably close to the aspirations of the ancient pre-Templar Guardians.

An interesting old book called *The Secret Societies of All Ages and Countries* appeared in 1875, and was revised and reissued in 1896. Its author, Charles William Heckethorn, reported on various claims made by early supporters of the group that came to be known as Rosicrucians. These claims included the discovery and reopening of Rosenkreuz's mysterious tomb in 1604 — a hundred and twenty years after his death.

This arcane tomb was alleged to have contained many strange things, including lamps that were either still burning or that had been so cleverly constructed by the ancient alchemists that they ignited themselves as soon as fresh oxygen entered the chamber.

There is a significant amount of material that is morally and philosophically commendable among Rosicrucian teachings, and much of it coincides with the ethics of leaders like Alexander and Charlemagne, as examined in earlier chapters. The question arises persistently: Were these shared moral precepts an indication that the ancient pre-Templar Guardians were working with several different secret groups, like the Rosicrucians, as well as with the medieval Templars of Jerusalem?

More speculative and less accessible to researchers than Rosicrucianism is the so-called Prieuré de Sion — rendered as the "Priory of Sion" in English, sometimes with the variant spelling Zion. Theories range from its being merely a harmless but elaborate hoax to its being one of the most ancient, powerful and sinister secret societies in the world. In 1956, Article IIIc of what purported to be the Statutes of the Priory of Sion maintained that the organization took its name from Mount Sion — not the one in the Middle East, but the one that was close to the little French town of Annemasse, near the Swiss border, where Pierre Plantard and André Bonhomme lived at that time. The official registration was made by them in the subprefecture of St.-Julien-en-Genevoise on May 7, 1956. Plantard's critics would argue that he was an impostor rather than a genuine Merovingian descendant — but that is an issue between him and them. Certainly assertions were made — perhaps implicitly rather than explicitly — that he was a claimant to the throne of France, and perhaps of Europe as well, via his Merovingian ancestors. In their world-famous *Holy Blood, Holy Grail*, Baigent, Lincoln and Leigh made much of *The Secret Files of Henri Lobineau*, described by its detractors as a pseudo-historical document. This, together with Plantard's own assertions, led to the hypothesis that the Priory of Sion dated back at least to the time of the medieval Templars of Jerusalem, that it was one of the powers behind the Templars, that it wanted to re-establish a Merovingian monarchy in Europe, and that the Merovingians were deserving of this because they included the descendants of Jesus and Mary Magdalene. Considering the slow but resolute progress of those federalist Europeanizers who seem to be working towards a European superstate rather than a simple, but commercially useful, common market, a perceptive political observer might wonder whether the priory's dream of a new version of the Holy Roman Empire, perhaps restyled the Holy European Empire, could really be on track. If it genuinely aimed at worldwide peace, prosperity and justice — rather than domination, control and exploitation — it might perhaps have some commendable qualities. It might also be part of what the ancient and mysterious pre-Templar Guardians are steering towards.

One of the most contentious aspects of the priory — if it exists as anything other than an elaborate hoax — is its supposed list of grand masters. This list is not universally recognized by Priorists; some of them support different versions of the priory's history. Plantard maintained that the priory had been founded in 1681 at Rennes-le-Château — where else? — and Dan Brown's use of the idea in his best-selling *The Da Vinci Code* has done a great deal to revive interest in it. Just for the record, and on the outside chance that there is a glimmer of reality behind the smoke-enshrouded myths and legends concerning the priory, the list of alleged grand masters included: Bertrand de Blanchefort (1156–1169), Jean de St. Clair (1351–1366), Leonardo da Vinci (1510–1519), Nostradamus (1556–1566), Louis de Nevers (1575–1595), Isaac Newton (1691–1727), Victor Hugo (1844–1885), Claude Debussy (1885–1918) Jean Cocteau (1918–1963) and finally Pierre Plantard (1963–1981).

Both Plantard and the priory claimed that their motto was "*Et in Arcadia ego.*" Wherever the real truth about the arcane and diffuse Templar secrets may lie concealed, it is always remarkable how the various quests for it are circular in nature — they inevitably curve back to Rennes-le-Château, to Poussin's paintings and to that curious Latin text, "*Et in Arcadia ego.*"

* * *

If the priory is hard to track down with any degree of accuracy, the job of researching into it is relatively open-cast surface mining compared with the task of investigating the deep and almost impenetrable seams of the Illuminati. One of the earliest uses of the term, which is based on the Greek root from which the English word *illumination* is derived, was in connection with baptized Christians in the early church — they had "received illumination," or "seen the light." The Alumbrados, who were religious mystics in sixteenth-century Spain, were also called Illuminati, as were the followers of Adam Weishaupt — who seemed to have gone in an entirely different direction and aimed to replace religion with rationalism.

The easiest way in may be via Weishaupt's life and work. Weishaupt, who was born in 1748, simply referred to himself as Brother Spartacus. The Abbé Barruel spoke of him as a devil, while Jefferson regarded him merely as a harmless philanthropist. An accusation so vehement that it is close to being a paradoxical compliment came from John Robinson, a one-time professor of Natural Philosophy at Scotland's Edinburgh University. He described Weishaupt as "the profoundest conspirator that ever existed." Robinson sent a copy of his book on the subject of Weishaupt and the Illuminati, *Proofs of a Conspiracy*, to George Washington. Washington replied that he knew about them, and that some of them were already in America.

The background of the real, historical Spartacus is helpful insofar as it illustrates what Weishaupt would have identified as his brand of idealism. The defiant hero after whom Weishaupt named himself was a Thracian who had once served as an auxiliary in the Roman army in Macedonia. He deserted, but was recaptured and sold into slavery. From there, he became a trainee gladiator at Batiatus in Capua. He led a breakout from the gladiator school, involving almost a hundred fellow trainees, in BC 73, and they attracted thousands of runaway slaves as followers. After many battles, Spartacus and his men were finally defeated, and the Roman authorities enacted a bloody and terrible vengeance. Nevertheless, the name of Spartacus became synonymous with a fight for freedom and equality — and has been so for many centuries.

During his mid-eighteenth-century upbringing, Weishaupt lived in Ingolstadt in Bavaria, where he learned Czech, Italian, Latin, Greek and Hebrew. He would have had the ideal background to compile the strange, secret parchments that were allegedly found in Rennes-le-Château and which purportedly led Saunière to his enigmatic treasure. Weishaupt's parents had originally been Jewish but had converted to Roman Catholicism. Despite the powerful persuasion of his Jesuit teachers, Weishaupt avoided the role of overseas missionary that they recommended for him, and instead became Professor of Canon Law at Ingolstadt University. His high intelligence, linguistic skills and access to the university's library of interesting old documents brought him into contact with the occult, and he focused in particular on the mysteries of the Great Pyramid of Giza.

Counted among the Seven Wonders of the Ancient World, it is a unique structure, and it points to what is best described as the celestial North Pole with an accuracy that modern science would be challenged to equal. If its alignment is genuinely deliberate and not merely a remarkable coincidence, its builders were impressive technologists and astronomers — men and women in the same league as Pythagoras, da Vinci and Newton. It's also a quantitative masterpiece as well as a qualitative one: there are roughly two and a half million limestone blocks in the Great Pyramid.

Investigators and researchers from various scientific disciplines have put forward several different theories about the age of the Great Pyramid. One accurate and ingenious hypothesis put forward by Dr. Kate Spence, an expert Egyptologist from Cambridge University, points out that Polaris (the Pole Star), which is a very useful guide to the Earth's North Pole today, wasn't in its present position from the standpoint of earthly observers when the pyramids were allegedly being built. Instead, the ancient Egyptian astronomers would have had access to two stars, Kochab and Mizar, which together enabled north to be fixed accurately. The positions of Kochab and Mizar in 2467 BC would have been particularly helpful to Egyptian astronomers, and this could well have been around the time when the Great Pyramid of Giza was being constructed.

There is other intriguing evidence, however, that leads different researchers to suggest a far older date for the Great Pyramid: 10,000 BC, or even further back, perhaps. That suggestion would link up with the legends of Atlantis and Lemuria, and would point yet again to the influence of the ancient pre-Templar Guardians.

The Arabian historian, philosopher, scientist and mathematician Abu Raihan al-Biruni, who lived from AD 973–1048, was of the opinion that the ancient pyramids once had watermarks on them that indicated a flood of unprecedented proportions in that area in the distant past. Such a flood, possibly the same as the one described in Genesis and in the Mesopotamian account in which a hero named Utnapishtim plays Noah's role, actually seems to have occurred around 10,000 BC. Al-Biruni's evidence is well worth considering. He ranks alongside da Vinci as a great all-round scholar and as a profound thinker. Was al-Biruni one of the ancient Guardians, or just one of their very able human supporters?

So, what did Weishaupt find in the Great Pyramid? Where did his research into the occult lead him? He certainly had a close friend and collaborator named Franz Kolmer, who had lived in Alexandria and visited Giza on several occasions. The society that they founded together — unless it was actually a much older and more mysterious group into which they were initiated — had five major principles: the abolition of hereditary monarchies; the end of private property and legacies; the elimination of nationalism and the patriotism that accompanied it; the end of marriage and family life; and finally the abolition of religion — of all religion!

The Illuminati's progress came to a dramatic end when lightning killed one of their couriers — a sort of eighteenth-century James Bond type — and police found coded messages from Weishaupt sewn into the dead messenger's clothes. Weishaupt subsequently spent the rest of his life in exile in Gotha in Thuringia, now part of modern Germany. Even here there are strange links that seem more than coincidental. Princess Basina (mother of Mérovée the Twice-Born) came from Thuringia. It was also in Thuringia that Tannhauser had a whale of a time with Frau Hulda, the local version of Venus-Aphrodite, in her subterranean love palace deep in the Hörselberg.

Although the term *cognoscenti* may refer in general usage simply to those who know, to connoisseurs and experts in various fields such as music, drama, wine tasting, cuisine and art, it may also have a very special secret sense related to an actual undercover organization like the Illuminati.

In this connection, the remarkable Johannes Vermeer van Delft (1632–1675) has been suspected of belonging to a secret society — many of whose members were also artists — whose members were referred to as cognoscenti. Very little is known about Vermeer's life, and he may have taken care that it was kept as secret as possible. His remarkable paintings are thought by some of the art experts who are intrigued by the apparent geometry of Poussin's paintings and their connections with the Rennes-le-Château mystery to be based on the same, or very similar,

"Grail geometry." In these enigmatic canvases, some simple object, such as the shepherd's staff in Poussin's *Shepherds of Arcadia*, can apparently be used as an indicator that leads to a complex geometrical construction. In Vermeer's case, one very significant painting is his *Little Street*, in which the gutter — which is unusually prominent in his composition as a whole — may be the keyline for a Grail-geometry construction. On occasion, when his work has been X-rayed, there are hints of figures that have been painted out. Such instances may signify nothing more than that a talented painter changed his composition as a better idea occurred to him; but on the other hand, they may be highly significant.

Just as Templar codes were frequently associated with the Knight's Tour on chessboards, so checkered floors have considerable significance in other contexts. It is therefore interesting to observe that the tiles the woman is apparently cleaning in Vermeer's *Little Street* are arranged as a checkerboard. The checkerboard patterns in the Church of St. Mary Magdalene in Rennes-le-Château may also be meaningful in this context.

Another very powerful and well-concealed secret society seems to have been in the hands of Francis Bacon, one of the most mysterious characters in sixteenth- and seventeenth-century history. Born in 1561, he supposedly died in 1626 after a bout of pneumonia. Bacon's keen interest in all branches of science and philosophy — as well as his great literary achievements — had led him to experiment with food preservation using snow and ice. The details of the episode that was said to have led to his death are his experiment with a chicken. In bitterly cold weather, with snow falling heavily, Bacon ordered his coachman to stop so that he could gather up a quantity of snow to pack around the chicken he had just bought from a nearby butcher and poulterer. Exposure to the severe weather gave him a chill, which developed allegedly fatal complications.

There are researchers, however, who tell a different story of the end of Bacon's life. For reasons of his own, and those of the secret society in which he is believed to have played a prominent part, Bacon's recovery from the pneumonia was kept secret and he was smuggled out of Britain. There was a mock funeral, and it would have been characteristic of Bacon's generosity and gentle humour to have sent the body of an unknown pauper into a dignified resting place in St. Michael's Church in Gorhambury, where Bacon's family had their home. That someone was buried in Bacon's coffin can be argued from an episode in which a Dr. King of St. Alban's allegedly disturbed Bacon's skull during the interment of Sir Thomas Meautys, Bacon's loyal old friend and secretary, who had expressed a wish to lie near his former employer. King had attended Meautys during his last illness in 1649. More disturbances were to follow some thirty years later. According to John Aubrey's account in *Brief Lives*, Sir Harbottle Grimston, who was master of the rolls in 1681, ordered Bacon's coffin to be moved in order to make space for his own!

If these accounts of Bacon's mock funeral are true, where did Sir Francis go in 1626? The evidence points to his having enjoyed a long and happy life in Germany under another name, where he was well cared for and protected by powerful and influential members of his secret society.

The mysteries surrounding his supposed death are equalled by the mysteries surrounding his birth. A reasonable case can be made that Francis Bacon was the illegitimate son of Queen Elizabeth I — not by Dudley, Earl of Leicester, the rather effete and unpleasant murder suspect in the death of his young wife, Amy Robsart, and the man who is sometimes said to have been Elizabeth's lover, but by the dashing, bold and fearless Sir Francis Drake, who would have been much more attractive than Dudley in the queen's eyes, although he was a few years younger than Elizabeth.

There was a very delicate religio-political balance in England at the time. If Elizabeth had produced an illegitimate son, her Protestant throne would have been in peril. Francis Bacon's ostensible parents, Sir Nicholas and Lady Bacon, were enthusiastic Protestants and were totally loyal and dedicated to Queen Elizabeth. It might just have been possible for Lady Bacon to have spread the word that she was pregnant in advance of the birth of Elizabeth's son. Elizabeth is known to have visited the Bacon family at Gorhambury — was it on one such visit that the all-important baby switch was made?

Between the mysteries of Francis Bacon's birth and death came the mysteries of his secret society and the codes they used.

Chapter 20

MISCELLANEOUS
TEMPLAR MYSTERIES

From the mists of time emerge the strange, shadowy figures of the pre-Templar Guardians. Their true nature and origins remain a mystery, but just because we can't see them clearly doesn't mean that they're not there! Were these powerful superhuman entities, as some dualist philosophers and theologians have suggested, a morally mixed group? Perhaps some were benignly motivated towards the progressive development and happiness of humanity, while others were oblivious to us, neutrally unconcerned about our wants and needs, and still others may have been negative and malign: a malevolent and dangerous reality underpinning the colourful and dramatic images of so-called evil spirits and demons described in early religious thought. There also seems to be evidence that these groups of powerful, superhuman entities quarrelled and fought among themselves. In almost every ancient pantheon, the so-called gods have had different aims and objectives, and have formed shifting alliances with one another and with human beings as it suited their transient purposes of the moment.

It seems likely, therefore, that whoever the ancient pre-Templar Guardians really were and wherever they originally came from, they had some specific, hidden purpose involving the nine pioneering knights of Jerusalem who formed the nucleus of the medieval Templar Order. It also seems likely that there were intermediaries between the ancient pre-Templar Guardians and normal human beings — wise, talented and powerful men and women like Alexander of Macedon, Princess Basina of Thuringia, Charlemagne and Bernard of Clairvaux. These outstanding human leaders would probably have been given some of the minor powers of the superhuman Guardians, and have been party to a number of the aims and objectives of their paranormal mentors.

Mysterious secrets — and perhaps mysterious artifacts, too — might have been entrusted to groups and societies as well as to individual leaders. What ancient secrets were guarded in the shadowy, enigmatic, southern European province of Septimania? Did the benign Prester John of legend really exist and rule some powerful distant land with the guidance and help of the Guardians? Or was Prester John just a coded synonym for the grand master of the medieval Templars? Was his "kingdom" their diffuse order and powerful fleet — impossible to locate specifically because it was everywhere? Were the enigmatic troubadours, minnesingers and minstrels used as agents and messengers by the Templars and by other powerful earthly leaders who were in contact with the Guardians?

Where do Solomon and the queen of Sheba fit into the whole mysterious Templar gestalt? Did the beautiful, black Queen Makeda of Ethiopia visit Jerusalem and later bear Solomon's son — whom she called Menelik, meaning "son of the wise man"? If so, how did this royal trio fit into the legends of the beautiful Black Madonnas and their strange, secret cult, evidence of which is still found today in many shrines and sanctuaries in France? Is there also a connection with Moses and his mysterious black, Ethiopian princess — who may be the same lady as the Ethiopian Woman described in the Book of Numbers?

Wise men like Solomon had important moral codes — the wisdom contained in the Book of Proverbs in the Bible is attributed largely to Solomon — and these valuable ethical principles are also found in the teachings of Alexander the Great, Charlemagne and Leonardo da Vinci. It has been suggested that the benign ancient Guardians not only taught these moral and ethical behavioural codes but also used them as a means of identifying and networking those earthly leaders who were promoting what the Guardians wanted to achieve.

Whatever intricate codes Leonardo da Vinci actually used to preserve and transmit at least part of the ancient, secret wisdom that had come his way, some strange mysteries were almost certainly concealed in his paintings — especially in *The Last Supper* and *Madonna of the Rocks*. Other enigmas were probably to be found in his many notebooks. As well as his outstanding artistic ability, da Vinci was also a formidable mathematician, and mathematics is an extremely useful instrument in the hands of a gifted code-maker. Euler's remarkable mathematical work enabled him to create a "magic square" Knight's Tour of such complexity that each row and each column added up to 260. The Templars used the chessboard knight as their symbol. Letters laid out in the pattern of the unique Euler's Knight's Tour could be found and deciphered by Templar cryptographers while other cryptographers might still be searching for whichever of the many possible knights' tours the encipherer had used. Numerous strange symbols, codes, ciphers and mathematical enigmas can be observed today among the amazing complexity of the mysterious designs in Roslyn Chapel near Edinburgh, Scotland.

The noble Sinclairs, who were responsible for Roslyn Chapel, clearly had Templar help and advice, and there is every possibility that the good and wise Glooscap — a Micmac hero who came over the sea to visit them in Nova Scotia — was actually Henry Sinclair, one-time ruler of the Orkneys. If the Sinclairs had befriended the Templars — as they almost certainly did after Philip le Bel had done his worst — and if the fearless Templars had gone with Henry Sinclair across the cold, wild reaches of the North Atlantic, then there were Templars in Nova Scotia at around the right period to create the mysterious Oak Island Money Pit. There, too, the coded stone may have been only a treasure indicator — but, if Professor Barry Fell and our friend George Young were correct, it could have been very much more important than that. Was it a connection linking Coptic Egyptian mysteries with something of great significance hidden in an ancient labyrinth far below Oak Island?

As already suggested, mathematicians like Euler and Bernoulli seem to have had a hand in the mysterious Templar codes and ciphers — especially those that involved chessboards — but how far were ancient mathematicians like Pythagoras involved as well? And what about the mysterious, medieval, all-round Arabian genius, Abu Raihan al-Biruni? He was also an outstanding mathematician.

It was not just a few gifted individuals, but mysterious secret societies (of which those individuals were often core members) that kept the Templar secrets alive, carefully wrapped in their preservative codes and ciphers. What mysteries did those codes and ciphers conceal for the secret societies that employed them?

There are five major probabilities: first, the Emerald Tablets of Hermes Trismegistus, alias Thoth, scribe of the Egyptian gods — tablets that may well have become the Urim and Thummim of ancient Israel; second, the cornucopia that became conflated with the Christian Grail legends;

third, the Rod, or Wand, of Power, which became the Christianized Lance of Longinus or Spear of Destiny; fourth, the Ark of the Covenant, which could have been an ancient Egyptian artifact that Moses took with him at the Exodus; fifth and finally, the Robe, Fleece or Cloak of Power that was later Christianized and conflated with the legends of the Seamless Robe of Christ, the Mandylion and the Shroud of Turin.

In the previous chapter, some of the mysteries of a few of the world's secret societies were surveyed briefly. Many more are hidden out there, and conspiracy theory suggests that not all of them are innocuous. A conservative estimate suggests that well over half of these secret societies have Templar connections of one sort or another, perhaps Templars who survived the attack of 1307 founded them or the societies have received — and are, perhaps, still receiving — secret information from the ancient pre-Templar Guardians and their human intermediaries.

Having looked analytically at the mysteries of the pre-Templar Guardians, the great men and women of history who were probably connected with them, the secrets of the troubadours, the enigma of Prester John, the riddles associated with the cult of the Black Madonnas, Leonardo da Vinci's strange codes and symbols and the mystery of the Five Great Artifacts, there are still a number of strange, arcane conundrums with Templar connections which demand further investigation. These miscellaneous mysteries form the subject matter of this concluding chapter.

* * *

One of the strange geniuses who strode across the pages of sixteenth-century medical history was the amazing Paracelsus. Born in 1493, his full name was Auroleus Phillipus Theostratus Bombastus von Hohenheim, and his father was a renowned grand master of the Teutonic Order — as well as a doctor of medicine who was a long way ahead of his contemporaries. That Teutonic Order was almost certainly connected with — or derived from — a group of surviving medieval Templars.

Manly Hall, whose opinions are always worth careful consideration, described Paracelsus as "the precursor of chemical pharmacology and therapeutics and the most original medical thinker of the sixteenth century." But why are Manly Hall's views so important? He was a very interesting and unusual writer and researcher, with access to many curious and informative old manuscripts. Born in 1901, Hall and his family travelled from Canada to the United States in 1904. Manly settled in Los Angeles in 1919 and became involved with the American Federation of Astrologers, the Freemasons, the Rosicrucians and the Theosophists. His excellent collection of occult books and manuscripts enabled him to produce his own textbook, *Initiates of the Flame*, as early as 1922. The following year he became the minister of the Church of the People, with a congregation that was principally interested in metaphysics and the occult. Largely for his congregants, Manly then published a magazine called *The All Seeing Eye*. In 1928, he produced his magnum opus, *An Encyclopedic Outline of Masonic, Hermetic, Cabbalistic, and Rosicrucian Symbolical Philosophy*. Before his death in 1990, Hall had written a great many erudite tomes, all dealing with these mysteries. It seems probable that Manly Hall had access to many of the deep secrets that pertained to the ancient Guardians, and which they had in turn entrusted to the medieval Templars of Jerusalem. This is what makes Hall's comments on Paracelsus so relevant and interesting.

Paracelsus was taught by the Abbot Trithermius, who was an acknowledged adept in a very senior order, and who initiated Paracelsus into what was then regarded as the all-important science of alchemy. Unfortunately, Paracelsus extended his studies into the weird, dark fields of necromancy, and when this came to the attention of the authorities the young genius had to leave Basle in a hurry! It goes without saying that travel increases knowledge and broadens the mind, and this was certainly the case with Paracelsus. While more or less on the run from his enemies in Basle, he went through Sweden, Germany, Hungary, Denmark, the Netherlands, France and Russia. Taken captive by the Tartars, he was handed over to a ruler known as the Grand Cham. His next adventure took him to Constantinople, accompanied by the Cham's son. In this ancient and mysterious city, it is alleged that Paracelsus was shown the secret of one of the classical alchemical objectives — a universal solvent known as the alkahest. This arcane knowledge was allegedly passed to him by an Arabian wise man.

From Constantinople, Paracelsus travelled to Italy, where he joined the army as a surgeon, and by all accounts did excellent lifesaving work beyond the competence of most medical men of the day. From here he went on to become a professor of medicine, but his many jealous enemies continued to hound him until his death in 1541 in the White Horse Inn in Salzburg in Austria — following what seems to have been a scuffle with professional assassins hired by his jealous rivals.

Paracelsus almost certainly met many wise old medical helpers and advisers during his extensive travels. They probably imparted to him many of the ancient healing secrets that they themselves had acquired through the good offices of the ancient pre-Templar Guardians or their earthly representatives.

* * *

Medical history is filled with unusual healers like Paracelsus who were ahead of their time and ahead of their contemporaries. The existence of such avant-garde physicians seems to point towards reservoirs of advanced medical knowledge that did not come their way by chance, but by virtue of secret wisdom. The Welsh folklore and legends concerning the physicians of Myddfai fall into this category.

Two strange legends are conflated here. The first concerns a widow's son (which in itself is highly significant and symbolic) who lived with his mother in Blaensawdde in southwest Wales. One day while guarding his mother's cattle near Llyn y Fan Fach, he saw a mysterious, but irresistibly beautiful girl rise from the waters of the lake. After the usual trials and tests imposed by traditional folklore, the young hero gained the necessary marriage permission from her father, the Lord of Llyn y Fan Fach. For many years they lived happily and prosperously together, and raised a fine family, but when certain conditions were broken, the mysterious Lady of Llyn y Fan Fach went sadly back below the water to her father's kingdom.

The history of the physicians of Myddfai concerns a highly successful and knowledgeable healer named Rhiwallon, whose three sons — Cadwgan, Gruffydd and Einon — were as able as their wise old father. These men made a comprehensive collection of efficacious herbal remedies and other medicines, which are still respectfully referred to today as the Recipes of the Physicians of Myddfai. These Welsh formulas were acknowledged to be centuries ahead of other

European medicines available at that time. Where did this mysterious medical knowledge come from?

Rhiwallon was employed by Rhys Gryg, who was master of the castles of Llandovery and Dinefwr during the first half of the thirteenth century — a significant part of the medieval Templar period. Was Rhys a Welsh Templar? Did he have Templar friends? Did they bring him Arabian medical secrets from the Middle East, which he passed on to the wise and discerning Rhiwallon? How do these Myddfai physicians link up with the mysterious Lady of Llyn y Fan Fach and the widow's son?

Taking the magical folklore elements out of that story leaves an actual historical probability that the people living on the uplands above the lake had access to different herbs and plants from those that grew lower down near the water's edge. While not exactly hostile, the two social groups tended to keep themselves separate — uplanders did not marry lakesiders. The uplander widow's son is guarding his mother's cattle close to the edge of what both groups recognize as the informal, but accepted, boundary between their territories. The beautiful lakesider girl, daughter of their chieftain, is near the edge of her territory. They meet, are attracted to each other, and marry. He is able to tell his new wife, her parents, family and lakesider friends about the uplanders' medicinal herbs. She in turn teaches him about the medicinal herbs used by the lakesiders. This combined knowledge leads to new cures for both groups of people. Word spreads that there are medicines in Myddfai which are more effective than most. The wise Rhiwallon investigates and adds these curative herbs to the stock that he and his sons already hold.

Another of these miscellaneous Templar mysteries concerns the enigmatic Dr. John Dee, who was born on July 13, 1527, at Mortlake, near London. As great a genius as da Vinci, but in very different ways, Dee went to Cambridge when he was only fifteen and was awarded a fellowship at Trinity College by the time he was twenty. Like Paracelsus, Dee spent many years travelling around Europe, learning new things wherever he went, and lecturing on mathematics and astrology. His mathematical powers put him in the same league as Bernoulli and Euler.

One of Dee's specialties was a magical ritual concerning the convocation of Venus, which is particularly interesting. One intriguing theory about Rennes-le-Château and Saunière's unaccountable wealth was given to us by our friend Bremna Howells, who writes as Rosy Malone and is an advanced student of magic in many of its forms. Her very interesting hypothesis centred on the idea that Saunière and his attractive young "housekeeper," Marie Dénarnaud, were together performing the sexual magic involved in the convocation of Venus ritual. Theoretically, this ritual enabled the magicians involved to make forecasts and predictions that were accurate enough to be financially rewarding. Hence, Saunière's money supposedly came from selling predictions — much as the priests of the Delphic Oracle had done many centuries earlier.

Dee later became deeply interested in "angelic magic" of the type associated with Trithermius, one of the teachers who also helped Paracelsus. Allegedly, these mysterious angelic beings communicated with Dee using the enigmatic language referred to as Enochian. The Enoch after whom the weird language is named appears in the Old Testament, in Genesis 5:18–24. This passage gives Enoch's ancestry and his line of descent from Adam and Eve. The most remarkable fact in the passage is that Enoch did not die in the normal way: "and Enoch walked with God: and he was not; for God took him" (Genesis 5:24).

The so-called Book of Enoch appears to be an Ethiopic text associated with the Qumran Community and the Dead Sea Scrolls. How did Dee manage to see a copy in the sixteenth century? Had medieval Templars encountered Arabian scholars in the Middle East who had access to the Book of Enoch? Did the Templars even acquire a copy for themselves and store it with their other mysterious artifacts and treasures? One way or another, Dee seems to have known about the stories of Enoch and his travels with various angelic beings. Most curious of all in the light of the Templar fascination with codes and ciphers, is Dee's strange Enochian alphabet.

Working with his colleague, Edward Kelley, Dee maintained that the Enochian language and its alphabet had been revealed to him by strange, angelic entities. Various experts in magic, including Benjamin Rowe — also known as Josh Norton — have written in depth about the Dee-Kelley system. Wherever it came from — as a genuine revelation or as a deliberate construction — it has a great deal in common with the mysterious codes and ciphers used by the Templars, various secret societies and the enigmatic Francis Bacon. Some figures in his watermark codes bear a significant resemblance to characters in Dee's Enochian alphabet. Dee lived from 1527 until 1608; Bacon from 1561 until at least 1626 — and probably much later! These two men of mystery were contemporaries; how much secret information did they share? Were they both prominent in the same Templar-based secret society?

* * *

Another strange Templar-based mystery surrounds the enigmatic character known as the Count of St. Germain. The man who claimed to be the Count of Cagliostro was really Giuseppe Balsamo, born in Palermo, Sicily, in 1743. He claimed to be a soothsayer, alchemist, healer and purveyor of aphrodisiacs and elixirs of life. Cagliostro also claimed that he had met the mysterious Count of St. Germain, who had initiated him into an elite Masonic society. Whether his claims were well or ill founded, Giuseppe seems to have died ignominiously in the Apennine fortress of St. Leo round about 1795 (coincidentally, the year in which Smith, Vaughan and McGinnis discovered the Oak Island Money Pit in Nova Scotia).

Who was the amazing Count of St. Germain? Was he one of the ancient pre-Templar Guardians? One of their intermediary agents on Earth? Or something else again? How much evidence can we locate about this seemingly fabulous character? Those who encountered him in seventeenth- and eighteenth-century Europe often — with some justification — referred to him as the Wonderman. There is no concrete, definitive evidence regarding his parents or place of origin. The wildest speculations about him linked him with the legend of Cartaphilus, the so-called Wandering Jew. In one version of this legend, Cartaphilus is a Jewish collaborator in first-century Palestine, working as a doorman for Pontius Pilate. In another version, Cartaphilus is a Jewish onlooker who spits on Christ as he passes him on his way to Calvary. In the legend, Cartaphilus tells Jesus to hurry. Christ looks at him steadily and says, "I shall continue this journey — but you will remain in the world until I return in glory." The legend goes on to explain that what Jesus meant was not clear to Cartaphilus until he realized that his family and friends were slowly aging and dying — while he wasn't! The legend had been almost forgotten until the time of the medieval Templars, when strange stories began to circulate about meetings with a curious-looking stranger who admitted to being Cartaphilus, the Wandering Jew. In 1228, for example, an Armenian bishop visiting Britain claimed to have had a meal with Cartaphilus in St. Albans in England. Could this wildest of possibilities be factual? Did this strange, immortal being turn up again in Vienna in 1740, calling himself the Count of St. Germain?

The possibility of his being Cartaphilus from the first century was only one of the many strange myths and legends that clustered around St. Germain like bees around lavender. Some said he was immortal — or that he possessed such great longevity that he might as well be. This particular hypothesis held that he had access to the Elixir of Life — a major goal of the alchemists. He was also said to be a leading Rosicrucian — and a king, travelling and working incognito for secret reasons of state. One very curious reference to him dates from a letter that Horace Walpole (son of Prime Minister Robert Walpole) wrote to his friend Horace Mann. In essence, this letter said that the provost of Edinburgh had in custody a man calling himself the Count of St. Germain. This strange prisoner was a brilliant violinist, but no one knew where he came from. It was guessed that he might be Italian, Polish, Spanish or Mexican. There were no charges against him, apparently, and the provost duly released him. He appeared again in Versailles, near Paris, more than ten years later, and was presented to the nobles and courtiers by the marshal of Belle-Isle, who was convinced that the count had miraculously restored his failing health. Yet again, mysterious healing abilities that exceed the medical knowledge of the time are much in evidence — another curious parallel with Paracelsus and the physicians of Myddfai.

St. Germain also appears to have been blessed with unlimited wealth. Could this possibly link up with the strange Cathar testimony from the tragedy of the Montségur siege of 1244, when the boldest of the Cathar mountaineers escaped with *pecuniam infinitam* — unlimited money? There are records that St. Germain bestowed lavish gifts of diamonds on the many new friends he made while staying in luxurious accommodation at the Château de Chambord. Almost as mysterious as the Count of St. Germain himself is his valet, Roger, around whom several intriguing anecdotes have gathered. When asked how old St. Germain really was, Roger modestly replied, "I can't say for certain, sir, as I have only been in his service for the past 100 years." Those who spoke directly with the count himself were deeply impressed by his encyclopedic knowledge of history — surely a relevant attribute for a man who had apparently already enjoyed many times the normal human lifespan.

He was an accomplished linguist, credited with a fluent command of many languages. One of his most significant claims in the context of these present Templar studies is that he knew King Solomon and was actually in Jerusalem when Makeda turned up with her entourage.

King Louis XV and his mistress, the exquisite Madame Pompadour, had the highest regard for him. Louis entrusted him with important missions of state — notably one to Amsterdam. As with Paracelsus, St. Germain aroused suspicion and jealousy in those who were envious of him. Minister of State Choiseul disliked and distrusted St. Germain and tried to arrest him, but the wily count escaped.

Perhaps the most significant recorded comment from this period is one attributed to Voltaire — but is the great French wit being ironic, something he was famed for? Voltaire said that St. Germain knew everything, and was an immortal. When a humorist like Voltaire makes a remark like that, it is never entirely possible to tell whether he is being serious just for once.

The count turns up in Russia and is suspected of being behind the coup that put Catherine the Great into power. After the successes he achieved in Russia, following which St. Germain sometimes dressed in a Russian general's uniform, the mysterious and elusive count made tracks for Belgium. It was here that a high-ranking Belgian politician named Karl Cobenzl left some very interesting notes about St. Germain. Cobenzl said that he had seen St. Germain transform iron into what looked like gold, and that he had entrusted Cobenzl with the secret truth about his noble birth. Cobenzl, however, stubbornly refused to disclose the count's ancestral secret — was that because St. Germain had told him that he was a descendant of the Royal Merovingian line and therefore related to the children of Jesus and Mary Magdalene? If Cobenzl had believed that, it explains why he was so unwilling to pass on what St. Germain had said!

The arcane count's next appearance is in Bavaria in 1774, and from there he moves to Schleswig-Holstein, where

Prince Karl of Hesse-Kassel befriends him. The story of his alleged death in February of 1784 is as muddled and uncertain as the stories surrounding the alleged death of Francis Bacon. Like Bacon, St. Germain was said to have contracted a form of pneumonia that proved fatal — but his great friend and protector, Prince Karl, was mysteriously absent at an important Masonic meeting at the time of St. Germain's supposed death.

Various pieces of evidence suggest that he was in Egypt while Napoleon I was campaigning there, and that a later Napoleon kept a file on him. St. Germain was reportedly seen alive and well in Paris in 1835 and again in Milan in 1867. Someone claiming to be St. Germain turned up on French television as recently as 1972! One significantly strange piece of evidence came from an elderly lady who claimed to have seen St. Germain in Venice when she was young, some fifty years ago. She added that his appearance had not changed at all over the intervening half century.

The question of St. Germain's authenticity remains challengingly unanswered, but it is not totally beyond the bounds of possibility that he was yet another of the ancient pre-Templar Guardians, or one of their distinguished intermediaries.

And there, with St. Germain as the last — and perhaps the most intriguing — of these miscellaneous Templar mysteries, our investigation ends. The final words are some favourites of ours from the pen of the great Dr. Joseph Glanvill, a Fellow of the Royal Society who flourished in the second half of the seventeenth century and wrote *Saducismus Triumphatis*, from which this quotation comes: "Facts ought not to be denied because we cannot see how they could have happened. It is unreasonable to assume a thing is impossible and then to conclude that it cannot be proved. Every action should be judged by evidence, not evidence by our prejudices about the action."